PE[...]
FROM [...]

Chitra Narayanan is a Del[...] d
gaze on consumer behaviour. She is currently an editorial consultant
with *The Hindu BusinessLine*, and in her two-and-a-half-decade-long
journalistic career she has had stints with *BW Businessworld*, *Business
Today*, the *Economic Times* and *Business Standard*. She has also written
for *Mint* and the *Telegraph*. She has written widely on marketing
strategy, workplaces, travel and hospitality. A lover of crime fiction and
a fan of P.G. Wodehouse, she would love to write an old-world mystery
set in a hotel.

PRAISE FOR THE BOOK

'We have all stayed in hotels and have discussed our experiences of hotels animatedly in social groups. Chitra has written a gem of a book that traces the origins of the hospitality industry from the big three—Tatas, Oberois and ITC—to the international chain entry and the rise of the Indian entrepreneur. This is a book that gives a fascinating insight into the branding, the experience and the segmentation of each of the players. The segmentation from experiences around sleep, food and the Internet to the role of the coffee shop, the décor and the location, etc., this industry has pioneered diversity and inclusion with the recruitment of the LGBT community in one chain and specially abled people in another. This book is an excellent compilation of the history, the people and the strategies that make up the hospitality sector; it's a riveting read!'—D. Shivakumar, group executive president, corporate strategy and business, Aditya Birla Group

'Chitra Narayanan's deeply researched and reported book gives us the fascinating history as well as a glimpse of the future of the hospitality industry. From the first proper hotel that came up in Calcutta to the rise and rise of OYO, which has attracted enormous funding and expanded faster than any other chain in history, she takes a look at how the industry works, the business models, the personalities behind the success and failure of the hotel chains, and the ongoing wars for supremacy. Chitra has managed to accomplish the difficult task of writing a book that both provides enormous business insight as well as a fast-paced and colourful tale of the history and evolution of the Indian hospitality industry from pre-Independence to the current era of online aggregators, shared travel apps, and mergers and acquisitions as every hotelier chases scale'—Prosenjit Datta, former editor, *Business Today*

FROM OBEROI TO OYO

BEHIND THE SCENES WITH THE MOVERS AND SHAKERS OF INDIA'S HOTEL INDUSTRY

CHITRA NARAYANAN

BUSINESS

An imprint of Penguin Random House

PENGUIN BUSINESS

USA | Canada | UK | Ireland | Australia
New Zealand | India | South Africa | China

Penguin Business is part of the Penguin Random House group of companies
whose addresses can be found at global.penguinrandomhouse.com

Published by Penguin Random House India Pvt. Ltd
4th Floor, Capital Tower 1, MG Road,
Gurugram 122 002, Haryana, India

Penguin
Random House
India

First published in Portfolio by Penguin Random House India 2020
Published in Penguin Business 2022

ISBN 9780143428374

Typeset in Adobe Caslon Pro by Manipal Technologies Limited, Manipal
Printed at Replika Press Pvt. Ltd, India

www.penguin.co.in

Contents

I
CHECKING IN: INTRODUCTION

II
AT YOUR SERVICE: THE PLAYERS

III
ROOM FOR GROWTH: STRATEGIES

IV
ENTER THE BOTLER:
THE FUTURE OF HOSPITALITY

Acknowledgements

For someone used to closing a story at 1000 words—that's the average word count of a feature article—writing a book was incredibly hard. I started out with great enthusiasm thinking it would be easy as I had many tales to tell, but on several occasions I got overwhelmed and was ready to give up. I owe huge thanks to Lohit Jagwani at Penguin Random House and literary agent Kanishka for keeping me going. This book would not have got finished if not for their belief in me. I also owe a huge debt of gratitude to my former boss at *Business Line*, friend and guide, T.C.A. Srinivasa Raghavan for scolding and berating me to finish the book. Also thanks to my former editor at *Businessworld* and *Business Today*, Prosenjit Datta who read through the book, offered valuable suggestions and encouraged me. To all at Penguin Random House, especially Milee Ashwarya and Manish Kumar, many thanks for tolerating the delays, and the periods of self-doubts, and a big shout-out to the copyeditors, especially Hina Khajuria, who refined and polished the manuscript. If there are any shortcomings or errors in the book, I have to take the blame for those.

A huge number of people in the hotel industry were supportive. The starting point of my book was actually the annual hotel conference Hotel Investment Conference–South Asia (HICSA) organized by Manav Thadani and his team, where one heard fascinating anecdotes and got inspired. Special thanks to Dilip Puri, the friendly, approachable former chief of Starwood in India and founder of the Indian School of Hospitality, who was the first person I went rushing to during my research and who was always encouraging. Also Anjali Mehra of Starwood (now Marriott), who despite being away from India continued to send me interesting insights.

So many people—Ajay Bakaya of Sarovar, Rattan Keswani at Lemon Tree, Jean-Michel Cassé and Amisha Gutgutia at Accor, Aman Nath of Neemrana Hotels, Deep Kalra of MakeMyTrip, Ashish Jakhanwala at SAMHI—were so helpful. Thank you to the Lalit and The Park for opening their doors to me, welcoming and allowing me to stay and experience the properties. Both Jyotsna Suri and Priya Paul are inspiring ladies. Swati Jain at the Lalit and Ruchika Mehta at The Park, many thanks for the hospitality. To Bhavna at the Taj for always inviting me for lunches where one heard many delicious stories. Thank you Deval Tibrewala for bringing the regional players including the North East to my attention. Thank you Marryam Reshii and Samir Kuckreja for sharing food nuggets. Anu Kapoor, it was very kind of you to help me with contacts in Jaipur and help facilitate so many interviews.

There are just so many people in the industry who helped me with their time and anecdotes that I owe a debt of gratitude to. I may not be able to name them all here as the list is way too long. There are many unconnected to the industry—Jessie Paul, Sandip Ghose, Anaggh Desai, to name just three—who helped out by sharing interesting customer insights.

I also owe thanks to several associates in the PR industry, notably the Adfactors team, Alphabet Consulting and Fortuna PR. Ruchi Mehta Lodha for transcribing interviews very quickly when I ran into an emergency and lost some of my files. Special thanks to D. Shivakumar of Aditya Birla Group for reading the book during the final stages and providing some pointers on style—will keep these tips in mind if there is a next book.

Above all, thanks to all the editors/publishers at the various media houses I have worked or written for—R. Srinivasan at *Business Line*, Suresh Nambath and Mukund Padmanabhan at *The Hindu*, Annurag Batra at *Businessworld* and Pro and Rajeev at *Business Today* for giving me the space to write on hotels and also the permission to use some of these writings in the book.

I must also acknowledge the inspiring writings of Vir Sanghvi and Sourish Bhattacharya who probably know the hospitality industry the closest and have chronicled so much.

To my parents, family and friends—thanks for being around and lending constant support. Last but not the least, my husband Vijay, and daughter Eshna—you two deserve a big holiday for putting up with my mood swings during the writing of this book.

Foreword

I can think of no better person than Chitra Narayanan to chronicle the storied origins of India's hospitality industry and its transformation, with a bit of crystal-gazing into what the future holds. I have known Chitra for many years and her reportage on the industry gives her a unique vantage point into the nuances of what makes hotels and hoteliers successful, with a pulse on the changing needs of today's digitally savvy guests. In an industry ripe with disruption, Chitra lends her valuable perspectives against the backdrop of a uniquely Indian context and the emergence of the Indian traveller on the domestic and global map.

India stands unmatched with its rich culture and tradition in hospitality, which millions of international and local travellers have experienced over the years—with increasing choices, a multitude of hotels and brands to choose from, and new destinations and experiences. India's hospitality industry stands at an inflection point today with a bright future. In fact, since 2008, we have seen a two-fold increase in foreign tourist arrivals with domestic tourism growing three times as much. Tourism brings enormous economic benefits and socio-cultural impacts that benefit all of society and India's tourism industry has incredible potential ahead.

With a greater propensity to travel than ever before, a burgeoning consumer base and one of the largest millennial populations in the world, hotels and their operating companies in India need to continually drive innovation in order to cater to a new generation of travellers. Today's travellers know what they want and are seekers of authentic, immersive experiences. Hotels have to be at the centre of it all, designing the travel and lifestyle experience and providing travellers with a true taste of their destination. Hoteliers must stay ahead of the curve to anticipate the changing needs of their guests and thrive amid increasing competition and segmentation.

To truly carve a niche for itself as a world-class destination defined by the strength and diversity of its hotel industry, India must continue to invest in and train talent and embrace digital technology to better anticipate guest needs. Finally, a favourable macro-economic environment is a prerequisite— the industry needs all the support it can get from a regulatory and taxation view given the capital-intensive nature of our business.

India stands at the cusp of being an economic powerhouse in the world with an opportunity to build a truly world-class hospitality industry.

Jean-Michel Cassé,
Chief Operating Officer (COO) India and
South Asia, Accor

Preface

'They say it used to be a good hotel, but that proves nothing. I used to be a good boy. Both of us have lost character of late years.'

—Mark Twain, *Innocents Abroad*

Hotels, much like people, have tumultuous destinies. Some shine, others just trundle along, still others sparkle briefly before losing character and fading. A few rare ones lose lustre but manage to rise from the rubble to new glory.

Perhaps no one has captured the destiny of a hotel better than Arthur Hailey in his racy novel *Hotel*. Peppered with memorable characters, it's a gripping read, with ups and downs, suspense and an unexpected ending. But the star of the story is the hotel itself—the St Gregory in New Orleans. The British–Canadian author really unlocked the world of a hotel, capturing its inner machinery, its complicated workings. Reading it as a teenager, I was completely captivated by the world of hotels.

Then there was John Cleese's classic comedy series *Fawlty Towers*, the bumbling attempt of a short-fused Englishman to run a hotel populated by eccentric guests that reduced us to mirth.

More recently I read Bengali author Shankar's classic novel *Chowringhee* thanks to a wonderful translation now available in English by journalist Arunava Sinha. This only added to my fascination with the world of hotels. *Chowringhee*, set in Calcutta, is a story of grand depth that gives tantalizing glimpses of the comings and goings in a luxurious hotel, as well as its seamy underbelly.

In the 1970s and 1980s, my family rarely stayed in hotels. Army messes, PWD guest houses and homes of relatives were the norm then. I think that might have been true for most middle-class Indians. Holidays were spent at the ancestral home in the village. The rare occasion when we took a touristy break was to places such as Kanyakumari, Madurai, or Ajanta and Ellora, where our usual lodging arrangements would not be possible and we stayed at hotels. And these were terribly unprepossessing ones. In Rajasthan, we fared better at state tourism-run hotels that had great location and decent rooms, even if the service was snail-like and the restaurants had a stale odour.

But we never complained. Our expectations were fairly low. We stayed cheerfully in rooms where rats scurried and you could spot a cockroach or two in the bathroom. And we ate indifferent-quality food without grumbling.

Growing up in Delhi, Calcutta and Pune, the high point in our lives would be when well-heeled relatives or friends visited town and invited us over for a meal at the five-star hotels they were staying in. I particularly remember a dinner at the House of August Moon at the Taj Palace—for a while that was the zenith of our dining experience. Now, look how casually we treat lunches and dinners at five-star hotels, even finding fault with the exotic fare and preferring home food.

I can't pinpoint exactly when things began changing. Perhaps in the 1990s, when I started working and got to stay at charming hotels booked by my office—the Clarks in Lucknow and the Jehan Numa Palace in Bhopal are two that come to mind. But these paled in comparison to the hotels we got to stay in around the mid-2000s, by when the global brands had arrived, and when we began seeing good mid-market hotels that offered some of the frills of the five-stars.

Call it the liberalization effect. The Indian economy opened up in 1991, leading to high economic growth in the country all through the 1990s and 2000s. Breaking out of the shackles of socialism, India introduced policies that were market- and services-oriented and this led to a boom.

Perhaps due to this, our salaries improved and we could afford better hotels during personal visits too, without a twinge. At some point—valuing privacy and comfort over roughing it out with shared bathrooms and adjusting to our host's schedules—we stopped staying with relatives, however close, opting to stay in a hotel. And we began to get fussier and fussier about our stay, throwing a fit if the food was cold or arrived late, if the shower was not hot enough, if the Wi-Fi was slow, and so on.

On the business side, I began to understand (and my education is by no means complete even now) how the hospitality sector operated only when I began covering it as a journalist. This beat was given to me at *Businessworld* magazine. By then the Internet had arrived and the old world of hoteliering had altered completely. Online travel agents disrupted things in a big way. The way we selected and booked hotels changed. There was a new complexity to the hotels business, and it took a while to figure it out.

Suddenly the pace of business also stepped up. One minute you would report on a joint venture (JV). The next minute you would find the JV gone, broken. A new hotel would open, sporting a foreign brand's colours. But even before the ink on the hotel review had dried, it would be sporting another brand's flag. Competition got intense.

The hoteliers themselves still had smiling faces and charming manners when they met you. But behind their suave veneers you could sense the worry and tension. A drink or two down and general managers (GMs) would admit to anxieties about filling rooms, about motivating and retaining staff and angst about the one hundred and one things that could go wrong. Suicides in hotels, murders (remember the infamous Tandoori murder case?) and bad publicity all added to GMs' nightmares.

This is an industry with great surface glamour. But behind the sparkling white linen and shining dining rooms, there also lurks a sleazy story of egos at play, exploitation at work, dirty street fights, shady money, and whispered tales of how hotels are used for illicit goings-on and to obtain political favours. Any service profession is difficult, but hoteliering is undoubtedly one of the toughest jobs.

Today, in the digital age, there's a whole new dimension to the challenges a hotel faces. A bad review on Tripadvisor can ruin its reputation. If a hotel does not adopt technology fast enough, it is in danger of being left behind. Technology has also meant that the entry barriers to starting a hotel have come down phenomenally—so young, agile and geeky players are leaping into the fray with the brash confidence of youth that there is a gap that they can fill. And they are doing a good job of it. Technology has also put power in the hands of small, independent hotels that can now pose stiff competition to established chains in a particular location as they have become discoverable now.

In 2008, Airbnb was launched. But even as this start-up captured the world's imagination, hoteliers refused to acknowledge the threat. Globally, the big chains understood the threat faster and began trying to do different things to take on this disruptive challenger. But in India, the industry is still taking the threat lightly, pointing out how timeshares, homestays, service apartments and so on could not threaten them.

When I started research for this book and met hoteliers, many refused to acknowledge that Airbnb and they had the same target customers. Or even that young tech-enabled players like OYO or Treebo could impact them. That attitude is now changing—there is no choice really, it's adapt or perish.

In India, hoteliers face additional challenges. We might be a country with one of the wonders of the world and incredibly picturesque landscapes, but infrastructure to reach these places has not developed. The stunning Taj Mahal, India's best-known monument—which attracts travellers from around the world—stands in a dirty city with bad air-connections. A place like Khajuraho would deter any traveller because of its poor connectivity. There's constant hope that things will get better. But then comes yet another challenge—poor air-quality. To top it all is the geopolitics of this region—we live in a region brimming with tension that can impact tourism and hospitality. Witness how after the Balakot air strike in February 2019, Pakistan closed its airspace on its eastern border with India, disrupting travel.

But all these now look pretty minor challenges, compared to the pandemic that totally upended the world in 2020. The hospitality industry was, perhaps, the worst affected. For months on end there were no customers as a series of lockdowns were imposed, travel came to a standstill and people stayed at home. Even when the world started resuming old activities, it was no longer done the same way. In the new normal, people's behaviours have changed tremendously and hotels have had to reinvent themselves. One hotelier told me that the pandemic has set the industry back by at least ten years. They all had to go back to the drawing board. But amazingly, several hotel chains rose to this challenge and came up with new ideas and new models to greet the changed consumer, showing great resilience.

The idea behind *From Oberoi to OYO* is to capture some of the changes in the hospitality industry, the challenges that hoteliers face, and how the frenzied pace and need for speed has led to many of them making mistakes and stumbling. There's no denying that some of our hotels are far superior to anything that the West can offer—there is a warmth and personalization that beats the standardized but impersonal quality standards of international chains. So many corporate folk I talked to, who spend a good 200 days a year travelling, described how they have a favourite hotel simply because they know the staff well and get special attention. It's interesting to note that Britain may be regarded as the motherland of hoteliering, where it all began, but it's the Eastern chains that today give a better taste of hospitality—and when they are good, Indian hotels are there right at the top.

The beginning of the book has a bit of history, but the idea is to map out the disruptive forces at play as well as the stories of new innovations, and to learn about the people behind the changes. Since mostly everyone knows the story of the older chains, the focus of the book is more on the unknown players who now have a lot of skin in the game.

I have been asked about the title of the book. After all, the Taj is the first Indian hotel brand, predating the Oberoi Group. Certainly, India's hotel industry would not have been where it is today if not for Jamsetji Tata's vision to build the majestic Taj Mahal Palace overlooking the Gateway of India in Mumbai in 1903 and the foresight of the hotel group chairman and managing director Ajit Kerkar, who expanded the Taj empire. But then everyone I spoke to unanimously agreed that Oberoi may have started later—only in 1934—but it set the dizzying standards that even foreign chains struggle to emulate. As for OYO, there is no denying that it has shaken up the industry, even if many are still in denial and its business model has been questioned. In 2019, it had notched up a valuation of $10 billion—which was more than double the market capitalization of a leading Indian player like Taj Hotels—and expanded into the US market, ratcheting up fifty hotels in next to no time there. And yet, representatives of the Oberoi Group were far from pleased to be mentioned in the same breath as OYO.

Even as hoteliers are probably spending sleepless nights wondering how to get more heads in beds at their properties, it is exciting times for customers. We finally have a lot of choice, can be picky about where we stay and get great value at luxury hotels at half the prices of what a stay there would have cost twenty years ago.

For three years I travelled around the country, meeting hoteliers, checking out hotels and talking to guests. A large part of this book is based on observations and interactions during these travels. But equally, many chapters also derive from the articles I wrote on the sector in *Businessworld*, *The Hindu BusinessLine*, *Business Today* and *The Hindu*. I am exceedingly grateful to these publications.

I have attempted to write a business book, but there is also the emotional, experiential and non-business side. After all, hotels touch all our lives in some way or the other—the first date, the first job interview, wedding anniversaries, celebrations and many such memorable experiences are all linked to them. We all have a little soft spot or great memory of a hotel stay and I wish this remarkable industry well.

Chitra Narayanan
Delhi

I

CHECKING IN: INTRODUCTION

1

Behind the Glitter—Cast of Characters

'All the world's a stage,
And all the men and women merely players;
They have their exits and their entrances,
And one man in his time plays many parts.'

—William Shakespeare

Not so long ago, a common lament was that there were hardly any decent hotel rooms in India. There was no definition of decent, but that did not deter anyone. Today, there are lakhs of good-quality rooms that meet the best global standards at affordable rates. They are there in big cities, small towns, near the sea, in the mountains and in really unexpected remote places. You can stay in forts, in palaces, in lodges, in multi-storied edifices, in villas and bungalows. They are there in floatels, boatels and rotels (cruise ships, houseboats and caravans respectively), to use the industry jargon. But who really holds the keys to these rooms?

3

The layperson often confuses the brand on a hotel's facade with the ownership of the hotel. Few would know that the Grand Hyatt in Mumbai's bustling Bandra Kurla Complex belongs to the Sarafs of Juniper Hotels[1] while the Hyatt Regency near Manesar has been developed by the Piccadilly Hotel group of politician Venod Sharma.[2] Owners often choose to remain invisible; people assume that the Hyatt Regency near Manesar is a property belonging to the US chain but that is not the case. Hyatt is just managing it for the real owners.

Even the brands themselves are utterly confusing—a guest staying at the Radisson may not know that the company that owns the brand (formerly Carlson Rezidor, now the Radisson Group) also owns Country Inns and Suites. In 2018, Carlson Rezidor changed its name, adopting its flagship brand's name as the group's. Hotel brands like Pullman, Ibis and Novotel belong to the French group Accor. Just a handful of big hotel companies between them own hundreds of brands, but a guest staying in a hotel may not know which brand belongs to which hotel company.

Of late, at a time when customer loyalty is at its lowest, the branding strategy of a hotel has immense significance. In 2017, the world's most powerful hotel brand was rated as UK's Premier Inn, which really may surprise people in India as this was one brand that bombed here and had to pull out. The second most powerful hotel brand in the world, according to valuation and strategy consultancy Brand Finance, is Holiday Inn. However, the same report puts Hilton as the most valuable hotel brand in the world, ahead of Marriott and Hyatt—surprising for the Indian hotel industry. Hilton has met with indifferent success while the latter two hotels have done well. Clearly the brand values of these hotels have not been articulated well in India.

Patu Keswani, the dynamic founder of Lemon Tree Hotels, one of the most innovative new chains in India, points out that the hotel business in India today is three-pronged—who owns the hotel, who manages the hotel and who brands the hotel. Lemon Tree has several hotels that it owns, manages and brands but at the same time, it also manages hotels for others as well.

To better explain what Keswani means, take an old hotel like the Taj Connemara in Chennai. The actual building is owned by the Goenka family of the RPG group (it is privately held), coming to them through the acquisition of Spencer's. Since the Goenkas are not professional hoteliers they allowed the Taj Group, which had been managing the property, to continue running the hotel. In this case, the management and the brand are same.

Or take a case like the Westin in Gurgaon. The hotel was developed by the real estate group Vatika. The management company is Marriott, which acquired the Westin brand through its acquisition of Starwood Hotels and Resorts. Westin is just one of over thirty brands that Marriott has in its portfolio. This is one of the most common structures in which many of the branded hotels in India operate.

But there can be other models. For instance, the Radisson Blu in Noida is owned by the Malhotras of the MBD Group, which is into everything from publishing to real estate. The brand belongs to the American Radisson Group but Radisson does not manage the hotel. It is managed by the owners themselves as the model is a franchised one. Radisson in return gets a brand licence fee. If it were to manage the hotel, it would get a management fee as well, increasing its margins.[3]

Several of the Ramada hotels in India also operate on the franchise model. Wyndham, the owner of the Ramada brand, has just licensed the users to fly the Ramada flag. In the manchise model, a company has the management as well as the franchise.

Till the early 1990s, the structure of India's hotel industry was fairly straightforward. There was an owner, there was a manager and the brand. But in the majority of cases, the hotel owner simply ran the hotel without a brand.

Today, there are many different models and several layers of complexity to the hotel business and different kinds of partnerships.

Former McKinsey consultant-turned-entrepreneur Siddharth Gupta, who runs Treebo Hotels, a tech-based budget chain in India started in 2015, says that there are today five-and-a-half hotel models—OLMFD (Owned, Leased, Managed, Franchised or Distributed). Many hotels are actually not owned but leased for ninety-nine years or less. When they enter into these leases, people assume the lease will be extended for eternity but that's not the case as seen with the Taj Mahal Hotel on Mansingh Road in New Delhi.

The Taj Mansingh, as it is better known, one of the most prestigious hotels for the Indian Hotels Group Limited (IHCL)—better known as the Taj Group—got a rude shock when the government decided to auction the lease rather than allow it to be renewed automatically. After much drama and prolonged suspense, the Taj managed to retain the hotel.

Distribution is also becoming a big game-changer today. There may be boutique hotels that are run and branded by the owner, but it could have tie-ups for distribution. For instance, the Suryagarh Fort in Jaisalmer owned by the MRS Group has a tie up with Preferred Hotels & Resorts, a referral organization for hotels.[4]

Between the hotel owner and the manager is a broker—the consultant who lines up suitors and arranges the marriage. Consultants are now called in for valuations, asset management, sale and financing of hotels, and advise on a host of other matters.

Then there are lawyers who read the fine print and advise what should be on the contract and what not. Typically, a management contract is drawn up for fifteen to twenty years, though the deal can sour quickly and break up, or continue for a good hundred years if the relationship is nurtured.

There are at any given point several distressed hotel assets across the country whose owners are selling out and new investors buying in. In the old days, the buy-and-sell game was between high-net-worth individuals (HNWIs) or a hotel company such as ITC or Oberoi.

In recent times, there are few industrialists with the spare cash to buy hotel assets. Hotel companies want to follow an asset-light strategy. But luckily institutional investors have entered the fray. According to hotel consulting firm HVS, over $200 million of assets were bought and sold in 2015 by institutional equity. This means that a host of players such as Goldman Sachs, Warburg Pincus and APG Asset Management have a play in India's hotel industry. Over 30 per cent of the new hotel rooms being developed in India in fact have institutional capital—which shows a maturing of the market. Not surprisingly, institutional advisory firms are making hay in this sector.

In the twenty-first century, hotel-managing companies themselves come in a bewildering array of sizes and shapes. There are established hoteliers with decades of experience who run management companies but there are also a slew of start-ups, with no background in hospitality, who think they can manage things better than the old warriors.

Young entrepreneur Ritesh Agarwal's OYO, which in next to no time has become the largest hotel chain in India by the sheer number of rooms it has branded, is a famous example. But there are also many other first-time hoteliers like Gaurav Jain, an ex-McKinsey man who quit his consultancy job because he believed he had spotted a gap and set up Aamod Resorts; Siddharth Gupta, again ex-McKinsey, of Treebo Hotels; Prashanth Aroor of Intellistay; and Shruti Shibulal, daughter of Infosys founder S.D. Shibulal.

There are also several allied players who have had an important role in shaping the course of the hospitality industry. The biggest change-makers have been online travel agents, who have altered the equation and, many believe, caused the first disruption of the digital age by giving an equal playing field to smaller hotels. Additionally, technology companies such as Praxis provide reservation management systems and other software to hotels. There are reputation-managing companies, which are increasingly playing a bigger role now that social media can make or break a hotel's reputation. There are spa players who are taking over the management of spas inside hotels—and spas are becoming increasingly important for hotels to have. And there are the talent providers—a host of manpower agencies as well as hospitality training schools. The Indian School of Hospitality, former managing director of Starwood Hotels South Asia Dilip Puri's state-of-the-art new school for aspiring hoteliers, could be a positive game-changer for the industry.

According to the India Brand Equity Foundation, India's gargantuan hotel industry and tourism together is worth US$234.03 billion based on the 2017 figures, and is expected to touch US$492.21 billion in 2028. The Indian Hotel Industry Survey 2016–17 by Hotelivate and the Federation of Hotel & Restaurant Association of India, estimates that the Indian hotel industry will be worth US$13 billion by 2020, of which US$4 billion is the online value.[5]

The Grand Old Warriors

The badshahs of Indian hospitality, the Taj, the ITC and the Oberoi—often called the Big Three—have dominated the landscape for decades, with the over-100-year-old Taj having a significant market share in the branded-hotel segment. The Taj and Oberoi are iconic global brands, but their names no longer command the premium and undying loyalty they once did. Instead, post-2000, each of these players has had to work hard to stay relevant in a world where the customer has plenty of choice and is fickle.

To be fair, the Taj has tried several new things, taking some risks and changing strategies. Will its experiments pay off? The Oberoi on the surface looks aloof and impervious to the changes, but there's a lot going on inside. As for ITC, it has boldly taken some big bets on new positioning like sustainability and responsible luxury.

With regard to chains, the Leela Palaces Hotels and Resorts, the Lalit and The Park are the other old Indian sultans in the fray, desperately reinventing to stay in the game. The former, struggling with debt and having to sell out stake,[6] still has a strong brand name while the latter two have found some unique touch points. Some lesser-known warriors in the country—chains such as Clarks— have had their following in small pockets but never had the scale to make an impact. Some are trying new things, while others are giving up and handing over the keys to management companies. There are also the old boutique properties that have stayed single but provide exemplary hospitality, resisting being part of a chain, such as the Imperial in Delhi.

The Professional Turned Entrepreneur

As in every profession, some career hoteliers have decided to chart their own destinies. After serving with one chain or another, rising through the kitchens and front offices, these serious-minded entrepreneurs with years of operational experience have managed to spot a gap and carve their own empires. To name a few, Patu Keswani, who after years at the Taj Group founded Lemon Tree; Anil Madhok, who learnt the tricks of the trade at the Oberoi and started Sarovar; and Param Kannampilly, who gathered experience at the Taj and the Leela before launching his Concept Hospitality, with the Fern brand of hotels. There is also Kapil Chopra, former Oberoi president, who is bravely trying to reinvent the luxury space with the Postcard Hotels and Resorts, an intimate collection of properties. After years and years of experience in the trenches, they have a pulse on what the customer needs, and the ability to be fleet-footed.

Meanwhile, another set of entrepreneurs have also emerged who have hotel blood coursing through their veins and have inherited the industry knowledge from their fathers. These are inheritors such as Jose Dominic of CGH Earth and Chender Baljee of Royal Orchid, who gave a new direction to their family business. Dominic, in fact, took a radically new tack and has been one of the big innovators in Indian hospitality.

The Regional Satraps

Every region in the country has had its own regional boss who knows the terrain well and set up a hotel to fill the gap and cater to the local people. They could be running small hotels or big hotels but they have been content to remain in their state or region—take the Residency Group of Hotels in Tamil Nadu set up by Rishi Real Estates. Or take Polo Towers in Shillong or the Green Park chain from Andhra Pradesh. Or Mayfair in the Northeast, the Grand Dragon in Leh or the Kamats in Maharashtra and the Konkan. They have their own identity, are entrenched in their areas and have withstood competition from the big boys, some even taking them on at their own game as the Kamats have done. But how long can they sustain themselves?

The Global Goliaths

Hilton, Hyatt, InterContinental Hotel Group (IHG), Accor, Marriott, Carlson Rezidor and Wyndham are the foreign brands that have mounted a successful invasion with their branding power and global reach. Though they have deep pockets, they prefer the asset-light route to expansion and partnering with Indian builders. After initial mistakes of trying to replicate their global models here, they learnt the hard way that domestic the Indian traveller has unique demands. To their credit they researched and came up with specially tweaked models for India, and now actually are outgunning the Indian chains in terms of growth. The second-rung global players have also entered India now, making it a crowded battlefield. According to the India Brand Equity Foundation, the international hotel chains together accounted for a 47 per cent market in India in 2018 and this is likely to shoot up to 50 per cent by 2022. We owe our legacy of hotels to the British and Swiss who were the first to set up here, but it's the American chains that are the most successful today.

The HNW Hotel-Owner

Till a few years ago, hotels in India were built by HNWIs and family offices as a way of deploying their surplus funds and creating long-term assets for the family. Occasionally, there were business compulsions. For instance, if a businessman running a successful enterprise in a tier-two or tier-three town had visitors to their facility and needed a good hotel to put them up, in the absence of such a hotel, he would set it up. A large number of politicians would build hotels as a place to park some of their wealth. Some wealthy individuals built hotels out of sheer boredom or just to flaunt an asset or to indulge a family member and so on.

In recent times, however, with a slowdown in business cycles in general and the crackdown on black money, investible surplus has come down significantly and there are fewer such hotel owners. People today are more hard-nosed about a hotel, expecting returns. Though, of course, political connection will never go away if you see the Oberoi Sukh Vilas in Mohali, owned by the family of former Punjab chief minister Parkash Singh Badal.[7] In smaller towns particularly, the local MLA will often have a hotel tucked away.

The Real-Estate Owner

The Rahejas, the Chordias, the Bhallas of the Vatika group, the Brigade group in the south, the Singh family of DLF and the Ambience group are all into hospitality in an organized way. The synergies between real-estate play and hotels are undeniable. They could also combine with a mall or an office complex. Though many are serious players and have proper verticals to run them in a structured way, many also have their eye on the main chance, with their exit strategies firmly in place as this is just another buy-and-sell real estate play for them, with a profit motive.

The Asset Player

Many players who work in related areas such as travel trade and entertainment and the land banks have recently got into hotels. Examples are Ankur Bhatia of the Bird Group, the Sharmas of the Kuoni/Tui travel group and Southern Travels set up by the Raos. They have the linkages to smartly tap into the opportunity.

The Unhoteliers

Entrepreneurs with no background in hospitality who have jumped into the fray as they think there is a gap that the veteran players have not addressed include Ritesh Agarwal of OYO, Gaurav Jain of Aamod, Aditi Balbir of V Resorts, and Prashant Aroor of Intellistay. This new breed of hoteliers have the chutzpah and confidence to venture into this turf and the good news is that they have backing from venture capital and private equity players.

The Canny Consultants

Deal brokers marrying brands to hotels, negotiating contracts, advising pull-outs or doing audits is a category that was pioneered in the early days by the Daves—A.K. Dave and his son Uttam—but today, a host of companies such as HVS, Horwarth and Hotelivate founded by the enterprising Manav Thadani continually add new skills and competencies to advise hoteliers. In addition, several real-estate consultancies such as CBRE that have hospitality verticals as well as facilities and asset management arms are in the game.

The Institutional Investors

Institutional capital has begun to play an increasingly larger role in India's hotel industry. Goldman Sachs backs SAMHI,

Amsterdam-based pension fund APG backs Lemon Tree, Berggruen runs Keys Hotels, the Xander Group pumps in investments in hospitality, and Duet India Hotels has been formed by a JV between the hospitality arm of the asset manager Duet Group with IHG.

Whether institutional capital leads to better-run hotels is still debatable since the Keys experiment has had mixed results and IHG has exited the JV with Duet.

The Government

India Tourism Development Corporation (ITDC) and various state tourism departments and bodies like the Hotel Corporation of India (HCI) had an important role in the growth of the hotel sector in India. To them goes the credit of creating supply when the country had a serious dearth of hotel rooms, and opening up remote destinations. They may be in divestment mode currently and run their properties rather lackadaisically but there are some jewels in their crown—such as the Ashok in Delhi.

The government can also be disruptors in another way, especially in India. They can make the operating climate completely unviable by creating strange rules. Demonetization, the strange slabs in Goods and Services Tax (GST) and the liquor ban have all impacted the hotel industry. The government can just alter the status quo by a simple thing like not renewing a lease automatically or by suddenly opening up a new market.

To illustrate this, take the story of a chief minister of a north Indian state, who took the CEOs of the top six hotel chains on a helicopter ride to show a new scenic site, which he said he wanted to develop as a destination. He wanted the hoteliers to commit to an investment there. The hoteliers asked what if he did not return to power. The chief minister's replied that he had worked it out with the opposition as well.

The Heritage Set

When the erstwhile princes of India lost their purses and their kingdoms, some converted their forts, palaces and lodges into hotels. But not just the maharajas and rajas, minor feudal lords and zamindars have also turned their sprawling estates into hotels.

The Taj Hotels really tapped into this opportunity with its palace hotels. But it was creative duo Aman Nath and Francis Wacziarg who really started the big trend when they restored and nurtured a decrepit fort Neemrana into a thriving hotel. The Indian Heritage Hotels Association (IHHA), with membership from Rajasthan to Sikkim, is a body formed to discuss the problems and issues of heritage hotels.

The Digital Disruptors

Online travel agents such as MakeMyTrip, Cleartrip, Yatra and Booking.com that blazed into the digital landscape completely disrupted the hotel industry. They changed the way people chose hotels and booked and created a level playing field for unknown hotels that had no distribution muscle. Thanks to them, a small single-hotel company can now get 100 per cent occupancy while hotel chains with deep distribution networks may struggle to fill up rooms.

The Adjacencies

The hotel industry depends on a lot of adjacencies. Many an entrepreneur has become a millionaire by becoming vendors to the hotel industry—providing talent, software, supplying uniforms, managing spas, providing food solutions, doing event management and so on. At consumer durable companies, there are whole business divisions that look at the needs of hoteliers. For instance, Samsung has air conditioner solutions especially created for hospitality.

2

All Keyed Up—Setting the Context

'Room service? Send up a larger room.'

—Groucho Marx in *A Night at the Opera*

The energy and enthusiasm at the Mumbai office of Prashant Aroor, CEO of Intellistay Hotels, which owns the Mango, Apodis and iStay brands, is infectious. Despite the sultry heat—it's an afternoon in April 2016—his young assistants, Neha Bhatia, who looks after marketing, and Salim Shaikh, a project manager, are raring to get out of the air-conditioned office and see how iStay, a hotel their company has renovated, has shaped up. They want to take pictures to post on social media as well as for the launch conference that is due soon. Aroor urges me to go along with them, the pride in his voice palpable as he shows me a set of before and after pictures of the property.

The team at Intellistay Hotels has just transformed an old, unprepossessing budget stay called the Traveller's Inn in

Mumbai's Andheri district into a cheerful contemporary hotel with bright yellow walls. The old dorms of this railway hotel from where you had to traipse past the reception to access the bathrooms have been refurbished with smart TVs and smart locks. Now, the bathrooms are adjacent to the dorms. The renovated hotel has coworking spaces, a restaurant with wifi, graffiti on the walls and other trappings to attract the millennial traveller. Lovely magazine racks and plants lend an inviting touch.

Young Ebrahim Balwa, whose family owns the iStay hotel—they also own the Grand Hyatt in Goa and another property in Mumbai—describes how the value additions by the management company Intellistay have helped him scale up the prices of both the dorms as well as single rooms without worrying about occupancies being affected.

Aroor, who is now operating hotels for people like Balwa, has no background in hoteliering. His family, from Mangalore was in the transportation business and he founded a hotel management company because he spotted a gap in the room utilization model of many buildings. Luckily for him, his ideas resonated with a HNWI, who invested in his firm.

Not far from Aroor's office in Teligali, Andheri, a new ten-storey Ginger Hotel, with 142 rooms, has come up. Ginger is the Taj Group's budget offering and has been seeing many reinventions. The second floor of this hotel is reserved for solo women travellers. Unlike other hotel receptions, this hotel has a red-brick-walled coffee counter that doubles up as the check-in counter. You can literally grab a coffee as you are being checked into your room.

I am taken around by Rahul Pandit, at the time the managing director of Roots Corporation, the Tata company that runs the Ginger brand of hotels (Pandit has since quit the company). Pandit put all his energies into ensuring Version Next of the Tata Group's budget hotel offering is in tune with what young business travellers want.

The reception area has low networking tables and benches that are ideal to park your laptop on and work. A well-equipped gym has a Power Mill, which has the pride of place along with an elevated treadmill with steps, which general manager Arif Asmath thinks is the first in any hotel—it was set up after researching the exercise habits of Ginger guests.

A month before the hotel opened, Pandit, an old Taj hand and former president of Lemon Tree hotels, shifted his office to one of the conference rooms, supervising every tiny detail. For Ginger, one of the early entrants to the branded budget hotel category in India but which subsequently lost the plot, there's a lot riding on the new crop of hotels it is setting up. Pandit has even changed the uniforms of all Ginger employees to smarten up the brand.

Subsequently, in just two years, Ginger went through yet another iteration, showing how quickly the market keeps changing. But that's a story for later in the book.

Close to this Ginger, also in Andheri, is the office of Param Kannampily, the entrepreneur behind another exciting mid-market brand, Fern Hotels, which has taken a unique green positioning, setting up earth- and climate-friendly hotels. Concept Hospitality, the company he runs, has brands Beacon and Zinc in its portfolio as well. Kannampily describes how he spends the bulk of his time meeting new hotel builders from small towns like Dhapoli, Sholapur, Karjat and Satara in Maharashtra. His son is also part of the company and managing several aspects. He excitedly talks about how twenty-seven new hotels mostly in tier-three towns will be managed by Concept Hospitality, in which Nepal's billionaire Binod Chaudhary's company CG Corp has a stake. Zinc is a CG Corp brand that has now been added to the Concept mix.

Binod Chaudhary has a big play in Indian hospitality since he has a joint venture with the Taj Group as well, and is growing his group's presence in the country through strategic partnerships. His group has also created a hospitality fund to finance new hotel projects. Riding on Chaudhary's assets, the Taj has managed to grow its presence in places like the Maldives, Dubai, Nepal and Sri Lanka.

Coming back to the hotel development scene in India, it's not just Mumbai that's seeing a frenzy of action in the hotel space. Travel to the southern tip of India to the seaside town of Rameshwaram that boasts the magnificent temple with 1000 pillars, and a Hyatt Place proudly greets visitors.

Though Rameshwaram has a fabulous pull for tourists and pilgrims, it lacked good hotels. Most people would stay at Madurai and do a day trip to Rameshwaram. Kurt Straub, the Swiss hotelier who oversaw Hyatt's India operations till November 2017, describes how the chain is pushing into cities where even many Indian brands have been reluctant to enter.

Head to the ancient central Indian holy town of Ujjain, where time has great significance—*Mahakaal*, the god of time, is the ruling deity here—and a slew of new resorts greets your eyes. Most of these came up just before the 2016 Sinhasth Kumbh Mela, the largest congregation of Hindu pilgrims. Hotel Atharva, with amenities that can match with any branded hotel, stands out. The ladies of the city meet for kitty parties here even as well-heeled pilgrims are delighted by the high-speed wifi and special help the hotel extends in arranging night-trips to the majestic Mahakaleshwar Temple. Before these hotels came up, most comfort-loving tourists would stay at Indore and do a day trip to Ujjain. The hotels are independent properties, not affiliated to any brands. But they could one day become part of a chain, as development teams from the big hotel groups pursue every good opportunity they see to convert properties into their brands.

Opportunities are opening up everywhere in India. Take, for instance, Vijayawada, a sleepy town in Andhra Pradesh. When the old Andhra Pradesh state was carved into two, Telengana and Andhra Pradesh, Vijayawada suddenly became a busy town because of its proximity to the new capital city of Andhra Pradesh, Amaravati. In December 2018, a Novotel built by the Rs 4500-crore Varun Group and managed by Accor launched in Vijayawada. The then chief minister of Andhra Pradesh N. Chandrababu Naidu himself cut the ribbon of the hotel, watched by French ambassador to India Alexandre Ziegler.

Is it unusual for a chief minister to launch a hotel? Not really, especially when hotels are seen to be closely intertwined with growth in a new state.

'I want to see a lakh hotel rooms in Andhra Pradesh,' said N. Chandrababu Naidu as he formally launched the 227-key five-star Novotel Hotel. Local businessmen said they were willing to take the plunge and would invest in hotel projects.

All over India, hotels in all sizes and shapes—big 500-key business hotels, medium-sized 250-key properties, boutique leisure resorts and well-equipped budget stays—are coming up at a fast and furious pace, providing good accommodation in places that hitherto lacked decent options. Some are ritzy five-star edifices, others more modest, some are new properties and others are old structures that have been renovated and modernized.

Since the early 2000s, fuelled by booming economic growth in India—a result of India's liberalization programme—there has been a huge spike in building hotels. There's also been a lot of renovation and upgrading going on, with owners of dated looking hotels redoing their properties in a bid to stay relevant and offer more amenities than the hotel across the road. What's common to all is that they all have decent bed, baths, broadband and breakfast, the four products that the discerning traveller of today seeks. Competition is intense, almost insane. The old warriors of hospitality must be ruing the chances they missed.

Changing India

For many in India who grew up during the 1970s and 1980s, all this comes as a sea change. That was a time when the Indian traveller did not have a decent room to stay in. The only hotels were either poky places with poor hygiene or grand five-stars run by the likes of the Taj or the Oberoi, which were unaffordable. So, there was nowhere decent and affordable really that the large middle-class of this country could stay in. As a result, most travellers opted to stay with families and friends or in state-run tourist homes. If you had connections in the government, you would stay at Public Works Department (PWD) guest houses.

Deep Kalra, the suave founder of India's largest online travel agency MakeMyTrip, which is helping Indians discover many gems of hotels in unexpected places, recounts family holidays as a kid staying in government dak bungalows because these were the best places to stay in for a middle-class family. Even when he joined his first job at ABN Amro, he recalled a trip to Goa, where he stayed at a beautiful house that his bank arranged—it turned out to be film director Shyam Benegal's property. Today, his online travel agency is helping Indians find good and affordable hotels to stay, and for a brief while even experimented with homestay options through its brand Right Stay.

According to Pran Nath Seth in his book *Successful Tourism: Tourism Practices*, in 1962 there were just 186 hotels across all star categories in India, with barely 7085 rooms between them. So severe was the shortage of the hotels that the government had to step in and build hotels all over the country.

Jyotsna Suri, chairperson of the Lalit Group, who spearheads industry association Federation of Indian Chambers of Commerce & Industry (FICCI) committee on tourism, says that the credit for the spread of hospitality in the country really goes to the government. They put up hotels in the areas that were underserved, she says, pointing to the role of both ITDC and the state tourism development corporations. She also points to how they bagged the best locations. Private players began opening up destinations much later.

Till the mid-2000s in fact, India's hospitality industry was fairly unorganized, with erratic supply. Look at the shift.

According to hotel consultancy firm Hospitality Valuation Services (HVS), in 1995–96, the supply of branded hotel rooms (those run by professional chains) in India was just 18,000 rooms spread over 120 hotels. In 2016, there were 887 hotels, with a room count of 1,13,622. In 2017, that figure zoomed to 1,19,219 rooms and projections are that another 45,000 rooms will be added in next to no time. According to rating agency Credit Analysis and Research Limited (CARE) Ratings, as of 31 March 2018, there were 1,28,163 branded rooms in the country, and about 50,000 rooms could be added by 2023. And these reports do not include several hotels that we might consider branded. OYO, for instance, which already has over 2,00,000 rooms across 300 cities in India and abroad, is classified in a different category.[1]

However, many in the industry regard any hotel inventory sold by an online travel agency as branded. So branded room inventory is probably three or four times the figure put out by HVS and CARE.

Industry estimates suggest that there are over a million unbranded rooms in India today. With 500 cities boasting over a lakh population, that's a conservative estimate, to say the least. And the opportunity size is tremendous.

In its 2019 report on India's hotel sector, Hotelivate, a consultancy founded by Manav Thadani, who was formerly with HVS, estimates that there were 2.72 million lodging rooms in India as of December 2018. This includes branded, unbranded and alternative accommodation. If you look at only pure branded supply, then the figure was only 1,30,000 rooms, according to the Hotelivate report. Its projection is that by 2023 there will be over 3.33 million rooms in India.

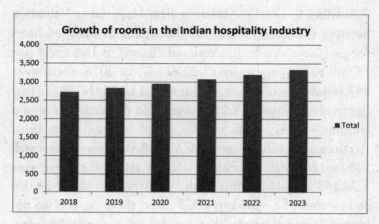

Source: The Ultimate Indian Travel & Hospitality Report: Hotelivate in association with Centre for Asia Pacific Aviation (CAPA) and World Travel and Tourism Council (WTTC)

Aditi Balbir, the founder of V Resorts, a resorts management company funded by private equity, and one of the bright young people who have entered the hoteliering arena, has worked out an ingenious method of calculating the potential. She points out that there are 6,40,867 destinations in India if you look at the number of villages and towns here. Even if you take just two hotels in each destination and multiply by an average of five rooms, that translates into over a million new rooms.

It's the Holy Grail to have a decent hotel room in every single village of India. And Balbir thinks it's not an impossible dream.

So, who are these people who could help India achieve this dream?

In the old days, only a small circle of people—the government, with its ITDC and state tourist corporations, industrialists, hotel companies, businessmen with spare cash, politicians, or real estate people—would set up hotels. In today's liberalized India, just about anyone is providing great lodging.

Ever since Airbnb made homestays fashionable, people like you and me who have a spare room suddenly have a stake in the hospitality and lodgings business in India. But even if you leave out homestays and alternative accommodations, a diverse spectrum of people make up the tourism and hospitality industry, that is getting bigger and bigger, and contributes nearly 9.2 per cent (US$247 billion) to India's GDP.[2]

Industrialists like the Munjals of the Hero Group are taking a plunge, with Marriott as partners. People like Virender Bhatia, an apparel exporter-turned-realtor who runs the Baani Group, have jumped headlong into hospitality. Bhatia has handed over the keys of his Gurgaon property to the Hilton to manage.

'I could have created my own brand or gone with one of the top three hotel brands in the world. In business, there is no need to reinvent the wheel,' said Bhatia, who was advised by veteran hospitality consultant Vijay Thackar of Horwath Consultants, Mumbai.

In south India, businessman Vijayawada-based Prabhu Kishore, owner of the mid-sized Varun Group, which is into auto dealerships and financing, chose to diversify into hospitality because that gave him visibility that his auto business did not.

Scions of zamindars and minor royals are converting their estates into hotels. Children of hoteliers are starting their own independent hotel ventures as, for instance, the sons of Royal Orchid's Chender Baljee, Keshav and Arjun. Rajat Pahwa, whose family arrived in Delhi from Lahore post-Partition and ran guest houses, now runs several hotels and is eager to get them branded.

Anybody with a parcel of land, some spare cash or a beautiful property seems to be building a hotel or converting their asset into one. And more often than not, they prefer to go with a foreign brand name on their signboards to attract the discerning new Indian traveller and get the distribution advantage. Not surprisingly, foreign hotel management brands such as Marriott, Accor (which owns the Novotel, Ibis and Pullman brands), Hilton, Wyndham (which has the Ramada brand), Hyatt and the IHG are all making hay.

Meanwhile, the old Indian warriors like the Taj, the ITC, the Oberoi, the Lalit and The Park are not sitting still. Faced with foreign competition and a new breed of demanding consumers who want more and more value out of their hotel stay, they are restrategizing. The venerable Oberoi shut down one of its prime properties, its flagship hotel in central Delhi, for nearly two years to rebuild it. Similarly, the Taj ruthlessly looked at all its assets and dropped those that it thought wouldn't fit into its brand portfolio. Tough times call for tough measures.

Add to this melange—and in some ways being a disruptive force—a rising crop of fleet-footed new Indian hotel companies such as Lemon Tree, Sarovar, Pride Hotels, Lords Hotels & Inns, Fern, Royal Orchid and Intellistay, each bringing a unique selling proposition to their hospitality offerings.

None more so than young Ritesh Agarwal of OYO, a twenty-something who came blazing into the hotel arena with the promise of offering a dignified stay to the masses. Like Aroor, he has no heritage in hoteliering but entered through a disruptive technology platform that aggregated rooms from mom-and-pop hotels all around the country. When he realized the drawback of the model, he pivoted fast and shifted to a franchise-managed model. OYO's stupendous growth spawned at least thirty-two similar companies, throwing pricing out of gear.

Disruption in the Air

If an OYO can offer rooms at Rs 999, then a Ginger or a Keys have to bring down their prices, impacting those above such as Lemon Tree and Ibis and so on, affecting the whole chain. The result is that formerly unaffordable five-star hotels are getting within the reach of the common man.

But as they come within reach, the five stars need to up their game to make them the exclusive preserve of the elite. Altogether, it has become a hard balancing game for them. Is it any surprise that traditional hoteliers regard OYO with great hostility and Ritesh as a young upstart?

And, mind you, OYO is not the only one—there are others like Treebo and Fab Hotels, which are all trying out new ways of managing hotels. They are not above breaking some of the stiff starchy traditions that have held hoteliers back as, for example, starting pet-friendly hotels, becoming flexible with check-in time and using apps to manage stays.

But are OYO and its peers the big disruptors of Indian hospitality? Views are mixed. Talk to the old hoteliers and they say the biggest disruptors have been the online travel agents—

MakeMyTrip, Yatra, Cleartrip, and now global players like Booking.com and Skyscanner, which have all started listing mom-and-pop hotels on their site. Online travel agents have put reach, distribution and power in the hands of small hoteliers who can now compete with the big boys.

This means a hotel with no website, which was earlier no competition for the big chains, becomes a competitor.

Also, several interesting tech start-ups—like Djubo and Hotelogix—which have property management systems have helped empower independent hotels. They help small hotels plan their rates and automate operations so that they can compete against larger chains. The balance of power which so far was residing with big chains thanks to their distribution muscle is therefore shifting.

Hoteliers believe that the biggest disruptors are yet to come. There's blockchain, threatening to change the distribution systems of hotels, before which small tech-players such as 6hourly.com came in offering innovations such as hotel rooms for a few hours—instead of nights, you could book a room for an hour or two. Imagine what this will do to the housekeeping department of a hotel as beds will have to be made every few hours instead of once a day.

Hotels cannot have any fixed rules or systems anymore. Flexibility is the need of the hour. Formats may have to be changed, processes overturned. But are they ready to change? Again, OYO has been showing the way, offering features like flexi check-in, allowing unmarried couples to stay at its hotels and creating women-only hotels, thereby expanding the market, while for the big hotels these are all strict no-nos.

Some of them have bowed down to the inevitable though and are becoming more flexible.

Even if the big hotels do change, this is one sector that is particularly prone to external shocks. In 2016 and 2017, just as the sector was in recovery mode, three big shocks were administered. The first was Demonetization. In November 2016, when Prime Minister Narendra Modi made this shocking move, changing India's currency, it affected hotels significantly. For three months, business slowed down. Then came a bigger whammy—a liquor ban on highways. Enforced on 1 April 2017, this baffling judgement by the Supreme Court affected hundreds of hotels located near these roads.[3] There were reports of hotel room rates dipping to ridiculous levels—a lavish five-start property like ITC Chola in Chennai was offering rooms at unthinkably low rates because of unavailability of liquor. Hotels in Tamil Nadu in particular were badly affected as the state took five months to denotify highways—Haryana and Maharashtra were very quick to do this as a way to get around the ban—resulting in very poor patronage by guests in the first half of 2017.

Then came the introduction of the GST, with its myriad implementation problems even if it will be good for the industry in the long run.

JB Singh of Interglobe Hotels, the joint venture that manages Ibis Hotels in India, points out that when GST was implemented, it was a nightmare for hotels as it impacted their investments. It was applied on a broad basis, and cost of construction went up by 10 per cent. He points out that for a chain like Ibis, which worked hard to bring its building costs down, GST came along and bumped it all over again. What it did to them is their return on capital went down by 1 per cent.

Despite all these troubles and challenges, hoteliers are still optimistic about the opportunity this sector offers. According to a report by KPMG and FCM Travel Solutions, business travel spending in India is expected to touch US$90 billion by 2030 by when the country will be ranked among the top five business travel market globally.[4] Is it any wonder that everybody wants to set up or manage a hotel? Or set up an adjacent enterprise around the hospitality enterprise catering to hotels—a spa business or a food supply business.

What caused the spectacular rise in supply? And as supply increases, how will traditional hoteliers, who were kings of their turf, stay afloat with discounting wars? More importantly, how are hotels evolving with the new guest profile? Today's hotel guest is a value seeker, wants the best of the best facilities and, spoilt for choice, is becoming fickle. How will hoteliers command loyalty from such guests?

What will the entry of so many players do to the dynamics of the industry? There will be consolidation for sure. But there is already a pressure on rates. How will hoteliers cope? We are already seeing job cuts. Hotels are now getting one person to do the work that two people used to do earlier. Room-to-staff ratio, which in the good old days used to be 1:3, is now dipping to 1:1 and may even go down to 0.5. This puts pressure on talent. How will the hotel industry deal with it?

Even as this book was being conceived, there was a whole new set of disruptions such as the global merger of Marriott and Starwood, two of the biggest hotel chains in the world, in a US$12.2 billion deal. Together they will control over

1.1 million hotel rooms over the world, and in India they have become a fearsome force as well.

In India, a big consolidation that has happened is mid-market warrior Sarovar selling out to French chain Louvre, which incidentally has a Chinese owner. Several such deals will happen. India is woefully short of hotel rooms by everyone's reckoning. And yet, there's not enough room for every player. Big brands like Premier Inn entered India and had to bite dust and go back.[5] Lebua from Bangkok, which launched in India in 2012–13, found the going rough and had to exit a hotel deal in Delhi's Dwarka area, reportedly over a difference with the owner.[6] Another Asian chain Banyan Tree too had a traumatic entry in India when its luxury resort in Kerala faced demolition even before opening.[7] French hotel chain Accor had to make three sorties before it got its India story right.[8] Even legacy hoteliers with home-turf advantage such as the Oberois and the Taj Group have had to go back to the drawing table to find new strategies to cope. The Leela Group has already crumbled under its debts and with financial institutions (FIs) picking up stake, it is a matter of time that consolidation happens—although industry insiders feel that the brand is strong enough to survive, whoever be the owner.[9]

Traditionally, the hotel industry in India has operated more on sentiment. Emotions and ego have driven projects and development, rather than cold logic. This means that financial viability goes for a toss. While emotions continue to play a big role in making decisions, there is some change in this aspect as well.

Read on for the action-packed happenings in India's exciting hospitality industry.

3

Laying the Foundation—History and Evolution

'As the bellhop closes the door behind him, you are left with a feeling of security and relaxation. Your mind starts to drift, and you wonder to yourself, who else has stayed in this room?'

—Ann Benjamin, Room 702

If only the walls of hotels could speak, there would be so many rich tales to carry forward. The Imperial in Delhi—which opened its doors in the 1930s on Queensway, now called Janpath—was a place where the subcontinent's history was shaped. It was in this impressive regal building that Pandit Nehru, Mahatma Gandhi, Muhammad Ali Jinnah and Lord Mountbatten met to discuss the partition of India and the creation of Pakistan.

The Imperial still stands in stately splendour, proudly showcasing its colonial legacy and heritage, notably through its Victorian, colonial and art deco interiors, the paintings and photographs on its wall and little details such as the menu in its coffee shop, 1911.

The story goes that Lady Willingdon personally supervised the interiors, deciding things like carpets, cutlery, chandeliers and even the lion insignia of the hotel. The hotel was inaugurated in 1936 by Lord Willingdon in the presence of 15,000 guests at a grand ball—a huge event in Delhi's social scene then, which goes to show how important a hotel opening was in those days.

At the Savoy in Mussoorie, the walls may not have spoken but the queen of crime Agatha Christie's very first detective novel was inspired by an incident at the hotel, which is now run by the tobacco and biscuits giant ITC.

In 1911, a forty-nine-year-old spiritualist Frances Garnett Orme came to stay at the Savoy with her companion from Lucknow, Eva Mounstephen. Soon after Eva returned to Lucknow, Frances was found one morning mysteriously dead in her room, which was locked from inside. The autopsy revealed she had been poisoned with prussic acid. The case created a huge ripple and Eva even got arrested but nothing could be proven. Author Rudyard Kipling was apparently so fascinated by the case (though he had left India by then) that he wrote to Sir Arthur Conan Doyle suggesting he write a story on how a murder could be inspired by suggestion. The creator of Sherlock Holmes in turn passed the story on to Agatha Christie and that's how *The Mysterious Affair at Styles* came to be written. At least so the story goes. The incident also inspired Ruskin Bond's *A Crystal Ball—A Mussoorie Mystery*.

If the Savoy in Mussoorie inspired some lovely detective stories, then Kolkata's Great Eastern India's oldest existing

hotel, established in the 1840s and now run by the Lalit
Group, was the muse behind one of the finest pieces of
Bengali literature. Shankar's *Chowringhee*, a timeless classic,
which is based on the goings-on in a hotel, is peopled with
memorable characters from businessmen to bartenders,
showgirls to snooty memsahibs, and cooks to receptionists,
bringing alive not just the property but Calcutta of the 1960s.

They say that nostalgia makes for a good host. It's so true.
One often visits hotels just to recall the good old days and get
charmed by the legends and stories provided the hotels are
smart enough to play them up. But there's a stronger reason
to delve into the history of hotels in India. As somebody said,
it's always good to know where we have been in order to know
where we are going.

Why did India's first hotel in Kolkata not survive, while
the second—the Great Eastern—has endured? Why did the
most luxurious hotel to come up in Mumbai—the Watson's
Hotel—fade away even as its competitor, the Taj, continues
to be ranked among the most famous hotels in India, if not
the world?

Delving into the history of hotels yields fascinating
insights. Sometimes location is a major factor in the destiny
of a hotel. When the market, say the business district or
the social scene, moves away to another part of town, it
spells doom for a hotel. Often it is the ownership and the
management of hotels that plays the role. The owner loses
interest, sells the property and goes off and it's never the same
again. Then there are hotels where the owner spent far too
much on the looks and interiors without paying too much
attention to service and ended up in trouble. We have many

such white elephants in India. And, sometimes, the political climate and fate plays a hand. For instance, during the Great Depression, several hotels in the West went bust. We saw that being played out in the recession in 2008 to 2014.

The Origins

In Europe and America, the precursor to the hotels were the inns and taverns. Or perhaps even the monasteries—especially in countries like Italy, which provided rooms to the travellers. In India, dharamshalas provided stay strictly on community lines to Hindu pilgrims. The Muslim equivalent was musafirkhanas while the Buddhists had their viharas. It is widely thought that in the olden days, hospitality was largely charitable.

However, Dr Kevin O. Gorman's book *The Origins of Hospitality and Tourism*, which studies charitable and monastic forms of hospitality, *serais* (an inn with a central courtyard typically found in central Asia) of the Mongol lands etc., finds that commercial hospitality existed as far back as nearly 4000 years ago.[1] Dr Gorman holds a doctorate in the history and philosophy of hospitality in the Greco-Roman World of Classical Antiquity, has studied forms of hospitality in various civilizations, and is the acclaimed expert on this subject.

According to him, laws existed concerning accommodation premises as far back as 1800 BC—these included diktats like burning alive women seen entering inns. He also talks about how Pompeii had several properties that could have been bars and restaurants or hotels, describing a hospitium excavated in the city that could have accommodated fifty guests and had a large secluded garden.

Moving on to the third century AD, he also highlights how a comprehensive system of caravan serais existed all across Iran and the Middle Eastern world, providing hospitality and care for pilgrims and merchants. [2]

From 1750 to 1825, English inns really set the trends when it came to providing boarding and lodging. Then there were the post-houses. Hotels as we know them started coming up in the 1800s. The advent of the railways in Britain affected the business of inns considerably.

Though many a fine hotel existed in England, and even in India, in the 1800s, the Victorian era edifices did not boast private baths. The first modern hotel of the world with a private bath and running water in every single room was by all accounts built by Edward Statler, who built the Statler Hotel in 1907 in Buffalo, New York.

India's First

Although the records are hazy, from what one can gather, the first-ever hotel in India was the Spence's in Kolkata, which was opened to the public in 1830 by John Spence. Many reckon that it could have been the first hotel in Asia as well. It stood where the Treasury Building, Accountants General Bengal, stands today.[3] Photographs of the building taken in 1851 by Fredrik Fiebig, a man who went about meticulously cataloguing monuments and people in India and Sri Lanka, show an imposing edifice with Gothic arches. Fiebig's pictures are beautifully archived at the British Library in London, where, incidentally, one can find so much distracting trivia about buildings in India—including the first-ever private building to have a lift—that it is hard to get any research done.

It's in this library that you find fascinating accounts of the Spence's Hotel which received many famous guests. Among them was Jules Verne, the author of *20,000 Leagues under the Sea*. Verne in his book *The Steam House* dated 1880 refers to the hotel when he writes, '. . . before dawn, on the morning of our start, I left the Spence's Hotel, one of the best in Calcutta, which I had made my residence ever since my arrival.'

Ten years after Spence's Hotel opened, the Auckland Hotel came up in Calcutta. An Englishman from the West Midlands county of Herefordshire, David Wilson, ran a bakery on that site. So successful was the bakery that he decided to set up a hotel as well, which he named after George Eden, First Earl of Auckland, who also served as governor general of India. The hotel opened with 100 rooms and a department store on the ground floor. In the 1860s, the hotel's name changed to the Great Eastern Hotel Wine and General Purveying Co. In 1915, it became the Great Eastern Hotel. Accounts from those days are hazy, but for a brief period of time, it was also called Wilson's Hotel.

It was a hangout for the East India Company's officers and even today, when you glance out of the Victorian wing of the hotel's windows, you will see much to your thrill a building sporting the name 'The East India Company'. In the mysterious, eccentric ways of Kolkata, somebody has preserved the board on the building, even as it houses some other offices. And now, the new owners are building exterior-facing retail stores in the hotel—things do have a lovely way of coming a full circle.

In 1883, the Great Eastern became the first hotel in India to be fully illuminated with electricity. A truly luxurious hotel, it hosted Queen Elizabeth II and several eminent writers including Rudyard Kipling who wrote in *The City of Dreadful Night*, 'a man could walk in at one end, buy a complete outfit, a wedding present or seeds for the garden, have an excellent meal, a burra peg (double) and if the barmaid was agreeable, walk out at the other end engaged to be married.'

American humourist Mark Twain called the Great Eastern 'the Jewel of the East'. But the glorious days could not go on forever of course, and once the British left, things changed. Over the course of the years, the Great Eastern changed many hands till the 1960s, when A.L. Bilimoria was the chairman; a legacy of his stint is a massive replica of a trophy cup that he got from Queen Elizabeth when his horse won a race. The trophy is beautifully displayed high up on one of the facades of the hotel.

Eventually the hotel was acquired by the West Bengal state government and managed by the state tourism department. As newer, fancier hotels came up, the Great Eastern went into terminal decline, but in an amazing turn of fortune was acquired by the Lalit Hotels (it was then called Bharat Hotels) and now has been lovingly restored to good health by its chairperson Jyotsna Suri.

When she bought it, she recalls that there were rats scurrying through the building and the emissary they had sent from Delhi to inspect the property came back in disgust, forbidding the Suris from buying it. But her mind was made up and she prevailed upon her husband, hotelier Lalit Suri, to bid for it. They acquired it in 2006.

In a tragic turn of events, Lalit Suri died a year later. But Jyotsna Suri made a special trip to Kolkata to reassure people that she was committed to the hotel and would get it opened one day. She fulfilled her promise admirably.

Today, the Great Eastern can claim the title of the oldest functioning hotel in Asia, even older than the Raffles in Singapore. It has been restored to its full glory and in a clever touch has been divided into three blocks. The original Edwardian and Victorian wings remain but a new contemporary block has been added in the middle (earlier this used to be a space for car park and so on). All the blocks are interconnected through corridors, and a basement car park created. A stay at the Great Eastern today is a bit like time travelling to the past—as you go through a quaint iron staircase to the Wilson Bakery, you learn that this narrow, circular staircase was reserved for natives. The grand staircase was allowed to be used only by the Whites.

Interestingly, in 2018, The Park Hotel has taken charge of the restored Denmark Tavern, established in 1786, which was a dwelling place for traders, clergy and travellers exploring Bengal. While it is not a typical hotel—it is far smaller and more intimate—if you go by the history books, it could be one of the oldest, branded hospitality-units. The Tavern was restored to its former glory by the Serampore initiative, a project by the National Museum of Denmark that has been documenting and preserving the cultural heritage of Frederichsnagore (today called Serampore), and handed over by the West Bengal government, which partly funded the restoration, to The Park Hotels to run. It's a handsome yellow and white building with a few suites and a cafe. [4]

A Gift from the British

During the colonial rule, everywhere the British went, they set about establishing marvellous hotels. Actually, we pretty much owe our hotels heritage to the comfort- and tradition-loving British, who set up hotels that conformed to their tastes in hill stations such as Matheran (The Rugby in 1876), Ooty (The Savoy), Simla, Mussoorie and in cities like Calcutta, Delhi, Madras and Bombay.

Many of the hotels have unbroken records. The Taj Connemara in Chennai, for instance, can trace its origins as a hotel to 1854, when it was called the Imperial Hotel and run by a gentleman named T. Somasundara Mudaly. The history of this hotel is fairly well-documented, in S. Muthiah's *The Tradition of Madras that is Chennai: The Taj Connemara*.

The Mudaliars acquired the property from one John Binny who bought it from the nawab of Arcot in 1799. It was renamed Albany in 1886 when it was leased to two other Mudaliar brothers, and re-established as the Connemara in 1890, named after the then Madras Governor Robert Bourke, Baron of Connemara (a place in western Ireland). There is a cheeky theory that it could have been renamed after Lady Connemara (who left her house in a huff after discovering her husband's extra-curricular activities and took refuge at the Albany).[5] It later came to be owned by the Spencer's retail chain.

In 1891, Eugene Oakshott, owner of Spencer's, which was then a little shop near Anna Circle, bought the hotel and its nine acres to build a showroom. Oakshott wanted to give Spencer's a facelift, so he decided to build one of Asia's biggest departmental store. In the 1930s, James Stiven, director of Spencer's, modernized the hotel, taking a good five years to do so. It sported an art-deco look when it was re-opened in 1937.

According to the first published tariff of the hotel, the cost of a room on single occupancy was Rs 10 with breakfast and that of a room with all meals was Rs 17.80.[6] A little while after the Connemara came up, in Mumbai, an architectural marvel of a hotel came up around 1867 or so. Watson's Hotel (actually Watson's Esplanade Hotel), was built in the Kala Ghoda area and was named after its owner John Watson.

Again, a treasure of details on this hotel can be found at the British Library in London, with reams of pages devoted just to the building plans alone. Believe it or not, this hotel was fabricated in England and shipped to India where it was constructed on site. Designed by the civil engineer Rowland Mason Ordish, who was associated with the St Pancras Station in London, the facade was very similar to many nineteenth-century buildings in England, such as the Crystal Palace in London.[7]

The main facade of the hotel featured wide open balconies on each floor that connected the guest rooms, which were built around an atrium, an arrangement like a courtyard. It boasted a sumptuous, top-lit ground-floor restaurant with attached billiard room, a first-floor dining saloon with another attached billiards room, and three upper storeys given over to 131 bedrooms and apartments, the uppermost of which were reserved for bachelors and quasi- single gentlemen.

Card rooms and billiards rooms were popular in hotels those days as were cabarets and these give an idea of what was trending in terms of entertainment. Actually, hotels often set the trends. For instance, on 7 July 1896, the Watson Hotel offered screenings of some of the Lumiere Brothers first films, including *Entry of Cinematographe*, *Arrival of a Train*, *The Sea Bath*, *A Demolition*, *Leaving the Factory* and *Ladies and Soldiers on Wheels* for the price of one rupee each. This was India's first taste of the moving image, just six months after their Paris debut. Of course, the screenings were for Europeans only.[8]

Although they may not have been private en suite baths, the hotel had over 120 baths fitted and at its peak outdid European levels of luxury. It also boasted India's first steam-powered lift. When it opened its doors, it was an exclusive Whites-only hotel, and very soon became the go-to place in the city. At its peak, Watson's hotel employed English waitresses in its restaurant and ballroom, inspiring a common joke at the time: If only Watson had imported the English weather as well. But to combat the heat, every room had a *punkahwallah*, an attendant who works a punkah. According to the accounts, each room also commanded breathtaking views across the harbours, bays and distant hills.

American novelist Mark Twain who stayed at Watson's during his India tour has some descriptions of the hotel in his book *Following the Equator*. Twain writes, 'The lobbies and halls were full of turbaned, and fez'd and embroidered, cap'd, and barefooted, and cotton-clad dark natives . . . in the dining room every man's own private native servant standing behind his chair, and dressed for a part in Arabian Nights.'

John Hudson Watson, who built the hotel, ran a successful drapery business in Bombay. His original plan for the building was to use it as additional office and showroom for his business. Somewhere along the line, he seems to have changed his plans, and he may have unwittingly helped in the creation of Mumbai's finest hotel.

The Start of an Indian Chain

A popular myth is that J.N. Tata built the Taj after he was denied entry to Watson's. However, many, including historian Sharada Dwivedi, dispute this legend and say that J.N. Tata built the hotel to elevate the city's image. Taj insiders say that the hotel got built because a newspaper editor complained to Tata that there were no good hotels in Bombay.

Whatever the reasons for Tata to build the hotel, it led to the foundations of Indian hospitality as we know it today. The Taj Mahal Hotel when it opened in 1903 had 400 rooms and was far grander than Watson's, with attractions like electric lifts, lights, bars, smoking rooms, an all-day dining restaurant and a hotel orchestra. It had American fans, German elevators, Turkish baths and English butlers. Lord Mountbatten gave his farewell speech from here and it was where India's Independence was celebrated, with Indo-French cuisine and cabaret.

The Gateway of India was only built two decades after the Taj Hotel came up. Till then it was the Taj's red-tiled Florentine Gothic dome that served as a beacon for ships coming into the harbour. In June 2017, the Taj Mahal Palace and Towers became India's first building to be trademarked for its architecture. Even grander than Watson's, it spelt the death knell for the Englishman's hotel venture.

In 1911, Watson's was savagely critiqued in the *Times of India*: 'Their majesties (King George V) will have to pass what we can only suppose is an experiment in garishness, Watson's Hotel, and that building is a good illustration of the dangers to which a sensitive public is exposed.'[9]

By 1920, Watson's had ceased to be a hotel. It had been renamed Mahendra Mansion and then in 1944, it was called Esplanade Mansion, subdivided and partitioned into small cubicles with independent access and let out on rent. Today, the fate of the building itself is uncertain, though there are plans to redevelop it.

Delhi Gets Going

When the Taj was opening in Mumbai in 1903, the same year saw the launch of the Maidens Metropolitan Hotel in Delhi, a lovely hotel in Civil Lines, with a sweeping driveway and European charm about it. The Civil Lines area was the hub of European-style hotels in the city until Lutyens Delhi came into being in 1911, and the Imperial was built in 1936. Englishman J. Maiden started the Maidens—he along with his brother had earlier run the Metropolitan Hotel from 1894 onwards in another location. The Maidens Metropolitan Hotel was the most expensive hotel in Delhi in the early 1900s.

The two other well-known hotels in Civil Lines were the Swiss Hotel and Hotel Cecil. Swiss Hotels later became residential quarters called the Oberoi Apartments. The Cecil was run by the Hotz family, which also owned Wildflower Hall and Cecil Hotel in Simla, as well as a hotel in Murree in Pakistan. The Hotz family lovingly created this posh hotel with over a 100 rooms on an 11-acre campus which had well-manicured lawns, and an amazing number of trees and flowering bushes. Strangely enough, even as the Hotz family sold off the Cecil in Simla to an Italian hotelier, in Delhi they wanted a buyer who would not commercialize it. So, it ended up with the Jesuits who bought it and turned it into a school, St Xavier's.

Meanwhile, the Cecil Hotel in Simla, one of the hill station's finest hotels and established in 1884, went into the hands of John Fratelli, who could well be called the first owner of a chain of hotels in India. Bachi Karkaria writes in *Dare to Dream*, the biography of India's most feted hotelier M.S. Oberoi that in 1916, Fratelli floated the Associated Hotels of India with a capital of Rs 6 million. It had some of the most sought after hotels in the north—the Maidens in Delhi, the Flashman in Rawalpindi, Deans in Peshawar, Corstophons and Longwood in Simla as well as a Cecil Hotel in Murree. It was at the Cecil Hotel in Simla that Rai Bahadur M.S. Oberoi cut his teeth. M.S. Oberoi eventually bought out the Associated Hotels—the way he managed to do so is a great story that has been fabulously described in Karkaria's book— and the Oberoi group he founded in 1934 is still rated as one of the finest luxury hotels in India. It was fortuitous for the Maidens and Cecil in Simla that they came to be owned by the Oberois or the East India Hotels as their company is called.

Rai Bahadur M.S. Oberoi can also take credit for the resurgence of one of the finest hotels in Calcutta, the Grand. This was originally one Colonel Grand's private residence, which was converted into a boarding house run by one Annie Monk, who then acquired some more buildings adjacent one of which was a theatre. In 1894, a young Armenian jeweller called Arathoon Stephen bought the theatre (he was soon to become a big real-estate baron) letting it run for a bit. However, the theatre burned down in a fire and he then acquired all the buildings, rebuilding a hotel on the site. Stephen incidentally had big ambitions as a hotelier and also went on to own (or lease for 99 years) the Mount Everest Hotel in Darjeeling. He built the Grand in Calcutta in an extravagant neo-classical style on a fourteen acre site around a green garden courtyard so that all the rooms were naturally cool and no punkawallahs were needed. The hotel was a great success and its New Year parties were especially very popular. After Stephen's death in 1930s, a typhoid epidemic struck Calcutta and six people staying at the hotel died. The hotel shut down as a result and management was at wits end and leased it at a very cheap rate to M.S. Oberoi, who managed to reopen it soon. He bought it outright some years later and turned fortunate with the hotel because thousands of soldiers were billeted in Calcutta during World War II and made the hotel their haunt.[10] The Darjeeling hotel, Mount Everest, which the young Armenian owned and which was designed by British architect Stephen Wilkinson, also came into the hands of the East India Hotels (EIH) in the 1960s in a circuitous way (Arathoon Stephen gave the lease to someone who in turn gave it to EIH). But the Oberois exited it in 2015, handing over the keys to a consortium of local businessmen. The hotel has been shut since 1984 and now a new hotel is likely to come up there.

Even as these hotels were getting established in the north and the east of India, parallelly in the south, several hotel developments were taking place. In 1912, Spencers started the Malabar Hotel at Kochi and the Mascot Hotel at Thiruvananthapuram. Later the Malabar Hotel was taken on lease in 1952 by Dominic Jose and three of his friends. In the mid-1950s, when the lease expired, in order to accommodate his manager who was nearing the age of retirement, Dominic started a small restaurant at Willingdon Island, an island in Cochin, now Kochi. Since beer licences were given only to hotels, he decided to construct a hotel that was called Casino Hotel and Restaurant. Today his son Jose Dominic is one of the finest hoteliers in the country, trying out radical new ideas and concepts that are almost whimsical.

There is much to be learnt from the growth and development of hotels, and the way these properties changed hands. The right buy at the right time—look at how both Fratelli and M.S. Oberoi made really good investments—could pay off wonderfully.

Also look at how hotels then drove occupancies. Back then they were already doing some of the things that today's hoteliers are trying out. For instance, the Imperial in the late 1930s, which was struggling to fill its rooms, converted the ground floor into offices. Not many people travelled to New Delhi then as there were no businesses or industries here. This worked well for a bit.

But the Imperial managed to drive up occupancy by focusing on food and events, with weekly dances in the ballrooms, and the finest of Western cuisine served. In the late 1940s, the room rate was about Rs 29.

Vijay Wanchoo, general manager of the Imperial, which incidentally for six generations has been with the family that built it, is a fount of stories on its history. He describes how if you look up the map of Lutyens Delhi of 1911, the spot where Imperial stands, the plot was earmarked 'Site for Hotel'. In the 1930s, when the top contractors chosen by the British were doing the construction of Connaught Place and Khan Market, the forefathers of the current owners were called and told to construct the hotel. When they said they had no experience of constructing a hotel, they said they would help with the design, and the lion logo was given by them.

And so this hotel was built. The fitment of the hotel till date has remained same. The hotel became popular in the 1940s and 1950s. The ballroom was very popular. The first cabaret performance in Delhi was probably held here.

'You will wonder why our corridors are so wide,' says Wanchoo. 'It is because of the diaphanous gowns that the English ladies wore in the 1940s.'

Two years before the Imperial opened, Delhi also saw the launch of two more hotels that still survive. The forty-six-room Hotel Marina in Connaught Place was built in 1934 by the Japanwala family—called so because of their business relations with Japan—and managed by an Italian family till the early 1940s. During World War II, the Italian family went back and the families of businessmen Sardari Lal and Girdhari Lal took over the management. An unusual feature of the hotel was that it had fifty-two servant's quarters for staff and private garages for guest's cars.

In 1934, Hotel India also opened in Connaught Circus with twelve rooms, a restaurant and a bar. This was started by the Nirula family's L.C. Nirula and M. Nirula and in later years became the go-to spot for fast food and ice cream. People still swoon over the thought of an HCF—Hot Chocolate Fudge—that only Nirula's served in the 1980s.

Pre-Independence, another hotel that came up in Delhi was the Ambassador, designed by British architect Walter Sykes George, who worked with both New Delhi's chief architects Lutyens and Herbert Baker. This hotel was a big hit with travellers and rocked in the evenings with its night club Jewel Box, which had strict rules of entry. Only men wearing tuxedos were allowed in. Today, the Ambassador sports the Taj brand, while the Marina in Connaught Place wears the Radisson logo, and both still have loyal repeat guests. Nirula's meanwhile is in danger of being forgotten altogether.

Post-Independence, one of the first hotels to come up in Delhi was the Claridges, a charming property created in Lutyens area by the Khanna family (they owned a jewellery business) with some political help—so the story goes—in getting the requisite licences. It was a Dutch manager who convinced the Khannas to open the hotel with a British style name and ethos.[11] Sadly, the property that was owned by a Hindu Undivided Family (HUF) got embroiled in litigation with some acrimonious succession issues. The Khannas sold the hotel to the Nanda family that is into the arms business and who in turn are reportedly scouting for buyers.[12] Despite being in some wonderful locations—Mussoorie and Surajkund, and getting a 40 per cent stake in Mumbai's Searock hotel—the Claridges chain never could rise above being a bit player.

The Government Steps in

No history of Indian hospitality can be complete without the role of the government, which still remains an important player in the hotels business—however carelessly it may choose to run its properties.

The India Tourism Development Corporation (ITDC), which runs the Central government's hotels, came into existence in 1966. There was a time when ITDC ran a sizeable number of hotels across the country, though in recent years it has been divesting most of them. 1967 was also another notable year in the evolution of India's hospitality sector because the government, recognizing that tourism had to play a bigger role in the country's economy, created the Ministry of Tourism and Civil Aviation that year.

ITDC may have been born in 1966, but the government's entry into the hotels business predates it by ten years. It got in because the first prime minister of India, Jawaharlal Nehru, fresh from attending a meeting of the United Nations Educational, Scientific and Cultural Organization (UNESCO), wished to host a session in Delhi. But to host the delegates, Delhi needed a very large hotel with superb convention facilities. That's how the concept of Ashok was born and the Ashoka Hotels was the name of the company that was incorporated.

Nehru wanted it to be a magnificent super-luxury hotel that would dominate the landscape. The whole idea was at odds with his socialist vision though. You couldn't spend public money on a lavish hotel like this. So Nehru went about tapping the rich princes of India. The maharaja of Nawanagar (whose clan cricketer Ranjitsinhji belonged to) made a huge financial contribution and Yuvraj Karan Singh, the son of Maharaja Hari Singh of Jammu and Kashmir, donated the land. Fifteen of the original twenty-three shareholders of the Ashoka Hotels, the company that was absorbed into ITDC, were royal princes.

The Ashok in Delhi has quite a riveting history, much of which has been lovingly preserved.

'It is the first-five star hotel built in independent India,' said Vijay Dutt, general manager of the Ashok, pulling out some fascinating drawings that show the construction of this palatial edifice.

After Independence, the Ashok was the first structure of the scale of North Block and South Block to come up. It was built on part of the Raisina Hill, with the contours of the land incorporated beautifully in the architecture. The lobby is almost two levels above the ground, while one of the restaurants and the convention area is at ground level. The original drawings of the hotel in the general manager's room also show a tall tower, which somehow got subdued in the final design. Legend has it that Nehru personally supervised the construction of the hotel, riding on horseback around the estate.

Spend some time at the general manager's sprawling room which is filled with records from the past and there's so much of nostalgic trivia that delights. For instance, there are the ledgers from 1957 and 1958 that show the check-ins and check-outs during those days. Most guests appear to have been foreigners though there are several film stars from Bombay too, with Sunil Dutt's name popping up prominently.

The Ashok is perhaps the first hotel in India built on such a massive scale. For those who visit Las Vegas or Genting Island in Malaysia, where hotels with 7000 rooms are par for the course, a 500-room hotel may seem laughably small. But for decades, this—along with the Taj in Bombay—was the largest hotel in India. The Taj though cannot match the Ashok's gardens.

Spread over 25 acres, the Ashok is like a mini-city that needs major upkeep. It takes 1000 employees and Rs 3.5 lakh to run the hotel daily. When the Ashok first came up, it was just a 100-room hotel. It expanded in 1967, when an annexe came up, and more floors were added in the 1980s. The hotel's last major renovation, which cost Rs 70 crore, took place in 2010, when it was one of the family hotels of the Commonwealth Games.

What's nice about the Ashok is that unlike most other ITDC properties that are decaying with neglect—the Janpath in Delhi is a case in point, though it has been handed over to the Ministry of Urban Development—this property is periodically refurbished and reinvented. And though ITDC is now on a selling spree, insiders say that this is one property that the government will never divest.

In the late 1950s and 1960s, the Ashok attracted the party set of Delhi who would assemble within its bougainvillea-covered boundary walls. In 1968, the then prime minister, Indira Gandhi, hosted a banquet for a thousand guests there to celebrate her son Rajiv's marriage to his Italian fiancée, Sonia. The feast comprised Parsi, Kashmiri and Italian cuisines.

It played host to many other luminaries as well. In 1959, when legendary rebel Che Guevara came to Delhi, he was a guest at the Ashok. But it is Cuban President Fidel Castro's visit in 1983 that sent the security in a tizzy—they had Castro lookalikes at the hotel to confuse potential assassins.

Some people, even without staying at the hotel, became known to the staff. A famous story at the Ashok is how a Mumbai-based yarn trader would often arrive at the hotel and leave his luggage with the clerk at the reception, saying he was doing a day trip. It was only later that Dhirubhai Ambani could afford to reserve a room at the hotel for his trips to Delhi to meet ministers and bureaucrats.

The hotel gave the city its first French speciality restaurant (Burgundy), its first Japanese speciality restaurant (Tokyo) and its first Korean speciality restaurant (Kumgang). The Taverna Cyprus used to be the only place in town for Cypriot food, long before Mediterranean fare became the go-to cuisine in the Capital.

The Ashok was quite the dining hotspot among Delhi's elite, with its buffet lunches at the restaurant Peacock Room being very popular. It cost Rs 26 in 1959. The hotel's Rouge et Noir restaurant was known for the cabaret. And it had Supper Club, one of Delhi's earliest nightclubs, where Usha Uthup, Sharon Prabhakar and Vijay Benedict used to perform.

A veteran Air Force officer's wife Mohini Bhargava recalls how even in the 1980s she and her husband used to frequently visit the Ashok. 'People used to stay there a lot and we had to go and meet them. It was so Indian. I always went there to do my hair. People there always knew us and there was Dilbar Singh at the salon, and service was always good,' she remembers. In its heydays, the Ashok had a post office inside the hotel (the Clarks in Jaipur had one too) as well as a bank.

Though ITDC officials are categorical that the Ashok will never be sold to a private player, its future is a bit uncertain. As a consultant who advises the government points out, one can't ever say never. All the USPs on which the Ashok manages to get its occupancy—large conference facilities, proximity to the government offices are all now fading as other hotels come up in the vicinity.

Vijay Dutt admits that it is not easy to fill a 550-room hotel. But he says they have 330 rooms occupied the year around. Government officials currently make up a bulk of the guests, but is depending on that one segment sustainable?

Though the Ashok is the jewel in its crown, ITDC has several other noteworthy properties, notably the Mysore Palace. All the ITDC properties enjoy locational advantage.

The ITDC has also groomed some formidable talent who have had a good innings in the private sector. Take the hugely respected K.B. Kachru, chairman of Radisson group, who prides himself as probably the first person in J&K to have done a hotel management course, or his successor Raj Rana, who joined ITDC soon after his graduation from the Pusa Institute of Hotel Management, and worked with the government body from 1984 to 1991.

'What a glamorous, beautiful hotel the Ashok was!' Rana exclaims. 'Every day was a joy to be there, to be rubbing shoulders with presidents, prime ministers, and state dignitaries at lavish banquets.'

Those days, of course, as Rana points out, the hotel was very well-positioned.

'I learnt a lot from ITDC. I think it is a very good grooming for initial years for any management trainee like myself because you understand labour relations, you understand guests services, you understand state banquets and style and all that has helped me lifelong,' he says. 'That stint held me in good stead through my years with Carlson Rezidor in Europe, Russia and the US.'

Other than the ITDC, various state tourism development corporations got into the hotel business too, setting up properties and connecting tourists. The other government player in the business of hospitality was Hotel Corporation of India, a subsidiary of Air India, which ran the Centaur chain. Air India decided to enter the hotels business in 1956 in keeping with global trends (remember Air France owned Le Méridien before it sold it off to Starwood).

In 1962, another important thing that happened was that the government decided to classify hotels. A hotel classification committee was set up and properties were accorded star rating depending on facilities. This was done to bring in standardization and to fix rates.

Today, the way we classify hotels according to stars—five star, four star, three star etc. may be a bit dated and the hotel industry wants to discard it, but it endures in our minds.

Private Players Get Going

Parallel to the growth of ITDC, the Oberoi empire grew too. Rai Bahadur M.S. Oberoi, chairman of East India Hotels Ltd (as his company was called by now), began expanding his empire in the 1960s. He constructed New Delhi's first modern multistorey hotel, and this was also perhaps the first time that a hotel in India was franchised to a big foreign brand—the InterContinental Hotels, which was till then called Six Continents).

By now the Oberoi portfolio consisted of the Cecil, Simla; the Oberoi Grand, Calcutta; the Oberoi Clarks, Simla; the Oberoi Palm Beach, Gopalpur-on-Sea. Somewhere along the way M.S. Oberoi exited the hotels in Pakistan.

The Oberoi association with the InterContinental group was the beginning of the association with foreign brands and it had some positive consequences for Indian hospitality.

What the entry of foreign chains—even if through the franchise route—did was that it led to the professionalization of hospitality service in India. In his book on the history of Indian hospitality, Amitabh Devendra says, 'The training of managerial and other personnel was an important franchise benefit, and the first few batches of managers trained by the InterContinental Hotel Company set a new trend of competent professional hotel management for India's Hotels.'[13]

The Taj Group was the next to follow this franchising trend in 1970, when for a brief while it adopted an InterContinental hotel franchise for its new hotel in Bombay. Simultaneously, the Oberoi Tower Hotel under construction in Bombay entered into a franchise and management agreement with Sheraton. This was the first of the Sheratons (a Starwood brand) to be seen in India.

Prior to that, in the 1960s, there are reports that J.R.D. Tata flirted with the idea of getting Hilton to manage the magnificent old Taj Mahal Hotel as it had been deteriorating. He famously said there was so much wrong at the hotel that he didn't know where to start. But the Hilton deal did not go through. Instead, J.R.D. Tata found a saviour in a young catering manager called Ajit Kerkar. He entrusted him with the task of righting the wrongs at the hotel. Kerkar not only turned around the grand old Taj, opening a new wing in 1972, but also was instrumental in convincing J.R.D. to start a chain of hotels.

J.R.D. was not really convinced initially. Columnist Vir Sanghvi describes how Kerkar then proceeded to create a chain almost by stealth. He didn't take any money from the Tatas for the expansion convincing businesspeople to invest in a hotel in Goa (Fort Aguada) and the Taj Coromandel in Mahabalipuram, Madras. To Kerkar goes the credit of opening up Goa as a destination by setting up a fine hotel there and for starting the trend of heritage hotels, getting the Lake Palace and Rambagh into the fold as management contracts.

By the end of the 1970s, the Taj had shot past the Oberois. Such was the growth of the Taj that there was a time when M.S. Oberoi wrote a curt letter to J.R.D. about why Air India was giving its business exclusively to the Taj. In those days Air India was run by the Tatas. J.R.D. wrote a polite reply back which in so many words just said that they saw no reason to change policies.[14]

The 1970s also saw the rise of another Indian chain. Tobacco giant ITC (the Indian Tobacco Company) decided to enter the field of hospitality in 1974 and opened its first hotel Chola (this was an acquired property) in 1975 in Madras. Initially, ITC Hotels had two divisions—Welcome Group Hotels and Indovilla Hotels, the first was in the luxury category while the second was low-cost. In 1976, it opened the Mughal Hotel in Agra and a year later the Maurya in Delhi. When it entered the fray many felt that ITC was not a serious player and it was just parking its surpluses (and these were huge) from tobacco into real estate, but, to be fair to the group, it brought several concepts to hoteliering, quite clearly owning the king of food, space and now more recently, the champion of responsible luxury. Despite nearly 100 hotels, it continues to remain a bit of an enigmatic player. The others are frankly envious of the deep pockets that ITC has and grumble that it enjoys unfair advantage as it can absorb huge losses without much of a dent.

Meanwhile, the franchising story of the foreign chains continued to grow. By now Holiday Inn also made its entry into India through franchising its hotel project in Bombay. The Advanis in Goa were the ones to spread the Holiday Inn franchise.

However, the growth of franchising of international chains was rudely halted when there was a rise of a nationalist movement in the 1970s, and all sorts of conditions were imposed.

In 1981, a new player burst into the scene when a self-made entrepreneur Captain C.P.K. Nair entered the fray, and very soon the Leela Venture was regarded as a formidable force in luxury hospitality. To start with, he set up Hotel Leela in Mumbai, initially entering into a collaboration agreement with the Penta Hotels Ltd for a period of ten years for sales, marketing and technical know-how. Penta, incidentally was a chain with investments in it by three big global airlines (British Airways, Lufthansa and Swiss Air). Ten years later, he ended the Penta partnership and signed up with Kempinski instead.

After Mumbai, Capt. Nair set up a hotel in Goa at Colva Beach. Leela had a golden run under Capt. Nair's leadership, but today it is in all sorts of financial trouble, buried under a pile of debts.

The 1970s and 1980s was a period when several individual entrepreneurs across the country entered the hotel industry, inspired in part by the fine hotels they saw in the metro cities and in part in a bid to fill the gap in supply. Both the metros and the small cities saw investments in hotels.

Delhi got a big boost when India decided to host the 1982 Asian Games. There was a huge need for hotel rooms and the government went out of its way to hand out licences—this was when the Hyatt Regency in Bhikaji Cama Place, the Taj Palace, Le Méridien, Surya Sofitel (today it is just the Surya) all came up. The government itself through ITDC built three more hotels on super-prime locations—Samrat cheek by jowl with the Ashok, Lodhi Hotel and Kanishka. Lodhi and Kanishka were later sold.

The rate of growth of hotels was fairly slow in India till the 1980s, when it began to pick up pace. There were many factors—in socialistic India, the average citizens were not really a consuming class. The government too discouraged the industry by being closed to the idea of foreign franchising.

It was only in 1986 that tourism was accorded an industry status. And it was in 1987 that the Indian government permitted an Indian hotel chain to franchise a three- and four-star hotel. These helped, but it was not until liberalization in the 1990s that things moved.

In 1991, the year when India liberalized its economy, tourism was accorded a priority sector status and the hospitality industry got a bit of a boost. Another interesting development in the same year was the adoption of a new classification—heritage hotels—the Eighth Plan of the Indian government. In a way, Francis Wacziarg and Aman Nath really catapulted this category when they lovingly converted the Neemrana Fort Palace, which dates back to 1464 AD into a heritage hotel. In 1986, this unlikely duo bought the crumbling fort for Rs 7 lakh (yes, doesn't it sound ridiculous?), invested love, passion and energy in restoring it and bowled over guests when they opened it.[15] By 2018, Neemrana Hotels was managing over twenty heritage properties. But it had competition as others followed the heritage trail too.

The heritage hotel classification covers running hotels in palaces, castles, forts, havelis and residences of any size that were built prior to 1950. Heritage hotels have been one of the big successes in India's hospitality story—given the appeal they hold for foreign visitors. But they come with challenges aplenty as Randhir Vikram Singh, general secretary of the Indian Heritage Hotels Association points out—apart from the maintenance and upkeep, now they have to contend with several faux heritage properties that have come up.

In 1998, rules were further eased, allowing the entry of foreign players. The floodgates opened only at the turn of the millennium. That's when India's hospitality industry story really picked up pace and we began seeing fast and furious action.

II

AT YOUR SERVICE: THE PLAYERS

4

The Badshahs and Sultans

'Common people have an appetite for food, uncommon people have an appetite for service.'

—J.R.D. Tata

Think Indian hospitality and the three names that come instantly to mind are the Taj, the Oberoi and the ITC. The big three between them control an impressive inventory (nearly 25,000 rooms as of 2018) and have set the standards for superior hospitality over the ages. They have pretty much laid the foundations, with each having their own unique strengths.

For decades the grand Moghuls who lorded over the Indian hospitality scene had things pretty much their way as there was not enough competition. Of course, there were other home-grown chains that blazed a trail—the Leela, especially, made a mark in luxury, until it got into a financial mess—but on sheer scale, vision and staying power, nobody could come close to the big three.

Today, the robes of all the three seem slightly askew. The entry of the global Goliaths, the rise of new Indian start-ups in hospitality, technology giving power to the single-hotel owner—all have shaken the big three. Also, today we live in an age of the fickle and demanding consumer where the power of the brand has diluted.

The Taj, which has seen many ups and downs in its century-plus journey, understood the new challenges and did a radical experiment in the late 2000s by creating segmented brands. Taj—at the upper end, Vivanta—to appeal to the vivacious, and Gateway—at the bottom. It also launched a budget brand, Ginger to appeal to new audiences, to get more people through its doors. It was a wonderful step for its time, though the execution faltered.

But just ten years later, it went back to the drawing board and decided to drop the segments relying on a concept it defined as 'Tajness' to draw in travellers. That was a short-lived idea and it decided to return to its segmented strategy. In hindsight, it was an unavoidable confusion created by the change in leadership, which caused disarray among owners of Taj properties. So much so that Taj might have lost out on new business as it could not make up its mind on its brand strategy.

The Oberoi, meanwhile, had its own dilemmas—should it be asset-heavy, should it go asset-light, should it look at other segments? In the end, Oberoi decided to stay true to its luxury ethos. Unlike the others who believe scale is a good strategy, Oberoi has also consciously decided to stay small, eschewing many a good partnership because of the fear of eroding its brand value. It is also fairly snooty and sometimes even stubborn about many things, radiating an English pukka sahib attitude. But is that wise in today's age?

Of the three, ITC is the most enigmatic hotel player. It has a seriously big advantage in this industry, of course. It has a vast surplus of funds from the tobacco-rich parent that can absorb experiments, absorb losses, and can fuel expansion.

'I don't regard them as hoteliers,' one industry veteran even said. They are just burning the money from tobacco here.

Be that as it may, ITC has taken a very strong positioning. It is the one hotel brand that is identified instantly with food. It took total leadership in terms of making its restaurants aspirational, go-to gourmet hotspots, be it Bukhara or Veda. ITC is also the first to talk about sustainability and responsible luxury.

There was a brief period when it looked like the Capt. C.P. Krishnan Nair–founded Leela Group would join the Taj, the Oberoi and the ITC as a formidable hotelier, delivering superb service. But overambition derailed Hotel Leela Venture's growth story. It got mired in debts and the second generation has had to sell off many assets (Delhi, Chennai, Bengaluru and Udaipur) to Canada's Brookfield Asset Management to rescue the group from insolvency. It had earlier sold its Kovalam and Goa properties as well.

Yet, there are many in the industry who believe that you cannot write off the Leela Group, because in terms of service, there is much that it has got right. And interestingly enough, though it sold the Goa property, it still manages the hotel for the new owners. Now that it has shed the white elephants, it can focus on its flagship property in

Mumbai and focus on new developments. But it all depends on how well the new ownership structure pulls along and which direction it takes the chain in. While analysts sound pessimistic about the Leela, given its precarious finances, those within the group and in charge of development for the group point that the Leela has won several management contracts, including the Mahatma Mandir, the gargantuan convention hall in Ahmedabad.

The Lalit and The Park are two other interesting homegrown chains that have seen some twists and turns and strategic changes. But in this chapter, we look at the big three whose individual contributions to Indian hospitality can fill up many books. Indeed, the colourful stories surrounding the Taj, the Oberoi and the ITC Group are documented in lovely books—Allen Charles' *The Taj at Apollo Bunder*, Bachi Karkaria's *Dare To Dream: The Life of M.S. Oberoi* and Habib Rehman's memoir *Borders to Boardroom*.

The Taj: The Pioneer

Soon after he took charge of Taj Hotels, new CEO Puneet Chhatwal addressed a gathering of hoteliers and he was first asked to share his impressions of India on his return. Chhatwal had spent the previous thirty years in Europe, and was CEO of Deutsche Hospitality (owner of Steigenberger Hotels) before being hand-picked for the job of helming the Indian Hotels Company Limited (IHCL).

'When I left India, the marketing was around the best bed, best shower, or best breakfast. But now, it is around projecting clean air!' he exclaimed.

The subtle subtext of Chhatwal was that there was practically nothing to choose between top hotel chains today in terms of the four Bs—bed, breakfast, bath and broadband. If competition is fierce and intense, the disruptions are everywhere—in government policies, in technology that wrests power away from hotels, and in customer behaviour. You have to find your differentiators elsewhere. In polluted Delhi, where Air Quality levels have been touching alarming levels, hotels like the Oberoi and the ITC Maurya have been pushing for their indoor air atmosphere as reasons to stay with them.

For unassuming and low-key Chhatwal, the job of keeping the Taj ahead of competition was all the tougher as his much-hyped predecessor, the flamboyant Rakesh Sarna, had left the group in a cloud and in much confusion. Sarna, who had arrived to lead the Taj after thirty years at the Hyatt, where he was group president Americas, had managed to pare the hotel group's losses with some ruthless letting go of assets.

In 2014, when Sarna took charge as MD and CEO, the Taj's losses were Rs 554 crore, but by the time he bowed out the net loss had come down to Rs 63 crore. The Taj cut gross debt by Rs 1,143 crore by selling some overseas hotels like the Taj Boston and its stake in Belmond (Orient Express). However, even as losses were checked, the revenues also came down from Rs 4188 crore in 2014–15 to Rs 4010 crore in 2017–18 as the overseas properties did bring in good revenue.

But the Taj Group is no stranger to suffering business losses or controversies over its leadership. In the 1940s it was terminally in the red, but bounced back. It had a severe leadership crisis when the seemingly invincible chief

Ajit Kerkar was sacked unceremoniously after a twenty-seven-year-long tenure.[1] Yet it flourished.

On 26 November 2008 (26/11), it bore the brunt of a dastardly terrorist attack on its flagship Mumbai hotel, an attack that shook the entire nation but it showed remarkable resilience in overcoming the tragedy, winning the hearts of the country with the courage its people showed during the crisis. The way the hotel was rebuilt, the way it bounced back, the way the employees rallied around—this is one property and group that will always have a soft spot in the hearts of its guests.[2]

The Beginnings

When Jamsetji Nusserwanji Tata set up the grand vision of a hotel in Mumbai, he might never have dreamt that it would turn out to be such a big chain. The credit for that goes to Ajit Kerkar, who had the vision to make it big and expand in all directions.

When Kerkar took over the reins of the Taj in 1962, it was a single-hotel company managed by the Tata Trust, with a revenue of Rs 2.7 crore. It had seen periods of acute struggle, notably during the prohibition years of 1939, then bouncing back in 1940 after it was lifted. During the two wars it made good profits with guests from the army staying at the hotel. But then again, post-war it had troubles, mostly on account of being badly run (then chairman J.R.D. Tata, nephew of Jamsetji, famously said that it was comical how stupidly it was run) and there are even accounts— exaggerated, no doubt— of a group of Swiss tourists finding the sofa they were seated in crumbling and the bed disintegrating.

Operations were a challenge until the dynamic Ajit Kerkar took charge. Can you imagine, at one point, the directors at IHCL even considered selling the hotel or tearing it down to build a new one. Thankfully that did not happen. A team of consultants was brought in to put things in order but it was Kerkar, Col Leslie Sawhny and Camellia Panjabi who together transformed the group.

If Kerkar was a dynamo, Camellia Panjabi was no less. She was the most formidable sales and marketing head for the Taj Hotels, sniffing out opportunities, scouting out new destinations for Taj to open hotels, talking to guests and understanding their needs and creating properties that would resonate with them. Today's development heads of various chains have much to learn from Camellia Panjabi, who had a gut for what would work.

By 1999, when Kerkar left the group, allegedly on charges of financial impropriety, it had forty-two hotels, not just in India but overseas too, with a turnover of over Rs 524.30 crore against the second-largest group Oberoi's Rs 440.42 crore, with a profit of Rs 140.57 crore. The dividends to shareholders of Tata had risen dramatically.

Although Kerkar had grown the hotel chain phenomenally, media was abuzz with reports about the charges against him of financial misdealings (the way he diverted IHCL shares into his son's business, etc.) being too grave.[3] Plus Ratan Tata, who had taken charge of the Tata Group, seemed keen to cleanse the Tata stables of entrenched honchos like Russi Mody and Darbari Seth and in the scheme of things Kerkar probably had to go too.[4]

The Taj has been a pioneer in India's hospitality story— not just because it was India's first hotel chain, but because it also introduced many new concepts and opened many destinations. Goa and Kerala opened up as destinations largely thanks to Taj Hotels agreeing to invest in these places. The palace hotels were a brainchild of Kerkar as were resort hotels. Maharaja Gaj Singh's Umaid Bhawan Palace at Udaipur managed by the Taj is one of India's finest properties as is the Falaknuma palace at Hyderabad. Also, IHCL was one of the first in India to start the segmented branded strategy.

After Kerkar's exit, despite the turmoil and divided employee loyalties, to the credit of his successors R. Krishna Kumar and Raymond Bickson, the group expanded rapidly. But in the 2000s, the Taj faced not an internal challenge, but one that came from a changing milieu— liberalized India could now afford to stay at hotels and was hungry for choice.

No longer could the Taj afford to play at just one traveller-segment point, the upscale luxury segment. Domestic tourists were a bigger opportunity than the global tourist and there was a need to cater to all price points.

The Taj was the first one to start with a more segmented approach, says Lulu Raghavan, India head of Landor, the brand consultancy that was engaged by the group to create different brands. Differentiation had become critical, as she said.

The thought behind the segmentation was to address both price point differences as well as traveller varieties. So, for a group that wanted contemporary unstuffy luxury, it created the Vivanta. For travellers looking for crisp service without any bells and whistles, there was Gateway. And for those seeking basic bed and breakfast there was Ginger. And, above all, at the top, were the iconic Taj classic hotels.

At the same time, the branding led to some confusion. Hotel consultant Manav Thadani points how Taj's Vivanta and Gateway just could not explain the differentiation well and there was a fuzzy line between these brands.

This confusion is what led the larger-than-life hotelier, former Hyatt executive Rakesh Sarna to decide to do away with the segmentation. He felt that there was nothing distinguishing about any of the hotels run by the Taj—in fact, some had become quite sloppy—and a defining value of Tajness had to be introduced.

He had a point. Camellia Punjabi, the legendary deputy of Ajit Kerkar, during a conversation on the sidelines of a hotel conference in Mumbai, describes how she was shocked to see how the flagship Bombay property's Food and Beverages (F&B) was losing all sense of reality in its operations. She felt this after seeing the pricing of some of the items.

Sarna came up with the idea of unifying all Taj properties through a concept called Tajness, distinctive Indian hospitality with a sense of warmth. The idea was to have rituals that would leave the guests with a clear memory of their stay at the Taj. As Chinami Sharma, chief revenue officer of Taj explained, 'It's a demonstration of the thought "we care for you".'

But embroiled in a MeToo scandal, with an employee alleging harassment at his hands, as well as caught in the power battle crossfire between new Tata boss Cyrus Mistry and Ratan Tata, who wanted to wrest back control of the group, Rakesh Sarna had to leave.[5] Given all the drama that Taj Hotels had seen, Chhatwal was lucky in the sense the expectations placed on him were not as high as those his predecessor had to bear. Also, Chhatwal has been fortunate that under his watch, the most prestigious Taj Mansingh property was safely kept in the IHCL fold. When the Delhi government decided not to extend Taj Mansingh's lease automatically but to invite bids, dragging it out into several suspense filled years marked by cases and counter cases, it became a matter of prestige for IHCL to retain control of this iconic hotel.

If you do a SWOT (strengths, weaknesses, opportunities, and threats) analysis of the Taj Group, the strengths far outweigh the weaknesses. It has legacy, it has the backing of the formidable Tata group, it has the scale and a great brand name. It has a massive distribution advantage as business flows in from the Tata Group companies like TCS, Titan, Tata Steel etc. According to a senior marketing executive in a rival chain, it's not just the Tata Group executives who give their business to Taj Hotels but also banks and other firms that have Tatas as their most important clients.

But above all these advantages, what's actually most important is that IHCL has the mindset to embrace change. Though it may not have been seen as taking action, but as Chinmai Sharma—marketing head of the Taj Group—said, the Taj was not sitting on its stately haunches. It was taking cognizance of the Airbnb wave and internally thinking about a serviced residence offering. It already had the, Taj Wellington Mews in Mumbai and 51 Buckingham in London, next to St James Court, which operated more like stand-alone units. The thinking within Taj was whether it could create a new division for these and if so, properties like the Ambassador in Delhi, which did not at all sit well with the Vivanta brand, could be converted into a serviced residence. But that line of thought was probably not pursued.

Eventually, Ambassador was placed under a new brand SeleQtions, created for unique properties that had a stand-alone identity of their own. Chhatwal explains that SeleQtions was created to celebrate individuality, by offering unique experiences through landmark hotels that have their own legacy and charm. Hotels like the President in Mumbai, the Cidade de Goa, a hotel that came into the Taj fold in 2018, and the Connaught, which it acquired in government auctions, are all under SeleQtions.

SeleQtions will allow IHCL to cater to a broader audience of travellers who prefer to stay in hotels with a distinctive character. Chhatwal says that SeleQtions also includes hotels that have a slice of history, defining location or a differentiated theme.

In addition, Taj created a brand called Expressions for its service retail brands like Chambers; F&B outlets like Golden Dragon; Wasabi; House of Ming; Thai Pavilion; Khazana, the lifestyle retail brand; and Jiva, its spa brand, to unlock their equity.

As for the apartments' idea, Taj chose to enter the homestay market instead, with Ama Trails and Stays.

Chhatwal, an MBA and a shrewd business brain, also launched a three Rs strategy—Restructure, Reengineer and Reimagine—to get better margins for the company. The target: to take the earnings before interest, tax, depreciation and amortization (EBITDA) from 17 per cent in 2018 to 25 per cent by 2022. From 15.5 per cent in 2017–18, he has ramped it up to 17 per cent in 2019.[6]

An industry insider describes how the Taj development team used to be quite laidback—but Chhatwal's first step was to drive them to go get hotel signings. And sure enough in the first year of his taking over, twenty-two hotels were signed.

At the budget end, Ginger too was reinvented, with more updated versions tried out. 'Customer trends and needs change over time. Hence, we needed to revisit the brand. The Indian consumer has evolved and, with the rising middle-class incomes, is more aspirational. We thus reimagined the brand and repositioned it in the lean luxe segment,' explains Chhatwal.

This willingness to experiment, some good leadership and a strategy that stays close to market trends will stand the Taj group in good stead as it negotiates the next 100 years. Plus, it enjoys enormous goodwill—there are well-heeled guests who have stayed at the Taj Mansingh in Delhi for years and years because it feels like home.

The Oberoi: The Service Edge

On January 1, 2018, the trendsetting Oberoi Delhi threw open its doors after a two-year shut down for a top-to-bottom overhaul of the hotel set up in 1965. The multi-million-dollar renovation of the hotel personally overseen by P.R.S. (Biki) Oberoi, the exacting son of the group's founder M.S. Oberoi, was eagerly awaited by everyone to see if there would be major changes in the hotel.

The verdict—a mixed one. Many felt the reincarnated Oberoi was too much like the old one—it was not an earthshaking alteration. Yes, there were acknowledgements to new realities of life in severely polluted Delhi. It had made clean air a priority putting in place purification systems using technology that was ahead of everyone else's.

But there were many surprising misses. It had not set up huge banquet areas. The business reality of today is that hotels in India need meetings, conferences and weddings to stay profitable. Yet, the rebuilt Oberoi still only had a hall that could seat a maximum of 175 people. Great effort and thought had gone into the decor and preserving privacy of guests—even the lobby was designed to be more private. In an era touted to be the sharing economy, where people like to intermingle, wasn't this an antiquated idea?

A very senior hotelier also points out that the refurbished Oberoi missed out on the opportunity to get millennials— the crowd that frequents Electric Bar at the Lodhi and Kitty Su at the Lalit—into its rooftop bar. What a miss. By not creating a spot that would appeal to the under-thirties with spare cash, the Oberoi may have lost out on connecting with a generation that might be tomorrow's valuable customer, says the hotelier.

This stubborn sticking to old values and ethos is considered laudable by some and foolish by others. Those who swear by the service ethos praise the Oberoi Group. But those looking at financial returns find it incomprehensible. Oversupply in rooms coupled with slower demand has led to weaker pricing of luxury hotels rooms. RevPar (revenue per available room that factors in occupancy) has been falling. So, every hotel needs to look at other revenue models. And catering to weddings and conferences is by far the most lucrative option.

Also, the opening of the hotel was not without its share of controversies. Kapil Chopra, the go-getting president of the

Oberoi and responsible for its financial turnaround, left the company the day before the relaunch. All sorts of speculative whispers did the rounds after the exit. Rumours had also been afloat about a difference in thinking between Prithvi Raj Singh 'Biki' Oberoi and his son Vikram Oberoi.

While Oberoi has a very loyal clientele—there are many people like Rajendra Pawar, chairman and co-founder NIIT, who says that ever since he was deemed worthy enough to be a member of the elite Belvedere Club back in the late 1980s, he stuck steadfastly to the hotel group—the question is: has it managed to attract new customers? Incidentally, till the time of writing this book the Belvedere is possible only if the chairman sends an invitation.

Also, in the two years that the hotel was shut, the Leela and the Lodhi in Lutyens Delhi managed to get a lot of old Oberoi faithfuls into its doors. It's always a tough challenge to get back someone who has found equal value in other places.

Compared to its Indian peers—Taj and ITC—which scaled to the 100-hotels mark in 2018, Oberoi had only thirty or so properties. And unlike Taj and ITC, which chose to expand out of the luxury segment, the Oberoi has not done so. That's not to say they did not consider the idea. In fact, the chain had protracted discussions with French hotel group Accor to bring the Novotel brand to India and four or five hotels were developed to Novotel specifications. But the deal breaker was Accor's refusal to customize to the Indian market. Accor wanted the hotel to stick to its global specifications while for the Oberoi group it was unthinkable to welcome guests without providing any services like shoeshine, etc.

After the talks broke down, the Oberoi explored a partnership with the Hilton. Finally, it decided to start the Trident on its own, with its own ideas. The result is that while Trident, a new brand, was born, the differentiation between it and flagship brand Oberoi is not evident at all.

An Oberoi insider who was privy to the discussions, however, feels that the group was justified in its stance. The Indian customer at that time was one who would not have liked a no-frills four star. He says that if you were going to do a price-point-value relationship for foreign guests, who would be just 20 per cent of the mix, and be disconnected with the Indian consumer's expectations, it wouldn't have worked.

The Oberois, as mentioned earlier, learnt a lot from the American style of hoteliering through its association with the Sheraton brand in Mumbai, focusing greatly on efficiency. But son Vikram's vision was grander—he upscaled the hotels his father had built. So, the Oberoi was pushed up to a grander level than five-star while Trident was at the five-star level.

Among the staff there is an impression that Biki Oberoi is too proper, and does not approve of irreverence. Culture whiz and now hotelier with his Neemrana properties, Aman Nath recalls his ad copywriting days many moons ago when he penned the copy for Oberoi campaigns. At that time Oberoi in Delhi had a restaurant called Taj—it was massive dining area, with a striking peacock made with beads capturing the eye. Since Taj Hotels was just launching its property in Delhi, Nath suggested a cheeky line saying 'At the far end of the Oberoi lobby, turn right into the Taj'.

Of course, the copy was not used. Ambush marketing was frowned upon by the Oberoi Group which considered it not kosher. But according to Aman Nath, the copy probably never even reached the chairman.

Another ad that Aman Nath wrote for the iconic Delhi hotel in 1985 when the hotel turned twenty-years-old, carried a picture of the Humayun's Tomb, which the Oberoi overlooks, and the hotel property. The line read: Fads come and go. Classics go on forever.

1565—Humayun's Tomb

1965—The Oberoi

So, what exactly has the Oberoi Group going for it? Why is it so respected and spoken about in hushed reverential whispers?

Every single person I met for this book mentioned the fabled anticipatory service of the Oberoi Group. Many say that once you stay at the chain, you are spoilt and no other place can match up.

Suresh Nair, general manager, India, Sri Lanka and Bangladesh, Air Asia group, says that he can never forget the service at Trident Chennai. He cites two instances: One day at breakfast he enquired of the hostess at the F&B station if there was pesarattu, a lentil and rice pancake preparation from Andhra Pradesh. She regretfully said it could not be made as the dish required presoaking of lentils. Next morning when Nair came for breakfast, he was astonished to find pesarattu served at his table.

The second instance he cites is when the hotel car supposed to pick him up from the airport was delayed by seven or eight minutes. When he reached the hotel, the front office manager was waiting to receive him—he apologized profusely and said they were upgrading his room to make up for the delay. That is service, says Nair.

So thorough is the grooming of staff at Oberoi that it's not surprising that many a general manager from the group has gone on to head rival hotel chains or form their own companies.

Biki Oberoi's eye for detail and design and his aesthetic sensibilities are universally praised as is his refusal to compromise on his vision. A story that a former Oberoi executive shares is how when the Trident in Gurgaon was being built, and the architect and designers could not translate what Biki Oberoi wanted, he didn't mind pulling it all down and redoing it, the couple of crores of additional cost notwithstanding. When the hotel was finally ready, it was a masterpiece. But guess who was paying for the cost of these redesigns. The owner. Very few owners would give the Oberoi so much freedom to experiment and that's perhaps one of the reasons Biki Oberoi didn't want to expand.

The quest for perfection notwithstanding, of the three Indian chains—the Taj, the ITC and the Oberoi—it is the Oberoi that looks a little shaky with the fear of an acquisition looming large.

In 2008, there was a hostile takeover bid by the ITC group, through a creeping acquisitions strategy. It needed a white knight in the form of industrialist Analjit Singh of the Max Group, to ward off that threat. Singh bought a 9 per cent stake in East India Hotels, which operates the Oberoi chain. And then, later in 2010, Reliance came into the picture as another saviour. Popular gossip is that Biki Oberoi requested Mukesh Ambani (the two are close and the Oberoi Group even manages Antilla, the towering home of the Ambanis) to help. As a result, Analjit Singh sold part of his equity to the Ambanis. Reliance owns 18.53 per cent of EIH stake, while ITC holds nearly 14.98 per cent stake plus another 1.15 per cent through its unit Russel Credit.

While the Oberois have maintained that Reliance's is a pure financial investment, there is often speculation on what the Ambanis might do with this investment. What if Reliance decides to get into the hotel business seriously? It is an uncertain situation. The fact that Nita Ambani attended the annual general meeting of the hotel group in Kolkata on 14 August 2019 increased market speculation that Reliance could possibly be acquiring ITC's stake and nurturing ambitions about entering the hotels business.[7]

And Oberoi, of all the people, should be cognizant—after all, in the late 1970s, it was exploring a partnership with ITC hotels to build hotels. That tie-up came to naught because Oberoi wanted ITC to remain a pure financier and let it handle the hotels. ITC, which then had just one hotel in its portfolio, decided to go on its own. And look where it took the Kolkata-headquartered chain!

With the growth of the Taj and ITC chains, a constant challenge for the Oberoi, as a former general manager in the group reveals, was how do you compete against the two on occupancy? It can battle the two on price and service, but both ITC and Taj get a fixed occupancy because they are business conglomerates with diversified interests. Industry reckoning is that at least 12–13 per cent of ITC and Taj occupancy comes from Tata Group and ITC Group employees, who pay market rates.

But this is a challenge that Reliance can undoubtedly help the Oberoi group with. After all, in 2019, Reliance Industries had nearly 30,000 permanent employees. And as mentioned, the Oberoi Group manages Antilla, the home of the billionaire owners of Reliance industries.[8]

EIH has been mulling over the owned versus managed model. It owns 70 per cent of the hotels in its portfolio, and manages the remaining 30 per cent. If it can reverse this ratio—which is its attempt—that could definitely help.

An ex-Oberoi executive points out that long ago the group figured out that it could not compete for growth and scale. Its single biggest differentiator would be luxury and service and so it would leverage that.

But the trouble with that is that consumer's definition of luxury changes with time and so does service expectation. Will the Oberois be able to adapt?

During a discussion with a passionate entrepreneur of a new-age start-up, not connected with hospitality in any way, he said, 'It is the duty of every company to try and scale. You owe it to so many—investors, stakeholders, employees—who have kept faith with you to try and grow. Looked at that way, some of Oberoi's decisions are disappointing.'

The Oberoi story now hinges on the next generation. Vikram Oberoi, Biki Oberoi's son, and Arjun Oberoi, his nephew, are joint managing directors. Will they be less rigid when it comes to running the show?

ITC: Responsible Luxury

Think ITC Hotels, and the first association that comes to mind is sensational food. Who has not tasted the famous Dal Bukhara or heard of it? A new association is responsible luxury.

Compared to the Taj and the Oberoi chains, cigarettes-to-paperboard company ITC entered the hotels business much later, only in the 1970s. And it did so in a haphazard sort of manner, building all manner of hotels with poached talent from ITDC and Oberoi. There appeared to be no apparent strategy to its entry into the hotels business and it seemed more like an asset game.

Cash-rich ITC had the money from the cigarette sales profits to build and buy hotels. Actually, the reason for it to enter hotels was because of the foreign exchange crunch during the License/Permit-Raj era and the growing challenges faced by the tobacco business. Ajit Haksar, the then chief of ITC, entered hotels with a view to earning foreign exchange as well as to own real estate assets, which he felt would appreciate hugely. The first hotel was created through an acquisition—the Chola Sheraton—in October 1975.

The change started coming about when Habib Rehman joined the group in February 1979. Just as Ajit Kerkar transformed the Taj, it was Rehman who gave the ITC Hotels (at that time it was called Welcomgroup) a character and identity. And this was shaped actually by his conversations with Ajit Haksar who was tired of borrowing from the West. All this is recounted in great detail in Rehman's lovely book *Borders to Boardrooms.*[9] One day Rehman told Haksar that his vision of an ideal hotel seemed to be akin to that of a Westernized Indian woman wearing a large bindi. A pleased Haksar responded: 'You have got what I am driving at.'

Till date the ITC flaunts all that is Indian, and plays up the country's heritage in a sumptuous and modern fashion. That in a sum was the identity that the low-profile

Rehman created. As Vir Sanghvi writes in his column in the *Hindustan Times*,

> If you've heard of Dum Pukht cuisine and convinced yourself that this is a throwback to the traditions of Avadhi Lucknow, think again: the cuisine was more or less invented by ITC under Rehman's tutelage. If you've been told that ITC is the Indian luxury chain, providing personalised service at distinctive properties, then that too is Rehman's contribution to a chain that wasn't even sure of its name (Was it ITC? Was it Welcomgroup?) till he took on the job of giving it an identity.[10]

An army major, Rehman had entered the hotel business late and accidentally, managing a property, the Rama International, in Aurangabad. But he caught the eye of then ITC boss Ajit Haksar, who was in Aurangabad to attend a convention. He got him to Delhi. The initial years with ITC were no picnic for Rehman as there was turbulence within the hotels division and within the ITC group itself. A large part of it was because there was no unified work culture in the hotels division. The folks who had come from ITDC had some ideas, while those from Oberoi had other. To add to the mess, Haksar brought in a Taj executive to manage the Maurya in Delhi, who promptly got in more people from the Taj Group. There was an inevitable clash of work cultures between these disparate group of people, leading to labour strikes and great turmoil.

By the time Rehman got his bearings in the organization— he had moved to Agra and handled the Mughal Sheraton there and then was in Chennai as regional director south—there was a new crisis with ITC. There was a huge battle between ITC and its principal shareholder British American Tobacco (BAT). BAT wanted ITC to exit all the diversified businesses it was in and focus exclusively on tobacco. The Indian management knew that this was not the right approach, given the trouble the tobacco industry was facing. By then Ajit Haksar had given way to his brother-in-law J.N. Sapru. And there were clashes between Haksar and Sapru too. In his memoir, Rehman describes the deteriorating relationship between the two brothers-in-law and ascribes it to the pressure that BAT was putting on Sapru to focus on tobacco.[11]

It was in these circumstances that the young and dynamic Yogi Deveshwar was asked to take charge of the hotels division. Deveshwar sent an SOS to Rehman to come to Delhi and take on the task of turning around the Maurya in Delhi. It was no easy task, given that the formidable Taj Palace was next door and Hyatt Regency had opened up in south Delhi and was getting significant business. But Rehman was equal to it.

He first transformed the kitchens and restaurants. Dum Pukht, serving Awadhi cuisine, became a huge hit as did the south Indian cuisine–format Dakshin. He templated the Bukhara formula and introduced it in other hotels with different names—Peshwari etc. Once the F&B had become established, Rehman set about transforming the hotels themselves.

It was by no means an easy task as ITC, at the corporate level, was facing trouble after trouble. J.N. Sapru had been succeeded by K.L. Chugh. Yogi Deveshwar had gone off on deputation to Air India. In 1994, a decision was taken to disband Welcomgroup and form ITC Hotels. All the staff had to hand in their resignations and join the new company. Many were alarmed. The transition was a trying time.

In 1996, Yogi Deveshwar came back to the ITC fold, inheriting a company in a solid mess. There were tax cases against the company, there were criminal cases, FERA violation cases. But he managed to fix it all.[12]

The Maurya in Delhi by now had found its mojo. A lot of renovation and restyling had been done, with a floor remodelled to suit the needs of the global political elite. A women's wing had come up. And the Indianness theme was going very well.

In his book, Rehman describes how Ajit Haksar once told him that each hotel that ITC built must be rooted in the city's soil and history. That's how the Sonar Bangla, ITC Maratha, ITC Rajputana and ITC Kakatiya took shape. All defined the culture of the heritage of the cities they were set in. His successor Nakul Anand followed it up with a Grand Bharat in Delhi, fusing all the elements of the different states in one grand property.

Rehman also launched the mid-scale offering, Fortune, and WelcomHeritage, which ITC markets, bringing under the umbrella hundreds of small hotels and havelis. He went a bit overboard in the Welcom branding with initiatives like WelcomTheatre (the group got theatre impresario Aamir Raza Hussain to stage royal plays).

What Rehman built, Nakul Anand pretty much expanded upon, taking ITC Hotels forward. Though the hotel chain took a hit during the downturn years of 2013–14, it kept investing in innovating and refreshing its product.

As the world keeps changing, we have to keep changing. Anand says, 'Never take your eyes off the changing trends.'

Anand's big emphasis was on investing in research on sleep. This was based on ITC's observations that people were sleeping two to three hours less on average. So, beverages packed with herbs that would induce sleep were placed on bedsides. Great focus also was paid to travellers' need for constant connectivity.

'First the traveller only wanted bed and booze. By "booze" I also mean food. Now, it's bed, booze and Internet,' says Anand.

But while these innovations only helped the hotel improve its product offering, Anand says they worked hard to find a differentiator that would improve the brand's image.

'The key differentiator is in gaining respect of the customer,' says Anand. And that led to the triple bottom line approach that ITC has taken. 'When we split our hotels into four brands, we came to crossroads—should we take the luxury route or be environmentally friendly? It was a tough call because those are in contradiction with each other. But then we decided to combine both.'

So, responsible luxury is the positioning that ITC has taken, chasing environmental sustainability. Every part of the service design, from the power transmission lines to the generators and the compressors, has been changed to make them energy efficient.

As for differentiating through its F&B approach, that has taken new strides. Joining the pantheon of Indian cuisine brands—Bukhara, Dumpukht, Dakshin—at the ITC hotels are global cuisine brands such as Pan Asian, Edo (Japanese) and Ottio (Italian).

'We don't just do F&B, but create brands. The driving principle behind our F&B approach is to create the globe's finest Indian and India's finest global,' Anand says.

The F&B at the ITC hotels also serves a larger purpose in the overall group's scheme. As part of its strategy to grow its non-tobacco revenues, ITC's big focus has been on FMCG, especially its packaged-foods business. And hotels are directly connected to this. As former ITC chairman Yogi Deveshwar explained during an interview with this writer, 'Which other packaged-foods company can have access to so many chefs who interact with so many Indian palates from morning to night. That's why our product development is absolutely many cuts above others. They will hire only one or two chefs. In our case we have a factory of chefs. They will be an endless source of product development. If one or two FMCG brands get created by the application of our hotels' business chefs, they will pay for their hotels forever.'

While ITC has managed to achieve product differentiation in a highly cluttered arena, observers still have some reservations about the way the group runs its hotels. There is needless wastage in the construction of its luxury properties. Everything is on a larger-than-life scale. While most other Indian hotels would stop at 350–400 hotels, ITC set up the 650-room Grand Chola in Chennai. Does the market warrant that kind of supply? It is doing the same in Kolkata.

It also takes risks, such as jumping into partnerships or acquiring assets that get into litigation, the Goa property being a case in point. In Kerala, ITC Hotels tied up with shipping tycoon Ravi Pillai to manage his properties in the state. Within no time, the tie-up ended.

At the mid-scale level, meanwhile, Fortune has no real personality of its own. Despite being quick to get into the mid-category, ITC has really not leveraged the potential of this category, though there has been some uptick.

However, on the talent side, the ITC story seems to be working well. It has a pipeline of talent all trained in-house, many of whom have come right up from ITC's own hotel management institute.

'For a hotel to become a great hotel, the differentiation comes from its people. If you were to build ten identical hotels that open on the same day around the same location, and take stock after ten years on how they are doing— they will all be performing differently. It's the people who make the difference. They are the software of the business,' Anand says.

What a far cry from the days when ITC just assembled talent poached from here and there.

ITC Hotels has also been lucky in its leadership. Group chairman Yogi Deveshwar, one of the most formidable faces of corporate India, took personal interest in the hotels division and supported it strongly. With his passing away, will the hotels continue to receive as much support?

While overall there has been much effort put into succession planning, things have not panned out as clearly in the hotels division, where an outsider, Sanjay Sethi, was brought in, but who left the company soon when Dipak Haksar was given an extension.

Summing up

All three chains—the Taj, the Oberoi and ITC Hotels—have history, legacy, some great people and rich experience. All of them have faced tough times and turbulence. On the face of it, it may seem that the Taj and the ITC may be able to withstand the future better than the Oberoi because they are part of large conglomerates that can absorb losses. But, if you look at their histories, that could potentially be a disadvantage too because when crisis strikes the mothership, it affects the fortunes of all the group companies. Their future ultimately hinges on strong leadership.

5

The Women's Touch

'Some leaders are born women.'

—Geraldine Ferraro, American attorney

Is there a difference in the hotels run by women? On the face of it, perhaps not. But just stay at two Indian chains that are owned by women, and you can immediately perceive how they stand out. More so, if you are a woman guest.

At the Lalit, you are escorted to your room by a woman guest-relations manager, your welcome kit in the room includes stuff like scrunchies, safety pins and those tiny little things that a woman traveller will appreciate. But quite aside from these cosmetic touches, it's the empathetic inclusivity at the Lalit that has made it a point to embrace the differently oriented which strikes you.

Jyotsna Suri, chairperson and MD, Bharat Hotels, who runs the Lalit, has a steely strength combined with unexpected sensitivity that has helped her turn around a run-of-the-mill hotel chain into a unique brand with its own special niche. To her credit, she has also listened to the voices of GenNext—most notably her son Keshav Suri, executive director at the Lalit and one of the petitioners against Section 377, and allowed him free rein to turn a stuffy hotel into a vibrant and inclusive one.

At The Park, run by Priya Paul, who is the first woman of boutique hotels in India, the things that stand out are the design sensibilities, the food and entertainment, the referencing of contemporary culture, and the mindfulness of the surroundings and context of the hotel. The Park was a distinctive lifestyle brand well before such things became fashionable. Over the decades, it did get somewhat subdued and seemed to be losing its way but, crossing its fiftieth birthday, it has emerged rejuvenated and is finding its mojo again.

Apart from Suri and Paul, there are several women now carving a space in the male-dominated industry. There is Amruda Nair, joint MD and CEO of Aiana Hotels and granddaughter of the legendary Captain Nair, who had the option of staying on at the family-run Leela Hotels but decided to give vision to her own ideas. There is the extremely confident Shruti Shibulal, daughter of Infosys founder S.D. Shibulal, who is creating a buzz with her niche hotel chain, the Tamara. There are the two sisters of the MBD publishing empire Monika and Sonika Malhotra who have displayed business acumen and chutzpah in the two Radisson properties they run and their aggressive bid to bring the Steigenberger brand to India. There are owner hoteliers like the Brigade Group's Nirupa Jaishankar, who are taking proprietary interest in how their hotels are run, with bright ideas on introducing more efficiencies. More on them later.

This chapter is about Priya Paul and Jyotsna Suri, who are undeniably the trendsetters. Both their stories have a commonality in that they inherited their enterprise, one from her father and the other from her husband, but made it their own, with their distinctive stamp and identity.

The Park: Anything but Ordinary

'It was 1988. A young girl walks into my office. Her card says Sales Manager, Park Hotels. My card says Sales Manager, SITA Travels. I had no idea who Priya Paul was, and she had no idea who I was,' recounts Arjun Sharma, chairman of Select Group and Le Passage to India, recalling his first encounter with Priya Paul, the chairperson of Apeejay Surrendra Park Hotels.

Sharma's family at that time owned and ran SITA World Travels, one of the most influential travel companies in India, and Priya Paul had just entered her father's hotel venture. The Apeejay Surrendra Paul Group was into shipping, plantations, FMCG and construction, and when Priya joined, there were three hotels—the flagship Kolkata property set up in 1967, the Visakhapatnam hotel set up in 1980, and the hotel in New Delhi set up in 1987.

'She came to sell Park Hotels. I as a buyer of hotels was very keen to work with the group,' said Sharma.

As it had happened, there was a big piece of business from Spain for which SITA was struggling to get a good hotel. For Sharma, personally, who had just joined the family business, this was the first big deal he was negotiating. The meeting clicked. The transaction was concluded successfully.

The Park Hotels, located fabulously at Delhi's Connaught Place, was just the kind of hotel SITA was looking for because as Sharma says there was a class of global traveller who did not want *desi* ethnic trappings, yet wanted a modern boutique hotel with cutting-edge design.

'The whole energy that Priya creates in the hotels is fabulous. There is a market for that in the global traveller who loves that,' he says. 'At the same time,' he says, 'The Park also embodied the aspirations of Indian travellers.'

'Long before global hotel companies discovered the merits of lifestyle branding, Park Hotels properties were always design-led and offered a differentiated guest experience,' says Achin Khanna of consulting company Hotelivate.

Indeed, from the very beginning The Park in Kolkata carved a name for itself as the cool place to go to for parties. Born the year the Beatles visited India, 1967, it was named after the fashionable Park Street where it is located, and was at one time, as ad man Swapan Seth put it, 'a haven of hipness, where Kolkata came to sing, dance and chill'.

'When we started we were disruptors in a way. We were doing hotels in a different way. When there was no social media, we were reaching out to customers and communicating directly with them through our events and fun parties,' says Priya Paul.

The Park was also a trendsetter in terms of its unusual interiors and creative use of spaces. It made art and design the talking point.

'We were very design-focused. Not just space design, but communication design,' points out Paul.

The Park was one of the first to talk about immersive experiences. For instance, The Park Chennai, which came up on the space that was erstwhile Gemini studios, made it a point to pay homage to the historic film studio, with photographs, paintings and posters evoking the silver screen.

But it was an easy job in the 1990s and early 2000s for The Park to stand out and be noticed. There were only a few great hotel brands then, the foreign chains were still not in. So, everything The Park did stood out as new, contemporary and refreshing. Things changed with competition. Amidst the multitude of brands jostling in the Indian market—many of them in the same boutique hotels niche space that The Park straddled—The Park's voice got subdued a bit.

For instance, despite being around for such a long while, the Park Group does not feature within the top twenty in India when it comes to inventory of rooms, whereas younger brands such as Lemon Tree have whizzed ahead.

'When looked purely from a size and scale point of view, the Park Group hasn't grown at the same pace as some of the other domestic and international hotel chains in India,' agrees Achin Khanna.

It's true that the Park has stayed away from the frenzy and aggression of expansion, and perhaps lost out on visibility due to that. But it has not been quiet. It would try and create excitement of a different kind by trying new things. For instance, it was among the first to introduce the concept of a designer room within the hotel, roping in Tarun Tahiliani to design the La Sultana Room, which pays homage to the women of royal courts. It sort of fits into the ethos of the Park

Hyderabad, where the overall design takes inspiration from the Nizam's jewels.

With changing times, the Park did go back to the drawing board and rethink strategy. It launched a new brand called Zone by The Park to cater to a new audience.

'We saw a new kind of traveller, who is about people and passion and created a different kind of hotel,' explains Priya Paul. This new segment of hotel is positioned lower than The Park, which has upscaled itself a bit more.

It's also gone the asset-light route, expanding through management of properties rather than building them. The strategy clearly seems to be to keep the Park upscale and boutique, while the Zone will give the group scale and presence, especially in tier-two and tier-three towns. Coimbatore, Raipur, Jammu, Jodhpur, Jaipur are some of the cities where the Zone has opened.

Park Hotels group also has invested heavily in design. At The Park too, especially its Hyderabad property, huge elements from the world of fashion and design were incorporated to give it a different look. Priya Paul roped in artists and designers for the project.

'I wanted to work with people from the world of fashion, furniture, product design and art to create spaces and objects that could reflect different ways of luxury living. So, it has an 1,800 square-foot regal room created by fashion designer Tarun Tahiliani called La Sultana that comes with a lake view,' says Priya Paul.

The centrepiece is an opulent canopied four-poster bed, and the room rate is Rs 50,000 plus. In Tahiliani's words, which The Park shared in a press release, 'I have created an oasis where guests will wish to keep returning. At the La Sultana Suite, one relives a regal past and stays in the present.'

It's also doing unusual things like launching The Park Collection, picking up heritage properties and tapping into the market for quaint holidays. In Chettinad, the chain has taken over and restored a 150-year-old heritage mansion, calling it the Vaadhyar's House. At Serampore, near Kolkata, the group has taken over the management of the historic Denmark Taven, an over 230-year-old property, lovingly restoring it.

The group has also entered into some interesting partnerships. For instance, it is developing with the West Bengal state government a Biswa Bangla hotel near the new convention centre at Kolkata.

Vijay Dewan, the chain's MD, points out that the chain is expanding, though they are in no race. 'You have to be careful when expanding that the brand values are not lost,' he says.

Priya Paul points out that in its fifty-year-journey The Park has seen five-and-a-half-brand refreshes, a couple of them done by her father. It started out as Park, then became The Park, then The Park Hotels, and so on. Currently, it is proclaiming itself as THE Park in black and white tones with emphasis on 'THE'. And with the tagline: 'Anything but ordinary'.

And how does it hope to be unordinary? By stamping quirkiness, an individual identity, clever interior design and a shining personality.

On 1 November 2017, on the occasion of its fiftieth birthday, The Park recreated some of its old magic with a really electrifying all-night long bash at its Kolkata property. The discotheques and nightclubs at the hotel—

Someplace Else, Tantra, Roxy—erupted in a frisson of pulsating music and tapping feet even as the chefs laid out a smorgasbord of cheese, fruit, exotic meat cuts and sushi platters. There were curated heritage walks, tram tours, river cruises and sundry other experiences laid out for the guests.

'Turning fifty is exciting and overwhelming. But fifty years is also four generations. So, just as every family changes in every generation, I would like to think that THE Park has changed,' says Paul, who maintains that through it all the brand has also remained consistent.

According to the art aficionado, the culture code at The Park is to be creative, daringly different and spontaneously joyous at work. She hopes these will translate into appearing so to the customer as well.

The Lalit: Passionate Developers

Jyotsna Suri calls herself an accidental business leader. She had to take over the reins of the company, Bharat Hotels, when her husband, the flamboyant hotelier Lalit Suri, died suddenly during a business trip in London.

When Lalit Suri ran Bharat Hotels, the properties he owned had no particular character and no brand strategy of its own. The Delhi property wore the flag of the InterContinental while the Srinagar property was called the Grand. It was Suri himself, an automobile engineer (his family owned an auto parts company called 'Subros') and a larger-than-life figure, who commanded a lot of media attention as a politician-hotelier who threw lavish parties. His nickname was the Luxe Moghul.[1]

Many of the hotels owned by the company had been acquired from the government-run India Tourism Development Corporation during its disinvestment spree between 1999 and 2004. Incidentally these acquisitions were not without controversy, as Suri was close to the Gandhis—though he was equally friendly with other parties.

In fact, the story goes that Suri got into the hotel line to create infrastructure for the Asian Games in 1982 in Delhi. Overrun by delays, it only came up in 1988.[2]

It was Jyotsna Suri who gave the hotel chain a character and brand identity. Till 2008, all hotels in the Lalit Suri group were operated under the brand of the Grand Hotels, Palaces and Resorts. Suri decided to end all its foreign tie-ups and brand associations and create a new brand that was a living tribute to its founder chairman, her husband.

She hired Mumbai-based agency Chlorophyll for the task. Describing the thought behind the eye-catching logo, the late Anand Halve said, 'We developed the new brand name to represent his legacy, hence the name "The Lalit". The stylized graphic representation in the logo is a homage to Mr. Lalit Suri's devotion to Lord Ganesh and the 'L' of the Lalit, becomes the trunk of the Lord's image! Lord Ganesh also represents new beginnings and change.'

When Lalit Suri ran the chain, it was a personality-driven hotel group, but under Jyotsna Suri it is the hotel that slowly emerged into the limelight.

Jyotsna Suri might describe herself as an accidental leader, but she has both the genes and traits to be a successful one. An early riser and highly disciplined, Suri is not above taking risks—not a surprising trait really as she comes from entrepreneurial stock. Her father moved from Rawalpindi to Delhi during Partition and built a profitable Mercedes Benz truck business in far-flung Kutch. He was nonconformist enough to send Suri to a co-ed boarding school, the Lawrence School, Sanawar.[3]

One of the first things that Suri did was to go and reassure the staff at Great Eastern Kolkata, which the group had acquired, that the project would go on and to not have any apprehensions on that count.

Today, the Great Eastern is a jewel in the Lalit's crown. Stay there and you can't help getting bowled over by all the nostalgia—for not only has the hotel been restored, but a great many of the original artefacts and tableware are displayed—old silverware, wine glasses and so on.

Since her husband died in London, Jyotsna was determined to have a property in the city and acquired a former grammar school St Olave's at a cost of £15 million and turned it into a seventy-five-room boutique hotel near the Tower of London. It may not sound like a logical reason but Suri is a quaint mix of pragmatism and emotion.

'I don't develop hotels because I am adding numbers, but because I want to make a hotel in a particular city,' she says.

Significantly, the profitability of the group also improved under her leadership.

Hospitality consultant Manav Thadani calls Suri one of the leading lady lights of the hotel industry in India.

'She took over the Lalit business under very difficult circumstances and has continued with the vision of her late husband and, in many ways, has improved upon it,' he says.

Suri believes the mid-segment is where the future lies and, keeping pace with the way the industry is moving, was quick to launch the Lalit Traveller brand, a mid-market offering. But she is playing it carefully, minimizing risks. In Ahmedabad and Jaipur, for instance, the Lalit has both its upscale and mid-scale brands in one building.

She listens to the ideas of her children (daughters Divya and Deeksha and son Keshav) who are part of the management, and has given them free rein to experiment. It is exuberant Keshav, who has infused quite a bit of vibrancy and fun to the group's hotels.

'I have got itchy fingers—just like my mother,' declares Keshav, who is responsible for F&B, entertainment and several other aspects at the chain. He is constantly introducing new things that will bring the young through the doors of the Lalit.

'Look at how Kitty Su changed the face of this hotel,' he says, talking about the flagship Delhi property in Connaught Place that was a boringly serious hotel frequented by lawyers and a business crowd. The nightclub transformed things as did novel concepts such as the Nannery at its Indian restaurant Baluchi. At the Nannery, chefs rustle up an assortment of miniaturized versions of Indian breads—from rotis to kulchas and naans—rather theatrically. These are paired with wine and served to guests accompanied by the signature Dal Baluchi and a few chutneys.

'I coined the term Nannery and now we have trademarked it,' says Keshav, grinning.

Keshav also floated the idea of food trucks that ply in Delhi and Gurgaon and have captured the imagination of diners on the move. He is also looking at managing the catering at large gala places like the IPL cricket VIP areas (the ITC does some of it) and, in fact, managed to do so at Bangalore.

Jyotsna Suri says she always looks at the big picture. Rather than just focusing on building hotels, she says that her strategy is to try and develop destinations, bringing to light uncharted terrains like Bekal in Kerala and Chitrakoot near Khajuraho.

'As we continued to develop hotels, I felt a responsibility to the people in the immediate vicinity of our properties and realized that what mattered was not just building hotels but also the destinations,' she says.

The Bekal experiment, where the Lalit was one of the first to set up a hotel but where the destination took over fifteen years to develop as accessibility was a big issue, does not seem to have fazed Jyotsna Suri. She continues to invest in places that seem illogical to any other hotelier. For instance, take Mangar, an Aravali wildlands between Faridabad and Gurgaon, totally off the beaten track, where the Lalit has set up an eco-friendly resort.

But Suri's plan is to bring this beautiful area into the limelight.

'It is a great place for a staycation, or for offsites. We have always created destinations, not hotels,' she says, pointing to how the idea is to play up local festivals and traditions and invest in cultural rejuvenation of the place. For instance, the group conducts the Shiv Vivah at Khajuraho, the traditional polo in Kargil, and so on.

Meanwhile, Keshav Suri who has become the face of the LGBTQ community, is driving in change at the Lalit in the way it recruits. At Oko, the Japanese restaurant at the Lalit Delhi, transgenders wait at the table. The Lalit is perhaps the first hospitality chain to endorse the UN's LGBTQ standards at work—it has funded surgeries of transgenders employed with it and hosts special nights for the community at its nightclub Kitty Su.

But ask Jyotsna Suri about what is the differentiator at Lalit and she says, 'We are passionate developers and passionate hoteliers. We are a homegrown chain not supported by anyone. Whatever we generate is ploughed right back into our hotels.'

6

The Global Goliaths

'Great companies are built by people who never stop thinking about ways to improve the business.'

—J. Willard Bill Marriott

They came, they saw, they failed to conquer—that was in the 1960s, and then again in the 1970s and 1980s. But if anything, international chains have been persistent in their attempts to occupy the Indian market. And eventually, most of them managed to crack the code.

By 2018, literally every big global hotel chain—Marriott, Accor, IHG, Hyatt, Hilton, Carlson and Wyndham—was present in India. Each took a different approach to making inroads into the market, making several blunders, but they learnt from their mistakes and slowly and surely carved a space in the Indian traveller's heart and mind.

The entry of the international chains has been a really important turning point for Indian hospitality because while the complexity of the Indian market may have challenged them initially, once they got their bearings right, they brought in some important ingredients—discipline, efficiency, transparency and strong processes—to the sector.

If India, with its myriad peculiar challenges, forced the foreign chains to learn and adapt, then the Indian chains benefitted a lot by learning from the models of the foreign chains. In the process, it's the customer who gained as a wide array of choices and better quality of rooms and service opened up.

The first international chain to make an entry into India was the British hospitality company IHG, which arrived in Delhi in partnership with the Oberoi way back in the 1960s. Starwood's Sheraton brand was probably the second when it partnered with first the Oberoi in Mumbai in the mid-1970s and then ITC in 1979, allowing it use of its brand name. The partnership between ITC and Starwood survived for nearly forty years and was renewed again in 2016. American firm Hyatt also got its flag planted early with a hotel in Delhi in 1983. But until liberalization in the 1990s, India was really not an interesting or attractive market for the foreign chains. Despite a large population, the number of domestic or international guests staying in branded hotels was not big enough to warrant serious investments from them.

Of course, many of them did fish around a bit here but did not really make much effort. For instance, in the 1980s, French chain Accor explored a partnership with the Oberoi Group to create a few Novotels in India. But talks fell through. The Oberoi Group then flirted with Hilton. But nothing came of it.

It was only in the early 2000s that the foreign chains began coming in packs. By now the ecosystem was conducive for hotels to thrive. Stock markets were booming, disposable incomes were rising, and Indians were travelling like never before, both overseas and domestically. Also, with the boom in IT services, companies like IBM, Microsoft and others were sending their executives to India in large numbers. IBM internationally is one of the biggest buyers of hotel rooms, and accounts for a large chunk of the rooms of MNC hotel chains. Hotels do tend to follow lucrative corporate accounts.

To begin with, the foreign chains set up development teams here to find partners. Most international chains operate on an asset-light management model, lending their brand name for a fee. By 2005, many had signed several contracts.

Accor, which arrived here in 2006, was one of the few exceptions to the rule. It came in as an investor. This was Accor's fifth attempt to enter India, and by now it had a modicum of knowledge of the Indian market. Wisely, it decided to come on a partnership with InterGlobe, the company behind the low-cost airline Indigo co-founded by Rahul Bhatia, a knowledgeable player in the travel industry.

A chat with Jean-Michel Cassé, chief operating officer, India and South Asia, Accor Hotels, on why the French chain succeeded in 2004 after five failed attempts is instructive. He describes how in the 1980s, a partnership was almost sealed with the Oberoi Group. It was a time when the Oberoi Group was looking at what foreign players were doing outside India. The business model they were keen on bringing to India was Novotel. Things moved, and four or five hotels were built in India—including one in Mumbai and one in Jaipur—that were replicas of Novotels.

But the Oberois wanted to make their hotel more luxurious than the Novotels usually were, and add more services. They felt that the Indian customer would not accept a model where there had to be so much self-service—if they were paying for a room they would expect a lot of bells and whistles. Also, the design sensibilities—tiles in contrast to granite—was not to the Oberoi Group's taste. All this was not agreeable to Accor, which refused to change anything in the hotel.

'Rattan Keswani (ex-Oberoi executive, now part of Lemon Tree's management) who was privy to the discussions, told us we were much too stubborn,' says Cassé. He says he agrees with that analysis.

'It was a great opportunity for Accor as they could have got an early mover advantage in India. It was also a great opportunity for the Oberoi Group—they could have had 500 Novotels up in the country by 2018 if they had done it then,' Keswani says. He says, however, that he can't blame the Oberoi Group as their call was that they were not comfortable doing it. '*Kuch cheez mere zehan mein nahin to main nahin chala sakta*—what is not in my soul I cannot do,' he sums up.

'That failed experiment, however, held many learnings, for both the Oberoi Group as well as Accor. What we learnt from that failure was that customization is key. We needed to adapt the product to the region,' says Cassé.

As for the Oberoi Group, it learnt how to improve their operating efficiencies in many little ways. 'Today, in Lemon Tree, where Keswani is part of the senior management, if you see those systems, it's a takeaway of the Oberoi–Accor lessons,' says Cassé.

Incidentally, the four or five hotels that were set up by the Oberoi Group then are what is known as brand Trident. The Indian chain decided to develop the brand on its own.

'Apart from bringing in an upgraded version of Novotel and Ibis into India compared to what they operate globally, there were two other important reasons why Accor's entry in 2004 was successful,' says Cassé. 'A big factor was that this time around it invested a chunk of money—a commitment of $200 million—when it entered. Also, it found the right partner in InterGlobe, a company that had set up a young exciting airline, had a start-up mentality and was hungry for growth. Why we didn't succeed before was because we lacked these two elements—the right partnership and readiness to invest,' he says.

This is echoed by another successful Western entrant into India, Carlson Rezidor (now renamed as Radisson Hotel Group)'s former boss in India Raj Rana, who talks of how having skin in the game helps, as well as investing in relationships. Early on, the group got into a strategic partnership with Bestech Hospitalities to develop forty-nine hotels in India, putting in some stake.

Similar was the case with Marriott, Starwood and Hyatt, who got solid Indian partners when they entered India with a serious intention and were less rigid.

Accor's was an interesting model of entry, and explains the group's slow and steady growth in the country. In terms of scale, it may not have blazed as rapid a growth as the Radisson Group and Marriott but the measured growth perhaps helped in the long run, seeing it through the downcycle of 2015–17. Accor and InterGlobe entered into a joint venture to build hotels in which InterGlobe had 60 per cent share and Accor 40 per cent. Another JV was formed to manage hotels with the stakes ratio reversed—Accor holding the higher share.

'This time, we were not just saying we want to be in India—but showing faith and investing,' says Cassé.

A few years later, Accor also entered into a threeway partnership called Triguna with InterGlobe and government of Singapore Investment Corporation (GIC) from Singapore to build seven hotels. Each held a third of the shares. It took ten years or so but all seven hotels came up—the Novotel–Pullman combo in Aerocity, Delhi; the Novotel–Ibis combo at OMR, Chennai; the Novotel–Ibis combo in Bangalore and a stand-alone Novotel at State Industries Promotion Corporation of Tamil Nadu Ltd (SIPCOT) in Chennai. This itself is big in India, where projects are announced and more often than not don't take off.

Though Cassé does not say it, the fact that he has been leading the group's operations for over ten years in India— he jokes that he has outlasted three Taj hotels' CEOs—is another important reason that Accor has been doing well. If partnerships have been an important element in the success of a chain, leadership contributed significantly too. The continuity provided by Cassé, who was open and receptive, was reassuring to owners who had seen rotating CEOs in many other foreign companies.

'In Asia, development of hotels is a matter of trust, of building relationships—and in India it is even more important,' says Cassé. It is not a matter of good marketing and pumping in money, but being able to bank on relationships.

This is strikingly similar to what the Radisson Group, which in 2015 was ahead of all the foreign chains in the number of hotels in the country, was doing too. Veteran ITDC man K.B. Kachru—a man of enormous talent and one who knew the country well, spearheaded the group since 1998 for fifteen years and was hugely instrumental in Radisson's early success in a very understated way. If one sees the HVS reports on hotels in India in the mid-2000s, it was the Radisson group that was ahead in terms of number of hotels. Kachru had become GM of a hotel when at ITDC at the age of twenty-four—no mean feat in a public service undertaking. His successor Raj Rana was another ITDC man.

Similarly, Starwood and Marriott did well when it had experienced Indian hoteliers helming their operations—the charming Dilip Puri and the suave Rajeev Menon, who could talk the same language as the owners. Meanwhile, a procession of expatriates unfamiliar with India led Hilton and IHG, which were struggling to penetrate India.

Unlike the US and other markets, where usually professional financial institutions held hotel assets; in India, ownership is with a motley bunch of people, mom-and-pop operators, big developers and institutional investors or businessmen with spare cash and large egos. Managing them is an art.

As Dilip Puri says, 'There's no one-size-fits-all approach to deal with them.'

Building Relationships

Marriott started off with a bang, riding on partnerships with predominantly real estate players like the Chordias and the Rahejas, who were big developers. Its journey in India started with a partnership with the Salgaocars of Goa. It built the JW Marriott and the Renaissance in Bombay with the Rahejas. It liked the model and stuck to it for some time.

It also helped that it had a brand that had resonance in the Indian market and was at the right price point. This was the case with Radisson too.

However, along the way, despite a good start, Marriott managed to annoy a lot of its assertive real estate owner–partners, who felt they were being shortchanged. Marriott would go by feasibility studies provided by consultants, which said a particular hotel in a particular area could only command a certain rate. And strictly going by its rates, it would decide on the brand allocation.

However, the owner would have overbuilt and made a lavish property. This was the case with Panschil Reality's Pune hotel which had bigger rooms and fancier fittings than a Marriott brand usually would have. But the US chain said the hotel on Senapati Bapat Marg did not warrant a JW Marriott, its more upscale offering. Owner Ranjit Bhatia was grumpy about it—'I admit I had overbuilt but why should I have settled for a $100 rack rate versus a $200 that a JW Marriott commands,' was his point. Eventually he got his way.

Similar was the case with a hotel in Chandigarh.

As a result of such situations, Marriott's portfolio was initially riddled with discrepancies creeping in between the brand values and the hotel. For instance, Courtyard by Marriott, a mid-market brand abroad, was almost upscale, commanding a rate of a five star. Also, it was a bit slow to push its economy warrior, Fairfield by Marriott. It really did not have a great product in that segment, actually.

And when it did bring in its super luxurious Ritz Carlton to India, the brand seemed to pale against the Indian luxury players—the Oberoi and the Taj's highest-end properties. Observers say that Marriott's mistake, for which it could pay for in the long run, was that it sacrificed brand sanctity.

On the customer front, however, Marriott was a preferred name, especially in Bangalore, where a lot of movement between India and the US happened and the brand had huge recall and recognition.

Even as the issues with the owners got smoothened out over time and Marriott was showing sizeable scale in India, thanks to adopting a humbler approach where it took trouble to listen to and talk out problems with owners, the global merger happened with Starwood in 2016. Interestingly, Starwood was doing pretty well in India, earning enormous goodwill even though some of its brands like Le Méridien were not living up their brand ethos, despite a massive marketing campaign. To make up, it succeeded with Westin, and Sheraton, despite having a tired image abroad, did well in India. The fact that Starwood had been here longer and had deep relationships with ITC helped.

Post-merger, managing local talent became a sticky point for the Marriott–Starwood joint entity. The fact that Marriott now had brands that competed against Starwood's brands and there was enormous confusion between the two only aggravated the issue. Owners were worried.

Craig Smith, president and MD Asia-Pacific of the merged entity, admitted that managing integration was tough. A lot of good talent had to be let go as there was duplication in roles and the morale went down.

'If I picked on somebody, I would be told, "Oh, you are picking on them because they are from Starwood." No, I would say, I am picking on them because they are not doing their job,' he said.

Owners with Starwood brands were also worried as to what would happen to their hotels.

'The mistake we made in the beginning,' said Smith, 'was that we took too long to make decisions as we were trying so hard to be fair and nice. We could have also communicated some of the benefits faster to the owners. We worried about Marriottizing the Starwood brands,' he said.

Global happenings do tend to cast a shadow on local operations and a chain that was doing pretty well here suddenly faced talent issues as well as trust issues as the merger created big confusion. Customers were worried about their loyalty points.

Meanwhile, global developments at Accor helped the French chain. In late 2013, the French chain had appointed investment banker Sebastian Bazin as its global chief to bring some financial discipline to the chain. But he brought in far more.

Bazin told me in 2014, during his first trip to India, 'I left investment banking to come to a human industry, which is the hotel industry—and not to do finance in Accor. It's a new job for me, a new life. But I will bring to Accor my financial discipline and probably a lot of methodology. But much more than anything else I am bringing to Accor the direction and big ambition to grow this company faster and better.'

Bazin was no stranger to the hotel world, having worked the night shift in hotels for three years while he was a student.

Soon after coming on board, he made changes to the operating structure of Accor. He separated the company into two different missions—those at the service of guests, and those at the service of the investor. Different missions, different expertise, different talents, different benchmarks. It makes it much easier for people to take decisions, as he explained. In each of the geographies, he also further segmented the business into luxury and upscale, mid-scale and budget, and economy. In India, he decided the focus should initially be largely on budget and mid-scale. So Accor invested all its energies on Novotel and Ibis though it did bring in Pullman, Sofitel and Grand Mercure here.

Bazin's decision-making was fast and closely in tune with global trends. Under his watch Accor made a huge number of investments, especially in technology companies, as well as got chains like Banyan Tree, Raffles and Fairmont into the fold. More on those later.

Among the other Western chains, the Radisson Group, Wyndham and Hyatt found stickiness with their owners, the former two because they were flexible with the product and focused on relationships, while the latter was not chasing scale, and only signing after deep thought. So, the same owner would do multiple hotels with them. For example, the Radisson Group did multiple hotels with Bestech Group, and Hyatt became synonymous with the Sarafs (the owners of the Grand Hyatt in Mumbai).

Raj Rana of Radisson proudly points out that the group did not lose even a single contract when the time for renewal came up after fifteen years. Every owner renewed.

'Imagine after ten to fifteen years of marriage, there is some wear and tear and some stress, and there is now plenty of choice for owners and yet the fact that they have come back to us shows the relationships and their endurance are critical,' he says.

Scale versus Quality

A common mistake made by international chains when they entered India was also that many began chasing scale at the cost of deeper study into the integrity and financial strength of owners. Now, scale was important to their models which was tied to distribution strength, loyalty programmes and so on. So literally, every foreign chain seemed to be engaged in who will hit 100 hotels in India first race. But in this race for scale, the hotel chains made compromises on the types of partners they were associating with—many of them had no real history of running hotels or were mired in debts. Also, because of the intense competition, the chains began discounting on their management fees. And many signed partnerships went nowhere. In 2006, Accor tied up with Emaar MGF to set up 100 budget hotels with an investment of US$300 million.[1] The same year Hilton formed a joint venture with realty major DLF to open seventy-five hotels and service apartments in seven years. Both alliances failed to take off. DLF bought back Hilton's stake in the joint venture in 2011.[2]

The InterContinental Group set up a joint venture in 2011 with global asset manager Duet Group, called Duet India Hotels, to develop nineteen Holiday Inn Express Hotels. But that venture had quite a rocky tenure and eventually IHG divested its 24 per cent stake in a span of eight years.[3] But IHG managed to make up for it by signing twelve hotels with SAMHI, a lodging development company.

Hilton, however, took a long time to recover from its India misadventures. In 2018, it had barely seventeen hotels in India, compared to the 100 notched up by Marriott or the fifty by Accor.

Ex-Marriott man Navjeet Ahluwalia, who took charge of Hilton in India in 2018, admits, 'Our previous JVs did not pan out the way intended. It was a case of missed opportunities. Several hotels that wore the Hilton flag—two hotels in Delhi's Mayur Vihar suburb for instance—moved to IHG.'

Even the owners they had relationships with, such as the Muthoot Pappachan Group in the south, they couldn't sign the next hotel that the group built in Kochi, losing out to Accor.

Ahluwalia, however, remained optimistic about Hilton's fortunes in India changing, especially with a strategy to focus on the gaps in the market—resorts, big box hotels and so on. Hilton's idea is to make India its third-largest lodging market after the US and China, he said.

Right from the start, Hyatt did not chase scale. Kurt Straub, former vice president of operations for Hyatt in India, said they had been mindful of expansion.

'Hyatt does not want to be biggest company in the world. We want to be the most preferred,' he said.

Unlike the other chains, which were very focused on the business market, Hyatt, in addition, was pushing to drive leisure more. This is reflected in its choice of destinations—Bolgatty Islands in Kerala, Rameshwaram. As Straub explained, 'There is a great opportunity we feel to tap into the religious pilgrimage market. We are going into places like Jaipur as well as markets such as McLeodganj in the Himalayas.' Even in cities, if you look at Hyatt's launches—the Andaz at a location like Aerocity is not a *business* hotel, but more catering to a crowd looking for a break.'

Hyatt also tapped into the opportunity for MICE (meetings, incentives, conferences and exhibitions). Although Kerala is predominantly a leisure market, in just one year since its opening in 2018, the Grand Hyatt at Bolgatty Islands in Kochi had logged 250 MICE events, the largest being a medical conference that saw 9000 delegates streaming into the hotel per day. According to Mausam Bhattacharjee, director of sales and marketing at Grand Hyatt, Kochi, 70 per cent of the hotel's revenues in the first year came through the convention centre attached to the hotel that it managed for the Lulu group.

Managing versus Franchising

For Wyndham, which has brands like Ramada, franchising has been one of the reasons for its successes in India. Several owners don't want to let go control and Wyndham early on recognized this and played on this. Deepika Arora, the bubbly regional vice president of Wyndham Hotel Group, says that they preferred to follow the franchising model because it gave flexibility to owners. It also works out cheaper for owners not willing to part with the huge operating fee.

'We were doing a different kind of expansion strategy through a different model which at that time the other brands were not following,' she said.

Wyndham was doing franchising only. Initially, franchising was also easier for Wyndham because as Arora points out the chain itself was not equipped enough to provide on-ground support to be able to do management.

According to her, most of the rival chains were adding hotels to expand their portfolio and purely to drive higher gross operating profits (GOPs). And they were signing up with owners who had absolutely no clue how to run the hotel. Wyndham instead looked for owners that did not want to relinquish control.

'Whenever I had interacted with owners, they said two things—"we need financial control and we should have the purchase control,"' Arora said.

Radisson's Raj Rana too bats for franchising.

'If you look all around the world, many companies have a very strong franchising arm. Management of course remains our core competency but, instead of having extensive wear and tear on a relationship, if there is a trustworthy partner whom you believe will uphold your brand standard—and many owners actually do because they are very proud of their own hotel—then why not franchise,' he said. 'They are not going to run the hotel down and so if you can provide the initial hand-holding—and these are hotels may be in the range of 100 rooms—it is a perfect plan if it's a successful brand, rather than having a relationship where there is so much pressure and that you are not meeting eye to eye,' he added.

Radisson also tried out manchising—a hybrid model whereby it would manage a hotel for a couple of years and then after that franchise it out. Almost 10 per cent of Radisson Group's hotels in India were on the manchised model.

Franchising does have one challenge—the chain does not earn as much as it could through management, getting just a brand license fee.

'But we are not cheap also,' Arora asserted. Also, she points that Wyndham then does not have the kind of operating costs of others. 'The team is very lean and mean. Otherwise it doesn't work for any business. Just eight people running forty-odd properties. Sometimes we outsource. You have to be very strategic in terms of how you are supporting,' she added.

Rattan Keswani points out that while franchising might not have the same yields as ownerships in terms of valuations, it benefits the operating company. 'Among the three models, ownership, managing and franchising, the former gets the most returns. However, risks are highest. In the case of managing, the risks are lower as are returns but you make up as valuation goes up. In the case of franchising, there is risk of brand erosion. However if contracts are drawn up well, the valuation multiple is higher, he said.'

The Distribution Battle

For the MNC hotelier, its distribution muscle, riding on technology, is its biggest strength and differentiator in the Indian market. All have very strong loyalty programmes (see chapter on loyalty). In India, hotel demand is primarily driven by corporate and conferences—almost 60 per cent of the bookings come through this route. A hotel with better distribution and a portfolio of hotels in different brackets is in an advantageous position when it comes to corporate clients. It can cater to companies at different levels, with rooms at different rates.

While the MNC chains have strong technology, India is one of those peculiar markets where foot soldiers are needed to close the account. Look at what IHG is doing. The group launched a national sales organization within the company comprising around twenty-nine professionals spread across India.

'We did this so that the people we do business with—the purchasers, the buyers, the bookers—don't have to talk to individual hotels as point of contact. We made the decision-making process very convenient for them,' explains Shantha de Silva of IHG. According to him, this move enabled them to leverage their scale better. 'If I as a buyer want hotel rooms, I don't have to talk to people in six cities but can talk to one person.'

This was primarily aimed at the corporate customer but it worked for leisure too where bookings were coming from general sales agents.

Hospitality consultancy firm HVS often does a sentiment analysis among owners on their preferences. HVS recently conducted a survey among hotel owners asking if they had to choose between Indian brands versus global brands which would they prefer. Fifty-five per cent said they preferred global brands, with forty-five choosing Indian.

The Second Siege

After the big global chains, the lesser chains from abroad too started making a foray into India. One saw brands like Swissotel, Kempinski and Fairmont making determined attempts. Kempinski came in on a tie-up with Leela and later tried on its own too. A few like Swissotel managed to sign properties—but then global consolidations happened, and it got acquired into the Accor fold as did Fairmont.

Soon after, the big guns of global hospitality—Marriott, Accor, IHG, Hilton, Hyatt, Wyndham, Radisson—dropped anchor in India, the Asian brands too began arriving. Around 2013 or so, one could see a slice of Thailand in New Delhi as brand Dusit made its entry through a tie-up with the Bird Group, which had interests in travel, luxury and aviation.

Hong Kong-based Shangri La Hotels, which was already present in Delhi, made a bid for Mumbai too, putting its flag on the posh property above Palladium Mall in Lower Parel. It had big plans to open several hotels in India.

Iconic chain Banyan Tree made a beeline for Kerala, with plans for a sixty-villa luxurious resort in an island in the southern state, the blueprint of a hotel in Goa and scouting opportunities for its Angsana brand in the north.

'We look for markets that are rich in cultural diversity—India fits us like a tee,' Abid Butt, global CEO, Banyan Tree Hotels and Resorts, proclaimed at that time, also pointing to shared affinities with the country.

With several Indians visiting Thailand and Indonesia are staying at Banyan Tree resorts, Butt felt that it would be easy to introduce the brand in India. The fact that India was a huge feeder market to its hotels in West Asia also lured Jumeirah and Rotana to India. According to data released by Dubai's department of tourism and commerce marketing, India topped international overnight visitors to Dubai, with 2.1 million Indians visiting the Emirate.[4]

As the Indian market boomed, Indonesian company Alila too came calling.

A huge number of Asian hotel companies sent emissaries on fishing expeditions. For instance, representatives from

Armani hotels (marketed by the Emaar group) and delegates from Peninsula Hotels could be seen at hotel summits like HICSA (Hotel Investment Conference South Asia), networking furiously. Aman Hotels put up its flag in Delhi at what was once ITDC's Lodhi Hotel, and for a brief while, it was the darling of the swish set in the capital. Lebua Hotels arrived with grand plans, putting up its flag in Delhi's Dwarka suburb and in Lucknow—and in fact many of us were taken on property visits.

Not only was the Indian market booming but, coincidentally, the Asian brands too were at that very time expanding out of their geographies, and venturing west. For instance, Shangri La had opened in Paris, while Banyan Tree had branched out into Greece and Corfu. India seemed nearer and a bigger market.

But for the Asian brands, just imagining that they were culturally compatible with India and so things would be easy in India did not prove right. Lebua and Aman got singed badly. Lebua Hotels, famous for the *Hangover* scene, had in next to no time a falling out with the owner of the Dwarka hotel. The owner was reportedly not willing to make the kind of outlandish investments that Lebua wanted him to make, forcing the brand to exit. Lebua's plans as outlined by its CEO Deepak Ohri sounded way too grand.[5] Not only did he talk about an ambitious pipeline of hotels in India but also of starting Lebua Air, a charter service, for its guests.

For Aman, the India outing went sour because real estate biggie DLF, which bought the Indonesian brand, got mired in financial trouble. Though its founder Adrian Zecha recovered control of the brand, the trophy property in Delhi went to

DLF. Banyan Tree too, which tried to come in 2008 with an Angsana property in Coorg, suddenly saw the developer changing his mind.

Of all the Asian brands that tried to make inroads into India, only Alila grew—though not at the pace it imagined. Its property in Goa and Bishangarh, Jaipur, have been fairly well-appreciated, going by TripAdvisor ratings.

When they came in, the Asian brands talked about how they were entering with differentiated products and scoffed at the myth of American distribution strength. Arjan de Boer of Alila went so far as to say, 'Whilst American distribution used to be very important, Asian distribution is becoming much more important with more affluent travellers from India, China and South East Asia.'

As for Banyan Tree's Abid Butt, he said that global Goliaths might have the distribution reach, but brands like his were actually not targeting that market. He said that their eye was on the leisure market and travel agents, and added that Asian designs and sensibilities were the rage the world over. Plus, on F&B, the Asian brands were better attuned to the taste buds of India.

Be that as it may, most Asian brands had to return home disappointed, while the West Asian brands never even got started despite circling around India quite a bit. The Banyan Tree Kerala project never took off as it got into environmental deep waters.

Dusit's tie-up with the Bird Group ended abruptly in 2016 when the latter decided to go on its own by creating its own brand. And quite suddenly the Dusit flag vanished from Delhi's skylines.

Round one of the siege of India clearly belonged to global brands. However, the Asian brands story is far from over in India. French chain Accor, which after getting the mid-scale story right in India and has started augmenting its luxury portfolio, will bring in Banyan Tree and the iconic Raffles brands. In 2016, Accor entered into a strategic partnership with Banyan Tree to co-develop the brand and in 2015 acquired Raffles, Fairmont and Swissotel.

By 2025, India could well see a plethora of new global brands, from the boutique to the big.

7

The Intrepid Explorers

'We're here to put a dent in the universe. Otherwise why else even be here?'

—Steve Jobs

For a long time India's hotel landscape had just a few branded players. The Taj, the Oberoi and the ITC dominated the scene with a few other impactful players like the Leela and The Park. Each had their differences but their core models were largely alike.

Although the big age of change in Indian hospitality, as Dilip Puri, former India head of Starwood, terms it, happened only after 2000, there were some early disruptors who tried something new and different. Many in the industry feel that Anil Madhok, founder of the Sarovar Hotels and Resorts Group, was a true change-maker as he tried to create a new category—the mid-market hotel—targeted at the middle class, thereby expanding the market considerably. While he opened the gateway, maverick hotelier Patu Keswani redefined the mid-market space much more flamboyantly, with his Lemon Tree hotel chain with a series of innovations.

Before that, down south in Kerala, the idealistic Jose Dominic was doing something utterly different—creating hotels that defied convention. He called it bare-bones luxury. A large part of the credit for Kerala emerging as a state famous for its tourism and earning the tag of God's Own Country goes to Dominic. His success on the backwaters spurred a number of private players to set up similar resorts, leading to a rush to the area.

In the 2000s, many Indian hoteliers took the risk of leaving their safe jobs with the big chains to try something new and different. Ashish Jakhanwala tried a new model of ownership, focusing on efficient finance management; Param Kanampilly decided to go the green route with his Fern hotels. The atmosphere was also right for many a player like Chander Baljee of Royal Orchids to ambitiously and bravely expand the family business of one hotel set up to many. He made many mistakes, but for sheer persistence and gamely taking on the big boys, his story is interesting.

Then there is the brash Ankur Bhatia of the Bird Group who forayed into hotels through a tie-up with Thai company Dusit and later created his own brand. Although there are sceptics about his model, he has the legacy of a travel and airline business and sky-high confidence (the Bird group actually put in a bid to acquire India's national carrier Air India).

In 2018, former Oberoi President Kapil Chopra decided to launch Postcard Hotels, convinced there was a gap in luxury that he could address with an experiential chain that would be both modern as well as old worldly. The hotelier whose motto is to challenge the status quo says people are looking at travel in a different way and his chain is there to cater to that.

*

The following are stories of a few of these hoteliers:

Jose Dominic: An Earthy Philosophy

Luxury is not built ostentation. It is the experience, asserts Jose Dominic, chairman of CGH Earth, a pathbreaking chain of hotels from Kerala.

'Even if it is a mud and thatch unit, it can still be luxurious,' he argues, pointing out that the strong ingredients for what he calls bare-bones luxury are respect for environment and respect for community.

That's the model and core value of this remarkable chain which has time and again defied the conventional way of operating hotels. Long before talking about sustainability became fashionable, long before hoteliers began talking of experiences rather than services, Dominic was doing it. While others were focusing on ramping up their F&B to offer the finest cuisine, focusing on their bars, and putting in bells and whistles in rooms, Dominic was mulling over the word 'holiday' and coming up with new definitions for it.

'My grandfather never went on a holiday. But he might have gone on a pilgrimage. And if you think about it, a holiday is nothing but a pilgrimage for yourself,' he says. For long, a holiday had come to mean wearing Bermudas, drinking and eating a lot. It was time to disrupt the concept, he says.

Although a reluctant hotelier, persuaded by his father through many plaintive letters to give up his job as a Chartered Accountant with A.F. Ferguson in Mumbai and take charge of the family hotel, Dominic had an instinct for the business, bringing in fresh ideas. Or perhaps it was because he was not a trained hotelier who had grown up through the kitchens and corridors but had an outside-in perspective that he could be different.

Dominic's father ran the Casino Hotel in Wellingdon Island in Kochi. Initially, it was started as a restaurant in 1957 as a partnership with friends—the name Casino being suggested by one of the partners who had returned from a Europe tour. In 1967, his dad decided to add rooms to the restaurant and make it into a thirty-two-room hotel. He also bought over his partners' shares.

Jose Dominic's baptism by fire came in 1988 when the Casino Hotels Group—the name under which his father operated—bid for the operations to manage a property at Bangaram Island resort in Lakshadweep. There were several big boys in the fray, all bidding for a foothold in this lovely virgin island. They all said they wanted months to do feasibility studies and anticipated crores for the project. But it was Dominic's pitch of not disturbing the island, using local architecture and methods and promising to have the resort ready in months at a budget of less than a crore that swung the deal. He got the lease for twenty-five years.

When the resort opened, the advertisement pitch was no telephones or television sets or swimming pools but an offer of nature in its most pristine form. And yet it pulled in people despite the tariff of $180 a night—which steadily climbed to over $400 a night.

Dominic's Bangaram association ended in a messy legal battle with the government, which terminated the lease before twenty-five years and put so many fresh conditions in the fresh bid that his group was not eligible.[1]

But says Dominic without rancour that the success of the Bangaram experiment was what led to the group's unique model of focusing on bare-bones luxury and keeping it as close to the local ethos as possible.

The next venture on the mainland in Kerala was the Spice Village at Thekkady. It was the first time that a private hotel group was setting up a resort in a remote location—till then the model was either city hotels or at Kovalam. There were only Kerala Tourism Development Corporation (KTDC) properties in the locations. Spice Village replicated a tribal village with the cottages made exactly the way the Mannan tribe built their homes, using elephant-grass roots. The staff at the hotel wore the Kerala dress of *mundu* (dhoti) and *jubba*—no bow-tie and pants and shirts here. The food served was *naadan* Kerala cuisine. The place became a roaring hit.

Coconut Lagoon, which came soon after in the backwaters of Kumarakam, again kept it as close to the local ethos as possible. On top of it, Dominic chose a site that was impossible to reach by road—the last mile had to be by boat. The cottages at the property were all created by reassembling old ancestral homes of people who were tearing these down to build modern structures.

'I got these for a song, and hired carpenters to reassemble them,' reminisced Dominic. Tourists were utterly charmed.

In 1994, plague hit the city of Surat in Gujarat and foreign tourists stayed away from India. That had an unexpected consequence. That was the year India discovered India, recalls Dominic. Well-off Indian tourists—especially from Gujarat began flocking to the backwaters of Kerala. So popular did Coconut Lagoon become that for couples about to be married, the joke was that a condition was the honeymoon had to be at the property.

Dominic kept charting an unusual path for his next projects, creating a faux colonial structure in Brunton Boatyard so that it could match with the setting of Fort Kochi which was dotted with Dutch-, Portuguese- and English-style buildings.

He again defied convention at the Kolangod Palace by opening a property where no meat or alcohol would be served. That was the precondition of the owners who were leasing it to him. So, Dominic restored the palace and created an Ayurveda resort at the palace—Kalari Kovilagam—charging €5,000 a night. The rate proved to be no deterrent and the palace hotel always had a waiting list—so much so that Dominic had to open another property, Kalari Rasayanam. This gave us the highest yield per room, said Dominic.

And as if that was not radical enough then, the group rolled out a one-key hotel, Chittoor Kotaram, the tiny palace that the rajah of Cochin, Rama Verma, built for himself in order to be close to the Guruvayur Temple. Only one family could make a booking. And there were lots of dos and don'ts for guests booking into the property. They needed to enter barefoot and stay that way. The menu is sparse— only one item a day. And yet people booked a stay in this unique hotel for the sheer novelty of the experience of being treated like a Kerala king.

In 2004, Dominic decided to rename the group to reflect the core philosophy of being one with the earth. Besides, Casino Hotels was a rather misleading name. Guests would come expecting a casino. Or guests would not book thinking there was a casino. And yet, a connect with the old name was needed. Thus the chain became CGH Earth, which could stand for Casino Group Hotels or for Clean Green Healthy. 'Those three words define us now,' says Dominic. After the new name, the group decided to exit all those properties that did not fit in with the philosophy—there was an Anjali Hotel, Pandal Restaurant etc.

The first venture outside the state was to Karnataka in Gokarna—a yoga retreat called SwaSwara.

Though most of the CGH Earth properties are owned or leased, Dominic is not averse to managing properties either, so long as they fit into the core philosophy. Eighth Bastion, a boutique property in Fort Kochi, is a managed property, for instance.

A pragmatic idealist, Dominic also thinks far ahead. 'Family-owned businesses rarely survive the fourth generation,' he says. So, now that the third generation—his children as well as his brother's children—are in the business, he has set in motion succession planning as well as a road map for the future. 'If on a table only brothers and cousins sit and talk, baggage will come in. An outside investor needs to come in,' says Dominic.

The lessons from Dominic's journey is to find a core proposition, believe in your product and stick to it, not look at the rules of the day, and be ruthless about exiting non-core businesses. It needs immense amount of courage and self-belief.

*

Anil Madhok and Ajay Bakaya: Mid-Market Messiahs

It's a cold winter afternoon in Delhi. The year is 2017. The press has been summoned to a hotel in Nehru Place for an important announcement. Anil Madhok, managing director, Sarovar Hotels is announcing sale of a majority stake to Lourdes group of France. Madhok, the founder of this mid-market chain, is waiting in the hall. Suddenly he bends down and picks up something from the carpet. It's a nail. 'Somebody will get hurt,' he says.

Madhok is the proverbial detail-conscious service-oriented hotelier, fussing around his properties, making sure everything is fine. He may be the promoter of a big chain but the old training will not go. Groomed in the Oberoi School of hoteliering, he is the quintessential hospitable host. Nothing escapes his trained eye.

Today every hotelier you talk to believes the pot of gold lies in the mid-market segment. But back when reforms started in the early 1990s, and the economy was just opening up, nobody was really interested in it. Yes, ITC had sensed the gap and set up its Fortune brand for this segment but it was taking its time moving in.

It was former Oberoi man, Anil Madhok, vice president for operations for the western and northern regions of the chain, who sensed the opportunity.

'I spent six months studying the market, assessing the chances. And I felt there was a huge scope as the big chains—Taj, Oberoi—appeared to have no interest in this segment,' he said.

Madhok started off his company Sarovar with a hotel in Goa. Ask him about the name and he laughs. He says that every other name he chose to get his company registered with got rejected until finally one day he saw a picture of a lake and came up with the name Sarovar and it clicked. Initially, he started the company in partnership with his friend Shailendra Mittal (who owns the Mittal buildings in Nariman Point).

'I went through the management route. I didn't have any money to own the hotels,' he said.

Whatever money Madhok had (Rs 50 lakhs) was spent on creating the basic infrastructure offices, hiring a few key people and investing in a sales force. That infrastructure multiplied about 100 times over the years as he scaled.

The first few hotel contracts came because of his personal equations.

Things began to move fast when in 1996, Ajay Bakaya—who had worked with him at the Oberoi—came on board. It was all due to a providential phone call.

'Had I left the office two minutes earlier I would have missed him!' exclaimed Madhok, describing how Bakaya after his stint at Oberoi had gone off to Australia where he worked at the Four Points by Sheraton among other chains. The phone call in question came from Amsterdam where

Bakaya had migrated on a sudden whim to try out a new line of trading, and where things hadn't worked out.

'I told him, "How long are you working for somebody? Come and have a chat." He flew down instantly and within an hour decided to join,' said Madhok.

For Bakaya, a suave, unflappable hotelier, the phone call was life-changing too. He had left hotels briefly and was in Amsterdam trying out new stuff as an entrepreneur.

'Somebody said to me, join and head the company and I will give you shares of the company. But the venture never took off,' he recounted.

But having tasted entrepreneurship, he didn't want to go back to a regular corporate set-up and hence had called Madhok.

'He was going out for lunch and I just caught him. He said he was starting something; why don't we talk? That's how we started off,' he recalled.

Bakaya was a risk-taker and the perfect foil for Madhok. After all, he had packed up and gone off to Australia without a job, he had jumped headlong into the opportunity in Amsterdam. He based himself in Delhi, while Madhok was headquartered in Bombay. When Mittal exited the company, Bakaya took some of the stake in Sarovar. He was the hands-on operations guy, while Madhok strategized from his Mumbai office. The duo complemented each other's strengths so well and together grew the Sarovar portfolio, with an average of six openings a year, though it picked up even more speed after ten years.

In any business in any industry, it is important that some people come along and want to change things because they see the scope for change, says Bakaya. When the Oberois started, there was no clear structured hotel-keeping in India. It was all run by foreigners. Mr M.S. Oberoi set the ball rolling. He built his company by owning restaurants and by providing hotel services and some exceptional products.

'When we started out in the 1990s, we simply said, look, there are some nice hotels that are not run well. Not every traveller wants four pillows and a bathroom with two wash basins etc. Travellers wanted a clutter-free, simple, functional hotel, which will give him clean sheets to sleep on, clean towels for a shower, proper facilities in terms of hygiene, basic cleanliness, a very comfortable bed, air conditioning that works all the time without the noise, water that has been treated well so it is neither very hard nor very soft etc. So that is basic and in today's world now, they want a wifi. But basically things where hotels do not make huge promises, deliver on what they promise or deliver a little more than they promise. That was our endeavour and I think to a large extent we have succeeded. We were at the right place at the right time; we thought a little bit ahead of our times. And in our case, I personally don't see it as a magical thing but I think that there was an opportunity and we saw that opportunity clearly and we said: let's jump in,' said Bakaya.

He explains further: 'Our model was simple. We wanted to be good managers for mid-sized hotel owners and we have maintained that consistently. And when the story went well in India, they decided to replicate it in Africa—an area that Bakaya was familiar with.'

'Sarovar were among the first to find the blue space in the mid-market,' said Rattan Keswani, ex-Oberoi man and 'one of the few to be successful with a pure management model.'

Madhok and Bakaya always operated in a very understated manner. This led to criticism from industry observers, who felt they were too low profile. The other criticism Sarovar faced was in its management model, where profits and margins are fairly low. They get just 2 per cent.

'Look at their operating profits—how low they are— whereas if you own the hotels, you get to keep 100 per cent,' points out an analyst. But as Keswani points out, often the management model can offset that by having a higher valuation. The valuer sees lesser risk in the model.

Bakaya points out that they do own a few hotels now— though that has nothing to do with change in strategy. The reason was to convince owners.

'In a lot of cases, quality standards were not met because the owner was not willing to put the money where we thought he should be putting it in so we thought let's do it ourselves, let's see how the model works and let's create hotels that become a benchmark hotels for us. So, this is how we started off with a hotel in Chandigarh. Then, we built Roorkee because Chandigarh worked so beautifully well so we thought let's do another one. Now we are not pushing that model,' he said.

When Sarovar started, they were the pioneers in the category. But by 2012 or so, the mid-market segment in India was no longer the barren playfield of past. By 2016, it got very crowded and challenging.

The decision to divest stake in the company to Louvre was a deeply thought out one.

'For Sarovar, the imperative to rope in an outside investor was in order to expand and cope with international competition,' said Bakaya. 'We were at a stage when it was difficult to compete with MNCs who can invest millions in distribution,' he added.

While Louvre gets to use Sarovar's expertise on home ground as well as its vast network (over seventy-five hotels in 2018), for Sarovar, Louvre's loyalty programmes, technology and its global distribution network, the second-largest in Europe, are useful. It also has the option of using Louvre's brands—Premiere Classe, Campanile, Kyriad, Tulip Inn, Golden Tulip and Royal Tulip—that straddle the one-star to five-star segments.

'We know we have a lot more competition. We need to be able to convince people in some other part of the globe that we can still deliver good quality. So somehow to that extent we have changed, but otherwise we have remained owner-loyal. We always put our owner on a pedestal. We believe in long-term relationships. We have maintained it since the start of the company,' Bakaya said.

As Madhok explained, 'Focusing on its relationship with the owners is important.'

'There are brands that push the owner out the minute the keys are given to them—we play ball with owners and keep their sensitivities in mind,' said Bakaya.

It may be a quiet, low-profile operator but the way Sarovar has turned around the fortunes of Marine Plaza in south Mumbai is much talked about.

'At times, Marine Plaza even commands higher rates than the Taj President,' said Madhok with quiet pride.

Though Sarovar has been conservative in the matter of debt, it was bold enough to venture overseas, expanding into Africa with properties in Mombasa, Dar es Salam and Nairobi.

Initially, operating with Park Plaza and Park Inn International, two brands it had licensed from Carlson, Madhok and Bakaya began focusing on their own brands since 2000 because the Western group had come into India too. Sarovar Premier, Sarovar Portico and Hometel, a brand born out of research, is limited-service, no-frills model. Apart from the hotel brands, it also has two F&B brands, Geoffrey's Pub and Oriental Blossom.

Out and out career hoteliers, their deep knowledge of operations is their big strength. Madhok can talk long on the innards of the air-conditioning systems, the plumbing systems and the operations. Their other big strength is the huge trust and respect they have earned and command. The understated manner, which is criticized by investors, is actually their big strength when dealing with owners. The lessons from their journey are to find a niche, do it well and stay focused.

*

Patu Keswani: Radical Reformist

If there were some strong gusts of wind blowing for change in the way hotels are managed and operated in India, Patu Keswani was an early typhoon. Outspoken, with a disdain for convention, he is not at all your average hotelier—though he spent several years with the Taj Group. His academic background—IIT engineering and an MBA—also made his early career in hotels a bit unusual. Later, when he did do a stint at management consultancy A.T. Kearney, an innings that was more in tune with his academic qualifications, Keswani with his ponytail and maverick ideas, again stood out.

Keswani's jump into hotel entrepreneurship was not at all surprising. He knew the operations, he knew the gaps, he got the funds and he had the ability and chutzpah of an entrepreneur who needed to move with lightning speed. Midway through the journey, he also got committed to a cause—embracing those with disability into the workforce, adopting stray dogs and making them mascots of Lemon Tree properties.

In 2002, after quitting A.T. Kearney, Keswani bought a plot of land in Gurgaon for Rs 1.2 crore and made a small fifteen-room hotel there, priced at mid-market rates. His logic was impeccable. At that time, the US was the most sophisticated hotel market, and it had 181 rooms per 10,000 room population. Globally, the penetration of hotel rooms per 10,000 population was just thirty-one. In India it was probably one or two. And most branded rooms in India were in the upper upscale category. So, should a product come in at mid-market price points, there would definitely be demand.

His other logic: 2,50,000 Indians travel by train by second-class AC every day. 1,00,000 Indians travel by air. There are 35,000 foreigners in India. Put all this together and there are 4,00,000 people travelling every day. They all need some place to stay.

Keswani also took a leaf out of the aviation industry. When the low-cost carriers came in, aviation exploded in India. With right pricing (between Rs 2000 and Rs 4000), the hotel market could explode too, was his logic. And sure enough that happened.

The question was: Could you run them at these affordable price points without incurring a loss? Keswani felt by ruthlessly paring costs in running hotels, it could be done. As he pointed out, 'Over 50 per cent of hotels in India were built with black money. These owners build hotels for return on ego. When you build hotels like that you build it to your specification and you cannot offer realistic prices.'

His solution was to create a mid-market hotel with right pricing and managed with ruthless efficiency, but having a standout brand appeal that would differentiate it from others. That is the core of Lemon Tree.

Keswani had some experience in managing costs and his confidence stemmed from that experience. At the Taj, at one time, he was in charge of twenty-two hotels, and his then boss, Krishna Kumar, told him to double profits. So Keswani broke down the hotel into 180 parameters.

For instance, at the Taj, one room boy would cover fourteen rooms. What could be the change in the design of the rooms so a room boy could increase productivity to, say, sixteen rooms?

He then set out to plot on an excel sheet these 180 parameters and study each of the twenty-two hotels on these. He would study what the hotel which performed best in each of these parameters did right. Interestingly, the Taj President excelled in quite a few.

'If I had set up a twenty-third hotel and introduced the best-performing model in each of these parameters there, its gross operating profit would surely go up,' he said. A lot of this has been applied at Lemon Tree.

A simple example—at Lemon Tree hotels, they don't keep soap bars in the bathrooms as each guest uses the soap once, and the soap is thrown. Instead they have liquid-soap dispensers, thus cutting wastage. Similarly, every little detail and aspect of running a hotel was looked at with a fine-toothed comb—almost like the way a householder would run a home on a tight budget yet make it very comfortable.

Rattan Keswani, deputy managing director, Lemon Trees, says, 'Patu is an incredible businessman. He knew that bells and whistles can bleed a hotel. And he also knew that customers could be understanding about the lack of frills if you clearly spelt it out to them. He got it absolutely right.'

He also had views on what the Indian consumers want. 'Eighty-five per cent of my guests are Indian, 15 per cent foreign. If you are rightly priced, you will get guys who step up from guest houses or step down from five stars, both staying with you,' he said.

At the same time, Patu also understood that five-star users and guest-house users, whom he was looking at to migrate to his budget offerings, had different expectations. Hence he created three brands—Lemon Tree Premier, a four-star product but gives five-star service; Lemon Tree, which is three star but offers four-star service; and Red Fox which is two star but offers three-star service.

Unlike Madhok and Bakaya of Sarovar, Keswani felt that only a truly integrated player— one who owns, manages and brands the hotel—can succeed in the mid-market play in India. If you are building your own hotel, you can keep costs down right at the time of construction.

Patu Keswani has decided views on everything—from pricing to location.

'Location is everything. Mid-market hotels cannot work in mofussil areas. When you come for business, the hotel should be in right location,' he says. 'Of course, land costs will be high, but business model should incorporate that and yet make money,' he added.

'Better occupancy is fundamental to the mid-market business model,' said Keswani, and scale is central to the game plan. In 2018, it had forty hotels spread across twenty-three locations, with 4500 employees.

To scale faster, Lemon Tree had also set up a joint venture with Netherlands pension fund APG, called Carnation, which would expand through management consultancy route. Carnation is spearheaded by Rattan Keswani.

'As a ratio, the management model may offer lower rupee value return. But because you have not risked your capital, from a stock market or banker perspective, your valuation is higher,' explained Rattan.

Scale could also come through acquisitions. The mid-market space in India has got quite crowded and consolidation is inevitable. In March 2019, Lemon Tree Hotels bid for a full stake in Keys Hotels, an India-focused mid-market chain funded by Berggruen Investments.

Lemon Tree's talent management abilities are another big differentiator. Since 2008 it has been hiring people with disabilities. In 2018, over 13 per cent of its employees were differently abled. In 2014 it began hiring people from economically and socially weak backgrounds as well and they added up to another 7 per cent.

This is in line with the new thinking in business—of inclusivity, of purpose and so on. But Lemon Tree has taken its disability hiring to audacious lengths. At its three-building complex in Sector 60 Gurugram, which houses a Lemon Tree, a Red Fox and a giant convention centre, it's aim is to make 70 per cent of the staff opportunity-deprived Indians (ODIs), which includes both people with physical handicaps as well as the economically weak. To make that possible, the entire complex has been made universally accessible, which means every single area—from the front desk to the kitchens to the inner recesses—has been fitted with ramps where necessary, and signages with Braille so that anybody can comfortably navigate.

Over the years, Lemon Tree has strongly got identified as a champion of people with disabilities and several guests began staying at the hotel as a result of that. Doing good is good for business. But it was serendipity that led to this focused hiring policy.

Like everyone else, Lemon Tree too hired the odd specially abled person. One day, however, Keswani got a surprise visitor at his office. It was the mother of one of his specially abled employees holding a wedding invitation card. She emotionally told him that thanks to his steady job, her son could now dream of supporting a family. Keswani checked with the NGO that had placed the boy and learnt that for many people with disabilities marriage was usually a mirage. That was the turning point for Keswani, who at once summoned his HR team and told them to study what would happen if the hotel could hire a large number of people with disabilities. Within no time, the project moved from a what-if stage and cascaded into a big initiative. A champion for inclusive hiring was created in Aradhana Lal. The sales and marketing executive was moved to drive the sustainability initiative.

'Sensitizing every single employee is core to the initiative,' she says. 'We don't want anyone to be treated as *hai bechara* (poor thing) and expect normal team behaviour,' she added.

An important part of the initiative has been job mapping. Kashaf Aziz, general manager explained that when they began construction of the Lemon Tree Sector 60 hotel, side by side they began to match abilities with functions.

'We could put a wheelchair-bound person in finance, but not in maintenance, and so on,' he explained.

Once the jobs are mapped, Lemon Tree reaches out to its NGO partners (Youth4Jobs, Dr Reddy's Foundation, Muskaan, among others) to recruit, skill and groom candidates. Training and trial runs come next. While the hearing impaired are hired first and then undergo normal induction and training, those with intellectual disabilities are first put on a six-month-long traineeship. Along the journey, many tweaks keep happening to workflow. For instance, at some restaurants, instead of the waiter taking the order, the guest writes it down. Now, technology is being deployed with a gadget placed at a table that lights up when orders are played. Then, shift timings were changed to suit those with Down syndrome who cannot be put on a night shift.

Currently none among the specially abled has reached a managerial level though quite a few are supervisors and several have been singled out as high potential. 'But it won't be too long before you see a specially abled general manager at a Lemon Tree,' proclaims Aziz confidently.

The takeaways from Patu Keswani's hospitality venture is that decisiveness and speed is imperative in a crowded field. It is also imperative to be value conscious but at the same time keep the consumer's needs at the centre. And, above all, conduct business with a big heart.

*

Ashish Jakhanwala: A New Type of Owner

There could be no hotel owner more vocal and outspoken than Ashish Jakhanwala, the founder and CEO of SAMHI, a private-equity-controlled hospitality firm that he set up in partnership with Manav Thadani of Hotelivate consultancy. GTI capital Group and US-based Equity International were early investors, putting in $100 million collectively, with Goldman Sachs later investing in $66 million.

It's an unusual company for India, for Jakhanwala—a Lucknow boy schooled in the hilly district of Nainital—has steered clear of operating and branding. He is clear he will only own. And since he has experience working for a hotel operator—he was in Accor group—Jakhanwala knows the ropes. In a short span of time, SAMHI, founded in 2010, became India's fastest-growing hotel asset business. In 2019, it had a portfolio of twenty-nine operating hotels, with over 4300 keys. Not just that, SAMHI also earned a reputation for being a turnaround specialist, picking up distressed assets and converting them into profitable properties. Of course, the company also built its own hotels too.

SAMHI was born because Jakhanwala, who had led hotel development for the Accor Group in India, spotted a gap in how the business functioned here from the ownership standpoint.

'Several people were looking at hotels as trading assets,' he said. 'What was needed was for someone to look not only at the long-term asset value but also the operational value that hotels have.'

'I did sixteen years of studies for my launch into entrepreneurship,' he said. The sixteen years refers to the time Jakhanwala put into hotel management degrees as well as his stint with Accor. He was the French hotel chain's first employee in India.

He also is very clear that hotel ownership should be separated from hotel management.

'The world over, stock markets don't like hybrid models,' he said, pointing out that while owners look at long-term asset appreciation, management objectives tend to differ, driven by gross revenues, return on capital employed and so on. 'It's hard to create differentiated returns on the capital,' he added, but he is trying to prove that it can be done.

One way is through scale. Since inception, SAMHI has been on an acquisition overdrive. The other way is to choose brands carefully. Most of his hotels are operated by global players such as Marriott, Starwood Hotels, Accor Hotels and Hyatt. It also has a joint venture with Marriott and Accor to develop budget brands Fairfield and Formule1 respectively.

'So far SAMHI has only worked with international brands because,' Jakhanwala argues, 'the Indian customer is international in outlook. There is no such thing as Indian customer versus international customer,' he said.

Jakhanwala is a keen student of various models, especially the financial discipline of the West.

'Western markets are mature markets. Look at aviation—low-cost aviation was created in the West and came here and became successful,' he pointed out. Similarly, he felt the way hotels are owned in the West by institutional investors who look at long-term inflation-adjusted yields with capital appreciation was a model we could do with in India.

'In 2004–05, private equity capital did enter hotel sector in India. But they started clubbing hotel projects like real-estate projects and operated with a seven-plus-one plus one time frame. Everybody thought they would build a hotel in two to three years, and five years later, sell it. They looked at hotels as a trading asset,' he said.

Jakhanwala says that the need was to look at the operational value of hotels too.

'We realized that somebody had to set up a business on the lines of the Western model. Raising funds was surprisingly easy,' he said and grinning mischievously added, 'Sorry, I have no sob stories to tell.'

He got the millions easily. Once the funds were in place, Jakhanwala started doing whatever was required to own the hotel.

'Right from owning the land and constructing it, to buying a shell and converting it, buying an existing one or acquiring stakes in a company, we have done it all,' he said. 'We looked at everything from extreme left to extreme right.'

Jakhanwala feels his brand's free style of functioning leaves him unfettered and in a better position to create more share value for his company.

'Brand-owning companies have to be present in certain markets—for instance, the Bombay market. Every brand has to have a flag for distribution purposes,' he said. 'I on the other hand have no such compulsion as I ride on somebody else's distribution muscle,' he pointed out.

Jakhanwala says cold hard logic dictates how he does business with brands.

'If I were to set up a hotel in an IT park, I would only go for an American chain—as the brand would have recall value with software types who would typically be my clients,' he reasoned.

He uses a similar sense when it comes to calculating returns.

'Returns can be defined in many ways. You can talk about ROE, return on equity. Payback period. Asset yield. Or return on capital employed. Effectively once a new hotel has stabilized what kind of yield you get on hotel investment. And this is inflation adjusted yield. Now we are not a fund, not looking at closing business and selling it, so we don't look at PE [Price-to-Earnings] multiples and other stuff,' he said.

Jakhanwala points out how for all practical purposes SAMHI began operations in 2012, but in the second year was already a positive-yield company.

'It helped that we set up business in a harsh environment,' he said.

When the downcycle happened in 2014 or so, and a lot of distressed assets came on to the market, everyone thought

SAMHI would buy, but Jakhanwala showed his shrewdness by waiting.

'We slowed down on acquisitions and people began writing us off. But I am not going to pay an unreasonable price for a hotel and would rather wait,' he said.

Jakhanwala is also betting mostly on mid-market and economy and pulls out slides to show how big the opportunity is here. He studies retail, aviation and other industries keenly to see market trends and applies them to the hotel industry. He is a man who relies on hard data.

The takeaway from this journey: In emotion-driven India, where often sentiments dictate business decisions—especially true for owners of hotels—the practical way in which Jakhanwala approaches his hospitality business stands out. It remains to be seen how this approach will work out in the long run.

*

Param Kannampily: The Green Hotelier

There was a time when India lacked good mid-market hotels. Today, the traveller is spoilt for choice with so many brands crowding the three-star and four-star categories. With Ibis, Hyatt Place, Four Points by Sheraton, Keys, Holiday Inn Express and Lemon Tree spreading roots across the country, we certainly have a lot of stay options. But for a hotelier, the dilemma arises: How do you differentiate your offering?[2]

Very early on, Param Kannampilly, the soft-spoken, affable chairman and managing director of Concept Hospitality, found a niche with his Fern brand of hotels or 'ecotels' as they are called. Everything in the Fern ecotel is built or created with a green mantra—from the core of the building, which is run on sustainable energy platforms, to the chilling units and tiny details such as recyclable pens, jute folders or hangers made of sawdust. India Inc. may have made Corporate Social Responsibility a buzz phrase today, but at Concept the slogan they promote is CER—Corporate Environment Responsibility.

Today, the pretty green frond logo of the Fern is travelling across India rapidly, with thirty-three hotels across the country and many more in the pipeline. According to Kannampilly, there's a lot of interest shown by hotel owners, especially in tier-two and tier-three towns. By 2020, the Fern will be adding another eighteen ecotels with 1500 green rooms, mostly in smaller towns.

Serendipitous Start

It was an accident of fate that brought the Burma-born, Indonesia-schooled Kannampilly (his dad was in the diplomatic corps) into hospitality. After his Inter Sciences in Bombay, he wanted to become a dentist and applied at Osmania University. He got a telegram saying he had been selected. I kept waiting and waiting for further news but there was none. Finally, he discovered that due to the Telangana agitation, the dental faculty was in disarray and the fate of the course uncertain.

'That year got wasted,' recalled Kannampilly. Since some friends were in catering college, he decided to join that in 1971, and stuck on to finish the four-year course, even though he got a job in the third year itself. Then came a long and varied career in hospitality, spanning the Taj Group, Spencer's, Leela, the Rahejas and a few independent hotel properties. In 1996, he decided to turn consultant and set up Concept Hospitality to manage hotels for other people. Restaurateur Dr Vithal Kamat took some stake in the firm, and Kannampilly joined the Kamats as technical adviser.

At that time, the Orchid Mumbai, a project by the Kamats, was in the development stage.

'We were brainstorming and I said that if you are doing more than one hotel, we need to think of a concept that will last not just a decade but through the next century,' says Kannampilly. Various ideas were thrown up—could they look at a non-smoking hotel and so on—until they hit upon the environment-friendly hotel positioning.

The Orchid Mumbai when it finally came up in Santa Cruz became Asia's first certified ecotel. There were many firsts at the hotel, said Kannampilly, describing how an ecopanel was created in all rooms to switch off lights that were not used, and an interactive TV spread the message of saving resources.

'We brought in the first screw compressors, energy storage systems and so on,' said Kannampilly.

After that he went about evangelizing green buildings to his clients. Among others, he was consulting for the Wall Street Hotel in Jaipur, Seasons Hotel and Service Apartments in Pune, and Uppal's Orchid in Delhi NCR.

In 2009, he decided to buy back the equity stake given to Kamats and create his own brand Fern.

'There were two or three reasons for the name,' he explains. 'It was the first plant that existed on earth. Second, environment consciousness is a concern of everyone and the brand would stand out. Third, it was a two-syllable word with easy recall.'

Concept today has other brands in its portfolio—there's Beacon and now, with Nepalese billionaire Binod Chaudhary-led CG Corp investing in the company, there's his Zinc in the mix as well. But it's the Fern that has been the clutter-breaking concept from Concept.

Kanampilly's son is now into the business.

The lesson from Kanampilly's experiments with Concept are to find out ways in which you can be unique and stay grounded.

*

Ankur Bhatia: A Flying Leap

There are many who are sceptical about Bird Group's Ankur Bhatia's foray into hospitality. But the tall, fit (he's a vegetarian and careful eater) Bhatia, who keeps up a frenzied pace of work, always appears confident. He is, after all, very conversant with the luxury space—the Bird Group has got Porsche design, Bally shoes, and other luxury brands into India. So, he understands the psychology of the high-end customer, which is where all his hospitality ventures are focused.

An urban resort, the Roseate, on the Delhi–Gurgaon highway and a contemporary business hotel Roseate House in Aerocity are Bhatia's creations and reflect his personality.

When he started, however, the hotels did not carry the Roseate name. In 2011, Bird Hospitality started off with a 50:50 joint venture with Thailand's Dusit group. The exotic 8 acre tree-lined urban resort was called Dusit Devarana and when it came up, wowed people with its purple-and-brown-with-hints-of-gold colour combination. The gardens were like an enchanted area with waterbodies. Designed by Thai architect Lek Mathar Bunnag, it has some rather flamboyant touches—towering wooden pillars, unusual sculptures and so on.

Bhatia is a typical Delhi boy. After studying at New Delhi's Modern School and computer science from London, he joined his parent's travel business. Dad and mom—Vijay and Radha Mehta—were travel industry entrepreneurs who founded the Bird Group and brought in the travel technology firm Amadeus to India. Before setting up the Delhi hotels, Ankur Bhatia had already wet his feet in the hospitality business by acquiring the Royal Park in London, a forty-eight-bed luxury boutique property near Hyde Park that he bought through Bird Hospitality.

The jump into hospitality was to monetize the family's land banks. Bhatia points out his family had a lot of private land—apart from Delhi, in places like Rishikesh and Goa too. The plan was to create the first five hotels on their own land and then look to manage others. Apart from the land bank angle, there were synergies with their travel and other businesses—Bird Group not only runs Amadeus India that provides centralized reservation services solutions and so on, it also runs Bird Academy, a training school for the travel trade. In the group fold is also Bird Marine, set up in 2008, a luxury yacht company that younger brother Gaurav manages. Another venture, Bird Retail is into luxury products.

There is a certain logic with which Bhatia expanded his businesses. Soon after the hospitality venture was conceived, Bhatia set up Bird Retail.

'The intent,' as Bhatia explained, 'was that they would eventually open luxury retail outlets at their hotels.'

Although Bhatia may have entered late, his chain can ride on the Global Distribution System (GDS) strength of his other businesses and his directorship of Amadeus India. Bird Group is into travel technology, and has a 'pulse on the traveller', he pointed out.

The plans are attractive on paper. Take, for example, the hotel in Aerocity. There are twenty hotels cheek by jowl and when the doors of these opened, there was no entertainment in the vicinity (it was only subsequently that a mall came up). So, Bhatia put in a fifty-seater multiplex in the hotel. Similarly, at the Dusit Devarana property, a serene temple—it is apparently the Bhatia family temple—comes as a surprise. Given the boom in wedding and renewal-of-vows travel, this is not incongruous. The idea is to get some of the wedding business into the hotel.

Unlike most in the hotel community who swear that all the new opportunity is in the mid-market or budget price range, Bhatia is taking a gamble on the luxury and upmarket segment.

'That's because,' he says, 'most of the land bank were in places suited for luxury.' A hugely finicky man and by all reports a very difficult boss, he personally supervised the choice of furnishings—some of which he got from Milan—and decor, with his wife chipping in too.

The lessons to learn from Bhatia's sojourn in hospitality is some of the outside-in perspectives he brings in, the travel business view, the luxury business view and his ability to offer interesting experiences.[3]

*

Chender Baljee: The Dogged Hotelier

If there is a prize for dogged persistence, Chender Baljee would surely get it. The Mr Nice Guy in hoteliering has found the going tough many times but through sheer hard work and persistence bounced back.

You could say hoteliering runs in his veins, hailing as he does from the Baljee restaurant family of Simla. After his BCom in Delhi, and MBA from IIM Ahmedabad (batch of 1972), he joined the family hotel and restaurant, but soon found there was nothing much for him to do as his father and brother were taking care of everything. That's when he began his own enterprise. He initially started out with a restaurant in Simla called Fascination, but then somebody told him about an opportunity in Bangalore where a hotel (the Metropole) was coming up for lease.

Baljee's bid was unsuccessful—but as luck would have it, he managed to get another deal in Bangalore acquiring hotel Stay Longer in 1973. Since then he has been based in the software capital. He renamed StayLonger Harsha and for ten busy years ran the hotel devotedly. In 1985, the expansion bug bit him—he wanted to go for an IPO but things didn't pan out the way he planned.

It was 1992, when he could finally start expanding when he acquired some land near Bangalore airport and started building a hotel. Initially, his plans were to set up a mid-market three-star hotel, but of course like every newbie hotelier he overbuilt and in 2001, it was a five-star property that he threw open—the distinctive purple Royal Orchids brand.

In 2004, the hotel Metropole (the hotel that first drew Baljee from the hills to Bangalore) came up for lease and he struck. In 2006, when the company had revenues of Rs 36 crore, he went public and raised Rs 130 crore. It was furious expansion after that.

Baljee echoes many other hoteliers when he says that one must have skin in the game. So, some of his hotels are owned, others managed. You must have credibility in the market before you can go the management route, said Baljee.

Owning, however, can be risky and he got into serious debt difficulties, though not on the scale of the Leela group. But he was quick to sell off the Ahmedabad Royal Orchids, leading to a lot of rumours that he was in trouble.

'It was rationalization,' Baljee explained patiently.

Ashish Jakhanwalla of SAMHI, who bought the company, endorses this. 'Mr Baljee was too asset-heavy—and it's right strategy to sell,' he said. 'Who does not get into trouble in challenging times,' he added.

Why would any owner want him to manage hotels in the face of so much competition?

'We are more approachable, more in touch with owners,' was the simple answer.

The future generation of Baljees is also into hoteliering. Both sons—Arjun, who studied hotel management in Cornell, and Keshav, who did his studies from Wharton and ISB—wet their feet by starting off their own independent chains—Peppermint and Spree hotels.

Baljee's expansion strategy involves getting more into tier-two cities as well as Africa. In 2015, it opened a hotel in Nairobi, as well as looked at a development in Tanzania near Lake Victoria and a wedding destination property in Dar es Salaam. In January 2017, Royal Orchid Hotels acquired Amartara Hospitality, to get a foothold into Mumbai.

From those days in 2015, when he was being written off, how Baljee kept calm and stayed focus is a story of resilience. His management mantras are to constantly monitor guest feedback, come back with fast responses and be very up-do-date on technology.

'The Indian customer wants a lot more personalized service—and we deliver that,' he said.

The lessons from Baljee's roller coaster journey is to have a never-say-die spirit and to maintain optimism.

8

The Owners—Visible and Invisible

'I don't know anything about running a hotel except what I don't like at other places.'

—Helen Hamlyn, philanthropist and hotelier

Rajat Pahwa, chairman, Gautam Hotels and Knife Arts Catering, is a walking encyclopedia on Delhi's booming hotel scene. Over the course of the last five decades, his extended family—uncles, cousins et al.—has opened around fifty hotels in Delhi–NCR.[1]

'Our family actually pioneered the guest house business in NCR. The first hotel in Paharganj called Nataraj, with a rooftop restaurant, was ours. The first hotel in Karol Bagh was ours,' he says.

And yet, despite fifty years of being in the business of hospitality, nobody in the family, until Rajat, had thought of creating a brand for their hotels.

'That's because the family treated it as a real estate play, investing in land, building a hotel and running it until the asset appreciated and then it was sold off,' he said.

Today, that outlook is changing, led by the younger generation like Rajat, who tried bringing five of the family hotels under an umbrella brand called Gautam Hotels. But now, he has decided to stop running these hotels and hand over the keys to professional hotel-operating companies so that he has the time to focus on scaling his F&B business. Two of his hotels—Gautam Residency in Greater Kailash (GK) in Delhi and Gautam Retreat in south city Gurgaon— have got makeovers and are branded as OYO Townhouse (OYO's upmarket offering).

Why OYO? The answer is surprising as well as insightful.

'Had traditional hoteliers been running OYO, I would not have given my keys to them. I was pretty much doing it the same way. But OYO has a very different, fresh approach, led by tech. That's the only thing that attracted me,' said Pahwa.

Pahwa in many ways epitomizes the change sweeping through the way hotel owners in the country of both large luxurious properties as well as tiny budget properties are now looking at their assets. They are upgrading rooms, putting in bells and whistles and handing them over to brands to operate.

More importantly, a growing band of owners, till now faceless and hidden to the guests who stayed in their properties, are now emerging from the shadows, and taking an active interest in how their hotels are run. They are very vocal and drive hard bargains with chains such as the Taj, Marriott, Hyatt, or Hilton that manage them. The balance of power is slowly tilting from these chains to the owners, who are banding themselves into associations. For instance, there is a Marriott Owners' Association that was spearheaded by Ranjit Batra of Pune-based Panschil Realty. By banding together, these hoteliers have managed to negotiate better deals with the foreign hotel management companies, giving away less commission, and even bagging some key money.

The entry of so many foreign chains, and the mushrooming of a lot of Indian hotel management companies has given the owners plenty of choices. If they are not happy, they can walk away and choose another partner—relationship building has become key in the hotel business today. How the management companies manage the relationships with the hotel owners will define their future.

The advent of online travel agents and technology companies like Djubo that have property management software also has given more power to the owners, who can now even choose to run the show themselves.

Only a small percentage of India's branded-hotel room supply of about 2 lakh rooms are actually owned by big hospitality chains like Taj, ITC, Oberoi, Accor, Hyatt, etc.[2] The real owners come in all shapes and sizes ranging from real estate barons, textile magnates, infrastructure majors, high net worth individuals, industrialists, politicians with loads of spare cash, former royals or simply small business families.

For many of these owners, hotels was just a side investment, more an asset to nurture a parcel of land. As Pahwa says, 'I can name at least 100 hoteliers in Delhi and its neighbourhood who have not visited their properties for six months despite operating them, because it is a second business for them.'

Several others built hotels as they saw them as easy means to curry favours with politicians and bureaucrats, who were given free use of their rooms for all sorts of activities. With CCTV cameras becoming ubiquitous, however, some of the activities are shifting locations.

For still others, it was an address to flaunt, an egoistic investment, if you please, to boast the finest hotel in town. For a few—especially scions of industrial families—it came down as a family heirloom, or accidentally landed in their balance sheets through acquisitions, such as the case of RPG group scions Harsh and Sanjiv Goenka, who own the Taj Connemara, Taj West End and the Savoy in Ooty. The RPG acquisition of Spencer's brought these three properties into the Goenka fold, but they choose to be invisible owners content to let Taj do the running.

Though the RPG group executives get to stay at the Taj as part of the business arrangements, Harsh Goenka says he himself rarely visits his properties and is totally hands off.

Till now, many of the other set of owners also preferred to remain discreetly in the background. All that is changing, however.

Take Prabhu Kishore, the founder of one of India's biggest auto dealer networks, Varun Group. His foray into hospitality was simply to find a use for his parcel of land, but then so hooked did he get to the business that he has become a serious hotelier.

'I got into the hospitality business not because I wanted to, but because I possessed a site that was apt for hospitality business at Visakhapatnam. It was a sea-facing land. In 2005, Vizag was not a great hospitality destination. I had a choice of making apartment complexes. But it was a hotel kind of site. An apartment would have messed up the seafront. So, I blindly dived into the project without any market survey,' Kishore said.

However, Kishore smartly built shopping arcades etc. into it for financial viability, and says that from day one of its opening, the hotel did well despite the recession from 2011 onwards.

The 225-key property had an inventory that equalled the Park, Taj, Grand Bay and Four Points by Sheraton. By 2014, says Kishore, I was enjoying the fun of the hotel. It gave me great PR unlike the auto business.

So, Kishore ventured into another hotel with a resort at Bhimli, followed by a hotel in Vijayawada, a town that was bound to grow given its proximity to the new capital of Amaravati.

Now, into his fourth hotel, he has the finances pat. He says when building a hotel, he manages to keep costs efficient. He is now entranced with the business and brimming with plans.

Up north, in Jaipur, Hari Mohan Dangayach is another owner who got into the business for unusual reasons. Dangayach's family was into trading grains. He himself got into the jewellery business and travelled a lot as a result. He says he got to stay in many good hotels abroad when he travelled for business and when he looked around Jaipur, he felt that nothing matched the standards he had seen abroad at the mid to upscale segment level. So, he set up The Park Plaza in Jaipur in 2000, followed by a Ramada. Then, he let passion take over and bought a heritage property, Chomu Palace. Now Dangayach is one of the investors behind Jaipur's biggest convention hall-cum-hotel, the Jaipur Exhibition and Convention Centre (JECC).[3]

In Kolkata, industrialist Harsh Neotia of the Ambuja Group has played around with hotels a fair bit too. He says that for him it was a passion. The nature of this animal is such that it is not very lucrative. Even if you see established players, for the investments and property they have, their profitability is very meagre. This is talking of top-notch brands with well-managed assets. There is a certain amount of passion play and only some amount of business. At least if you are looking at it as creating products of excellence.

Neotia started with a club in Kolkata, called the Conclave where businesspersons could meet. Then he built a riverside resort at Raichak, called Ffort, followed by a five-star hotel in Kolkata which is managed by Swissotel. Neotia, whose family sold off the cement business to focus on real estate, is no stranger to difficulties of running a hotel venture. His real estate investments along the Raichak took a long time to take off but he has the patience and passion to wait it out.

'I put my soul in these projects,' he said.

Now, he has tied up with Postcard Hotels—former Oberoi man Kapil Chopra's new luxury hotel venture—to develop hotels in east India.

If passion dictates Neotia's decisions, there are many other owners who look at hoteliering quite clinically from a pure business proposition.

Real Estate Owners

Many of the real estate companies that own hotels—the Rahejas, the Sarafs, the Jatias, the Brigade Group and the Panchshil Realty Group—are quite conscious of the balance sheet and consolidating assets, ruthlessly taking the operating chains to task if returns are not adequate.

And they have the scale and clout to do so. Take real estate giant K. Raheja Corp's Chalet Hotels, which in 2017 had 2700 rooms—mostly in the upscale luxury segment—including the JW Marriott in Mumbai, Four Points by Sheraton at Vashi and the Renaissance Convention Centre.

At that time, the group was the fifth largest hotel group in the country in terms of room inventory, and in terms of revenue the fourth largest. It compared favourably with ITC hotels in terms of revenue generated.

The secret of Chalet Hotels success,' said Sanjay Sethi, CEO of Chalet Hotels was that it had gone with tier-one locations and category A hotels.

And with scale comes clout. As Sethi points out, 'Chalet Hotels is the largest hotel owner of the Marriott brand in India. They would actually consult us on strategy.

'As an asset owner,' Sethi said, 'Chalet is playing a two-pronged role. One is driving performance. Our second role is growth.'

Another example of a very proactive real estate owner is Bengaluru-based Brigade Hospitality that in 2017 had 700 rooms spread across four hotels and is expanding quite rapidly with a long pipeline. What's interesting about this owner is its focus on building tech and software in keeping with the city of its origins. Nirupa Shankar, the young director of Brigade Hospitality, describes how they have set up an incubation centre for start-ups that can provide these solutions, pointing out that building material software could reduce wastage by 2 per cent.

The Relationships

These owners are so demanding that now management companies are actually investing a lot in nurturing relationships. As Raj Rana, former Carlson Rezidor boss in India said, 'The biggest pleasure in my job as a management company is when an owner renews a contract with me.'

Almost all the Indian chains one spoke to said they could do relationships better than the foreign chains as they were more flexible. But check with the owners and that's not actually the case. Many of the foreign brands have changed their approach, become more flexible and coming up with deals that will benefit the owners.

Take the Muthoot Pappachan Group from Kerala, who have been investing in hotels since 2000. For them, it is a pure investment game. They started with a Hilton in Trivandrum but when they built a property in Kochi, they did so with an eye on making it a Taj property, a Vivanta. But this was the time when the Taj Group was going through some turmoil and could not decide on its brand strategy—it was thinking of killing off Vivanta and Gateway and the Muthoots decided they could not wait. As George Muthoot explained, 'With all the changes and confusion within Taj, we decided to look for new operators and talked to Hilton and Accor. We found Accor a bit more proactive and chose to make it a Novotel.'

In the old days, Accor might have told the Muthoots that the hotel was just not meeting Novotel specifications—it was far more luxurious since it was built keeping the Taj in mind. But that they were willing to be flexible shows how far the operators have travelled in India.

Deepika Arora, regional vice president, Eurasia, of Wyndham Hotel Group says, 'I don't go and dictate to my owner. I want to nurture relationships with my owners, trust them for what they are doing and try and then see if I can give them the brand they want rather than the other way round.'

Arora says there have been opportunities that have come to her table but when she sits with her development team, she said, 'Listen we should not be doing this. Even though it's a big number for us, I don't think we will be able to justify the returns to the owner and should tell him accordingly. Also, there have been times where I have gone to the owner and said, "why are you doing a mall? Do a hotel." So, I believe in delivering what the owner wants. For me, the relationship with owners is very important, which is why when you meet my owners, I am either their daughter or a sister. I call my Lucknow owner "bade papa".'

Owner operators

Several owners such as the Malhotra sisters of the MBD Group are taking involvement to new levels, insisting that their names should be co-branded on the hotel property along with the chains they are partnering with, and even demanding they manage the property themselves. Usually, in hotels that carry its brand name, Carlson-Rezidor operates the hotel.

'It took me seven months of negotiations to get my way,' smiles Sonica Malhotra triumphantly.

The sisters run a thriving publishing empire, and yet Monica Malhotra and Sonica Malhotra are very clear that they will micromanage their hospitality diversification as well. Their farsighted father laid the ground for the diversification into hospitality, buying land in places like Noida, Greater Noida and Ludhiana, and picking up Kolkata's Ashok Hotel when ITDC was divesting it. The two sisters subsequently shrewdly sold it off, investing in a parcel of land in Bengaluru instead, which they are now building on. The first hotel in their portfolio was Radisson Malhotra Book Depot (MBD) in Noida, followed by one in Ludhiana. Next up is MBD Steigenberger Hotel, taking shape in Bangalore's Whitefield area, with luxury residences alongside.

Despite just two hotels in their portfolio, the two sisters managed to drive a hard bargain with German luxury hotel chain Deutsche Hospitality to operate, manage and franchise hotels in India under the MBD Steigenberger co-brand. Initially, the first few Steigenberger Hotels will be owned properties, but the two sisters are confident they now have the acumen to operate hotels for others as well. At a time when people are frowning at hybrid models, it is interesting to see owners take this approach.

Professional Owners

And then, finally, a new group of owners have emerged. Private equity-funded asset groups such as SAMHI Hotels or DUET Hotels that are changing the old ways in which hotels used to be run, bringing in financial disciple and transparency to a sector that has been opaque in its money dealings. You could call them professional owners who are hardcore hoteliers but are very clear that ownership and management have to be separate.

There is an inherent conflict between the two roles. Asset ownership is a long-term appreciation role. While management is about day to day revenues, said Ashish Jakhanwala, founder SAMHI, pointing out how global chains that both own and manage are increasingly separating the two functions.

'Today, as professional owners, we can demand more. We cannot tell the management company at what price to sell the rooms, but we certainly can give guidance, he says.

The ownership piece is getting quite interesting as an explosion of activity is taking place there. The move from unorganized to organized in India's hotel industry is a fascinating one to track. Till now mostly the credit has been given to the aggressive expansion drive of big global chains like Hyatt, Marriott, Accor as well as Indian brands like Taj, Ginger, Fortune, Sarovar and Lemon Tree that are frantically expanding by getting independent hotel owners to put their flags on their property.

But equal credit must be given to the owners' part in this story, and how their changing approach and growing professionalism is leading to a transformation in the sector and leading to a greater choice for customers. Most owners now realize that a well-known brand name on their signboards will attract the new discerning Indian guest who is conscious of things like service standards, and will also help them command a higher room rate.

There is a third reason too—the growing clout of the online travel agencies (OTAs) like MakeMyTrip and Cleartrip, which have given power to independent hotel owners all over the country. Jakhanwala says he would consider any hotel sold by an OTA to be a brand as the OTA too insists on certain hygiene and service standards levels.

And a fourth factor is the arrival of aggregators such as OYO, Treebo and others. OYO's disruptive approach of taking only a few rooms from hotels and not the entire hotel has helped convince owners who were sitting on the fence.

While most big brands are loathe to sit at the same table as OYO, feeling their brands are superior, former Ginger Hotels CEO Rahul Pandit admits that what OYO has done is create awareness among owners, which he thinks will help chains such as Ginger, which is seeking to scale from thirty or so hotels to 100 in a few years.

If there has been an explosive growth in India's hospitality story, it hasn't been just the brands and hotel companies driving it, but the owners who have scaled it up, brick by brick.

9

The Heritage Set

'When you walk into a Neemrana hotel, you walk into history.'

—Aman Nath

Heritage is an experience that money cannot buy, asserts Thakur Randhir Singh. Singh is joint managing director of the Mandawa Group of hotels and an office bearer of the Indian Heritage Hotels Association (IHHA), which has its office in Jaipur. More significantly, he is one of the pioneers who converted his family castle into a hotel, created a destination and a circuit in the Shekhawati region of Rajasthan. This was way back in 1980, when only Marwari businessmen with roots in the area visited the place.

Today, Shekhawati is a booming tourist destination with scores of ancient havelis converted into hotels. Flocks of visitors arrive to see the famous frescos of the region that adorns literally every wall in the place but which no local really paid any attention to until creative professionals Aman Nath and Francis Wacziarg—the former a writer and historian, and the latter a photographer and envoy—arrived there. Enchanted by the open art gallery that the place was, they seeded the idea of making the place a tourist destination.

The uniqueness of the region is its paintings, says Randhir Singh, who incidentally studied art. He knew nothing of hotel management, but decided to open up his ancestral home in this offbeat place to tourists. In ancient days, Shekhawati was on the Silk Route and several traders settled here, attracted by the prospect of doing business. The Rajput chieftains of the area—the thakurs of Nawalgarh, Mandawa, Sikar, Jhunjhunu etc.—had their palaces but the prospering Marwari businessmen too built opulent havelis and to give it a lavish look adorned the walls with paintings. When the British arrived and colonized India, promoting their imported goods, the old trading route fell into disuse and Shekhawati fell off the map. Many of the Marwaris from here migrated to Calcutta though they would return often to their havelis. There are over 2000 painted havelis in the area.

In 1980, when Randhir Singh and his family set out to restore their castle in Mandawa and convert some rooms for guests, things were not easy. Connectivity to the region was poor in those days and provisions and supplies were hard to get. Singh describes how for every little thing, from loaves of bread to toiletries, they had to send a car to either Jaipur, two-and-a-half hours away, or to Bikaner, three hours away, and it was a struggle to provide great hospitality. But foreign tourists arrived, entranced by the exotic splendour of the place.

Meanwhile, Aman Nath and Francis Wacziarg, who frequently crisscrossed between Jaipur and Delhi, happened to see a dilapidated fortress in the Aravalli foothills halfway between the two cities, and were so smitten that they bought it. This was the Neemrana Palace. The maharaja of Neemrana, who had lost all his wealth, was only too happy to let go of it. Nath described how while returning to Delhi from Jaipur their attention was captured by the way the sun was glinting on the fortress and they stopped to explore. It took them five years to restore the property they bought barely for Rs 7 lakh.

At first Wacziarg and Nath had no idea what to do with the place but after toying with several ideas, they restored it and converted it into a swish hotel with all the charm of its storied past intact. In 1991, Neemrana opened as a heritage hotel with twelve rooms. Every weekend, their friends from Delhi would arrive to stay at the place. Word spread and the hotel became a must-visit destination.

Nath and Wacziarg made two discoveries—first Shekhawat and then Neemrana—setting in motion the trend of heritage hotels in India.

Far before these developments, however, some large palaces in Rajasthan owned by maharajas were turning into hotels. Maharana Bhagwat Singh of Udaipur converted the picturesque Jag Niwas set in a lake into a hotel in the 1960s, hiring an American design consultant. In the 1970s, he asked the Taj Group—then spearheaded by the go-getting Ajit Kerkar—to manage the Lake Palace hotel. Kerkar felt it would be commercially viable for the Taj only if it had more rooms—and the hotel chain added a whole wing. In fact, credit goes to the Taj for creating marvellous palace hotels all over the country. After Udaipur, Maharaja Sawai Man Singh of Jaipur handed over the keys of the Rambagh Palace to the Taj. The Taj's formidable marketing team, headed by Camellia Panjabi at that time, sold these palaces and Rajasthan as an exotic destination to foreign tour operators and the state became much talked about in the luxury circuits abroad.

When the smaller havelis began opening up, at more affordable price pockets, it opened up tourism in the state to a larger segment of foreign tourists, as well as well-heeled Indians, and heritage became a sought-after niche. As demand grew, every other major and minor Rajput in Rajasthan began restoring family properties with a view to convert them into hotels. Their selling point—the chance for the visitors to interact with the owners and hear anecdotes about bygone days.

In the early 1990s, our newspaper office would be flooded with invites to visit one or new haveli opening up the other, and it was such a novelty then that we would go. Today, when there are thousands of havelis, most invites go into the bin.

In the 1990s, this writer visited the newly opened Alsisar Haveli in Jaipur but the real insights came on a trip to Samode Palace just outside Jaipur, with architect Pradeep Sachdeva, who had been charged with the restoration project. We were a jolly bunch driving to Rajasthan. We stayed one night at Samode Haveli in Jaipur, the family's city home, before moving on to Samode Bagh, a Rajput-style garden owned by the family.

Sachdeva's brief was to create tented hotels in the gardens. At that time luxurious tents were quite a novelty but he had managed to create splendorous ones with the peony motifs seen in Rajasthani textiles. The palace structure served as lounge.

Young Yadavendra Singh, the owner of Samode, epitomized the initiative and ambition of the Rajput royals. He had an additional quality—a passion for hoteliering. He said that compared to some of the properties that others were trying to convert, Samode Palace was an easier project as it was a lived-in palace. But still there were many challenges as these structures were not built for air conditioning or modern plumbing and it could be quite expensive to do all this without disturbing the original character. Sachdeva and his team who helped with the adaptive reuse, strengthening structure, redoing interiors, additions and alterations, managed to retain the old feel.

Twenty years later, Samode has stayed the course and lived up to its promise, consistently ranking among the top heritage hotel destinations in Rajasthan. Part of the reason is the constant evolution.

'Work carries on almost continuously,' Sachdeva says.

Randhir Singh of Mandawa echoes this when he says, 'Till today, I am doing something to my properties. At Neemrana, a sign of the evolving times, there is now a Selfie Mahal, where guests can take pictures of themselves.

The 1990s and early 2000s were heady days for the development of heritage hotels. Nath and Wacziarg got many commissions to restore properties.

'Every week, at least two letters would arrive,' Nath recounted.

They could, however, afford to pick and choose as the duo built up a formidable reputation for converting old properties into profitable enterprises. Not just royals like Thakur Mangal Singh of Kesroli Palace and Nawab Mansur Ali Khan Pataudi but the government has also approached Neemrana Hotels. Rajasthan Tourism Development Corporation has handed over the Tijara Fort on a sixty-year old lease to them. Neemrana owns some of the twenty-odd heritage hotels it operates but mainly operates on a lease model.

Meanwhile at Mandawa, Randhir Singh's family were on an expansion spree. When he threw open the Mandawa property in 1980, it was just six rooms.

'I kept converting my stables,' he says, 'gradually taking the number up to seventy rooms. The Jaipur city home was converted too.'

After the castle, they also created mud huts in Mandawa, where guests could stay. The idea was to give a 'village' experience to the guests who stayed at their Shekhawati hotel.

'You need an element of storytelling to sell heritage properties in the middle of nowhere,' said Singh.

And that—along with service—has been the differentiating factor between the success and failure of heritage hotels. Especially, as the unchecked development meant oversupply. In the beginning there were the actual owners who were going around refurbishing their properties, then came people who bought old properties. Take Hari Singh Dangaych, hailing from a jewellery business, who bought Chomu Palace. Then there were many who created faux heritage properties that resembled old forts or palaces.

The trend of converting old properties to heritage hotels was not restricted to Rajasthan. Gujarat, Madhya Pradesh, Uttar Pradesh, Kerala, Tamil Nadu—it spread everywhere.

As Randhir Singh says, 'The heritage association members come from all over the country. The entire country is studded with such jewels. But Rajasthan has been the frontrunner and grabbed the mind space. That's because the Rajput clans really spread out and built quite a number of impressive dwelling places—from palaces to hunting lodges. So, anyone looking to run a heritage hotel has amazing properties to choose from.'

And yet, many of the newer entrants are choosing to build faux palaces. The economics work out better, perhaps. You can build to scale, blending the modern into the traditional and you don't have to get into the expensive job of retrofitting. It may not be truly heritage but if done well, it can have takers.

In Jaisalmer, Mahendra Singh Shekhawat has built a truly impressive faux fort, Suryagarh. The former Gladrags model has built his hotel exactly like a fort with ramparts, turrets, courtyards and majestic doorways, and made it so luxurious that it's attracted A-listers from all over the world.

Many of the early crop of nobleman hoteliers are also busy expanding through faux havelis. Take Colonel Gaj Singh, who quit the army early and turned his family home in Jaipur, Alsisar Haveli, located bang opposite Randhir Singh's Mandawa Haveli, into a hotel in the early 1990s. His neighbour Gaj Singh also converted the family estate in Shekhawati into a hotel. Not content, he kept expanding his empire, and when he ran out of heritage properties, he built faux heritage ones as at Ranthambore, where the Nahar Haveli is a modern-constructed edifice.

The Challenges

The way everyone has jumped headlong into restoring old properties, one would imagine it is a lucrative niche. But far be it. Many of the properties are white elephants. They need huge amounts for the initial restoration and adapting to use as a hotel. And then once open, the hotels take far longer than conventional hotels to recover their investments. For one, there are fewer rooms; then the properties are located in far-flung places with limited infrastructure. Getting full occupancy tends to be a challenge, especially when you are in off-the-circuit places, even if it is an extraordinary property. If you are in the wilderness, the economics don't work, especially if you are not the owner of the property, Randhir Singh says.

Many are finding a way around that problem by courting big fat weddings or film shoots. Others are selling whole experiences, packaging more than a stay.

'Run of the mill won't sell,' Singh says bluntly. 'You need ideas to transform the heritage hotel into a different product. Make it high end. Create some kind of a story that will attract people. Just for coming and staying, however beautiful and well-run the property, people will not be interested,' he says.

He cites the case of Ananda in the hills above Rishikesh as a case in point of a heritage property that has sold a beautiful story.

'They created a destination plus spa. They created something special. That is one way of approaching a property,' he said.

Singh does not feel that oversupply is a problem though rates are affected. The Mandawa region has 600 rooms today so obviously pricing is a challenge. For him, however, marketing and strategy is a bigger challenge. Earlier, the bulk of the tourists were foreign guests. But now the mix is changing to domestic. While this is good, the ugly side of the Indian tourist is causing many a problem to the heritage property owner. There is no respect for breakfast-hour timings, there is a lot of drinking and loud noise which puts off some of the regular guests. It's a hard balancing act.

Neemrana Hotels has tried to address these problems by introducing an entry fee to discourage day trippers.

'There are so many Indias—there is the old rich, the nouveau riche, the yuppy rich,' Aman Nath points out.

When even the entry fee failed to discourage visitors, the hotel made it mandatory to have a meal at the place if entering the property. Now it has segregated its property into two different zones—one for the high-paying guests, who get more privacy, and the other for those paying ordinary tariffs.

An additional challenge these days is that the expectation of the visitor is sky-high. Exposed to fantastic food and beverage options, the guest at these small havelis expects more choice from the kitchen.

But as Randhir Singh explained, 'Serving a la carte at small properties in offbeat places is very tough. There are hardly walk-in visitors for lunch so fixed menus are the most viable option.'

The heritage hotels have their challenges—a lot of run-of-the mill properties are on the block, but they do have their charm and devoted guests too.

Going forward, India's heritage hoteliers will face stiff competition from chains, many of whom are venturing into heritage. Apart from Taj, Leela and Oberoi, which are all into palaces and have sumptuous old heritage properties, ITC has a line called WelcomHeritage, which straddles several tiers. Started as a joint venture between ITC Hotels and Jodhana Heritage, WelcomeHeritage manages palaces, old bungalows and havelis, forts and lodges.

Foreign chains have an eye on India's heritage properties also. Kurt Straub, former vice president for operations for India, Hyatt, excitedly talked of possibilities of bringing a newly launched Hyatt brand called the Unbound Collection to India as it is a flexible brand that can fit a heritage property.

'It gives us an opportunity to go into palaces, for instance. Unbound can take on fabulous old structures,' he said.

Asian brand Alila has already got into heritage spaces. It's a matter of time before others get in. This was inevitable.

As Aman Nath summed it up—the real India lies in its heritage properties. You cannot experience India staying in a hotel in Delhi.

10

The General Managers

'Being general manager is like being the de facto owner. It's like wearing the crown of "Restaurant Man" without being "Restaurant Man". You're trying to run the business, but you're running the ranch without riding the big horse.'

—Joe Bastianich, American restaurateur, winemaker, author and television personality

Think of a hotel as a city. And some hotels—the Ashok in Delhi and the Clarks in Jaipur, to name just two—are veritably like cities, with post offices and banks on the premises. The general manager is a bit like the mayor of the city, having to take care of people, utilities and services, and constantly managing crises. It is the general manager's lot to contend with quirky situations, much like those faced by short-fused Basil Fawlty, played by John Cleese, in that supremely comic television series *Fawlty Towers*. But it is also the general manager's lot to tackle grim and tragic occurrences like suicides in rooms or people jumping off balconies as happened at a hotel in Delhi.

It's a job with immense responsibility as the general manager is the custodian of a hotel's brand reputation in many ways. A hotel chain's image can be made or marred by the service at a single hotel, and it is up to the operations man on the ground, the general manager, to deliver on the brand promise.

When the Taj at Mumbai was attacked by terrorists, one of the most poignant stories was how the hotel's general manager, Karambir Kang, helped guests out of the building even as his own family remained trapped and perished in their living quarters on the top floor. Kang put duty above all else.

In the good old days, the general manager was literally the face of the hotel, a stately presence who lent an air of gravitas greeting guests. Old-timers recall industry veteran and founder of Sarovar hotels Anil Madhok at the Oberoi, greeting Indira Gandhi with great panache. He was also mentor to many of the big names in the industry, grooming them to great heights. The irrepressible Dilip Puri, former head of Starwood in India, who has now opened a hotel management institute, recalls cutting his teeth under Madhok at the Oberoi in Mumbai, and being shielded for his mistakes after being reprimanded firmly.

'He got up to all sorts of mischief, playing pranks,' Madhok recalled fondly.

Those were the days when you would have to do a twenty-year grind across various functions before rising to be a general manager and even then only those with spit and polish were chosen to be the face of the hotel.

Gone is that gentle era. With the proliferation of hotels—from mere thousands to lakhs across the country now—there has been a huge change in the general manager's profile. For one, they are getting younger and younger. Especially at the new budget chains you will see ridiculously young twenty-four-year-olds managing a hotel. Many hotels are now choosing their general managers from the F&B space rather than the traditional front office route. It's no longer rare to see women general managers. In Delhi, for instance, there are at least five women GMs across the five-star hotels, a couple of them expat ladies. There are also a sizeable number of expat general managers, especially in the foreign chains, bringing cultural diversity to the pool.

But the biggest change is in the general manager's job description today. A general manager has to now not only know about operations of the hotel, but be savvy about business and finance, marketing and social media, building materials and a host of other things. With sites like TripAdvisor having the potential to ruin a hotel's reputation, knowledge of ORM (online reputation management) has become essential.

Shantha de Silva, former country head of the InterContinental Hotel Group in India, sums up the change in the general manager's job best. 'Earlier in the good old days, a GM was like a very hospitable, affable person, a warm host welcoming guests to his house. Today, I think, the GM's role is more that of a business enterprise CEO,' he says.

It goes without saying then that the GM's job has got a lot more stressful. There is an added challenge to the GM's job today as many of them have to report to two bosses—one, the management company and the other, the property owner.

Sometimes there is conflicting advice from both and it becomes a tough balancing act for the GM to keep everyone happy.

However, de Silva felt that aligning the expectations of two parties should not be difficult if the GM were to run the hotel like a business unit. 'To me it is always about understanding the expectations and the priorities of your stakeholders. So, if you know what your owners want and your management company wants and if you align those expectations, then it is going to be very easy,' he said.

Also, unlike in the past, the general manager is no longer the face of the hotel, the celebrity figure. That status has been usurped by the chefs who are the ones that everyone wants selfies clicked with.

Given the kind of skills required to be a general manager today, it has become very tough for hoteliers to find the right person.

Retired hotelier Ravi Shankar, who has worked several years with the Taj Group as well as clocked time with ITC, points out that talent in hotels has always been a critical issue. But it has become an even bigger issue now as he says that in the process of trying to standardize operations, hotels have ended up robotizing their staff.

'In the earlier days, we always took great pride in the fact that service was more of a personalized affair. We would get to know the likes and dislikes of a guest in a very unobtrusive and casual manner. Not out of lengthy questionnaires. And a great effort was made to ensure it got put into practise,' he pointed out.

Ravi Shankar bemoans the placing of inexperienced individuals as hotel managers. 'As in probably any industry, it is imperative that individuals get a fair amount of experience working their way up the ladder. Especially, in a service environment, every day is a learning process. Having a twenty-something trying to respond to a complaint or trying to solve a problem and invariably bumbling through the process is certainly not going to give any confidence to his other staff. Responding to issues then becomes a full-time job whereas an experienced hand would have foreseen the problem,' he says.

What Ravi Shankar says is true. But do hotels really have a choice? The speed with which they are opening up means you need to have a really large pool of talent, and there is a serious dearth of experienced hands, so the only choice is to trust the young. And, frankly, who better to understand the millennial guest than a younger general manager. It all boils down to training and many seem to be rising to the challenge.

Take Shubhanshu at Lemon Tree. He became GM in just five years, at the age of twenty-seven. He joined the group as an associate in 2004 after doing his hotel management from Chennai and a couple of jobs here and there.

'The advantage of working in a rapidly growing brand like Lemon Tree,' he said, 'is that the growth does not stop at GM. You could go on to managing multiple properties (a supervisory post providing guidance to younger GMs), or you could get a corporate role.'

As GM, Shubhanshu said that a typical day in a city hotel starts around 7.30 a.m., with a quick round of the breakfast arena to see if it is laid out and meeting some guests who are breakfasting to gauge whether they are happy with the service. A round of the lobby follows and then it's time to go and bury one's nose into the hotel's MIS—management information system.

'In half an hour I get to know what is happening in the property and create reports that need to be circulated,' he said. Once that is done, he shuttles between lobby, restaurant and the banquet if there are business meetings happening.

At 10.30 a.m., it is time for stocktaking with the staff on maintenance and service issues as well as going through the daily business report that provides occupancy figures of the hotel and customer feedback, gleaned both from guests as well as social media. Social media is really a double-edged sword for hoteliers. As one general manager ruefully points out, most service problems in a hotel can be sorted out with a quick phone call. But nowadays guests tweet first and then only think of calling the front desk, and it is so difficult to undo the impression created by the tweet.

Shubanshu says from customer satisfaction to customer acquisition, the GM has to straddle a lot of responsibilities. The afternoon hours are usually spent on sales calls. Often the GM will accompany the sales team on calls.

At 5.30 p.m., there is a small ten-minute debriefing to see if there are any issues pending, any new fires to douse.

'By 6.30 we are all free but a general manager's job never ends really, we are always on call,' Shubanshu said. 'You can delegate of course, and should—after all how will the executive assistant general manager learn—but many GMs still prefer to be hands on.'

If you think Shubanshu is a fairly young GM, then meet the GMs at OYO. They are even younger, many hired laterally from the retail arena. Take Sukhraj Singh, a GM at barely twenty-five. He worked at Dunkin Donuts in Chandigarh and at a five-star tea lounge in a Delhi mall before being headhunted for a role as a customer manager at OYO. Since Singh had experience of being in pre-launch teams at both Dunkin (when it was just entering India) and the Manjushree Birla tea project, he was considered an apt choice for overseeing new hotel launches.

Singh does not think his youth is a handicap and expresses confidence in his ability to manage a hotel. Then again, as he points out, the OYO properties are fairly small units (thirty to forty rooms) as compared to Lemon Tree hotels or Ibis, which could run into 200 rooms-plus.

Apart from the big challenges of customer acquisition and social media, Shubhanshu points out that keeping staff happy and motivated is another challenge. Especially as some customer behaviours can really stress staff. Take managing room service in the evening at a business hotel, especially in tier-two cities, where guests tend to bring their own liquor and order room service. These guests tend to order room service just before the kitchen shuts down and tend to have lots of demands. To provide service and yet be firm about the closing hour and keep staff happy is a fine balancing game.

The second challenge is extending credit limits to business clients. For many a hotel, corporate clients account for nearly 50 per cent of the occupancy and often they take ninety or 120 days to clear bills. There are travel agents too who keep defaulting. Budgeting, planning, all get tricky in such a scenario.

But general managers at chain hotels still have it easy when it comes to customer acquisition and business development. There is a well-oiled machinery, web platform and loyalty.

Hilton and Marriot, for instance, gain through their redoubtable loyalty programmes. For standalone hotels there is a bit of a challenge here.

Tejpreet Singh Oberoi at the Clarks in Jaipur points out how chain hotels inevitably show up on the first page of search on the OTA platforms. For a hotel like Clarks, the search would have to be more refined.

'If you search by star category or by ratings, you might find us,' Oberoi says. 'So, huge effort and energy has to be expended to make sure you are on top of ratings. However,' he says, 'the solution is to personalize both product and sales. A big chain will have to sell rooms in twenty properties, while our team has just three properties so know each product as well as the target constituency very well,' he says.

For Vijay Wanchoo, general manager at the stately Imperial in Delhi, selling one property is not difficult, he insists. His challenges are more to do with keeping his flock motivated—a single hotel means that career growth is limited for the employees at the hotel. But Wanchoo invests a lot of time in team-building activities—every so often cricket matches are organized. Once in a while, Wanchoo will shoo out the chefs from the kitchen, don an apron and rustle up a meal for his staff.

The approach of every general manager is different. It is best summed up in Habib Rehman's memoir *Borders to Boardroom*. He writes:

> There is a stark difference in approach of the astute innovations driven manager with a wealth of experience and insights, and those managers who are driven by their suppliers and vendors often at the cost of the hotels under

their charge, or are prone to extending disproportionate hospitality, often self-serving.

Women Managers

Increasingly, the industry is seeing women general managers, who bring a special touch to the property. At the Taj Vivanta Ambassador property in Delhi when the dynamic Suman Gahlot, was its GM, you could see meetings of the All Ladies League and Women Economic Forum (a global sisterhood of women professionals) held.

Speak to the women managers and they say that for all the challenges (the timings are exacting), they love it.

Nita Brid is the gregarious general manager at the 207-room five-star deluxe resort Cidade de Goa.

'I do not think I would have done anything other than hoteliering,' Brid says. 'In 1988, after my class XII, my parents were keen for me to pursue Engineering or Medicine. I got into a regional engineering college too. However, for some reason I chose to get an admission into a Hotel Management Institute. It was a very new stream and I had the support of my father who backed my decision and I have never looked back since then. I started my career as a Kitchen Executive Trainee and went to become a Sous Chef. Thereafter an opportunity came along to head the Food and Beverage department in a five-star deluxe hotel in Goa and I took up this challenge too. As a lady in this hardy industry I did not face any hurdles or challenges,' she said.

From operations, which is a demanding job, Brid moved to sales when her son was born, eventually becoming GM. 'It has been a fabulous journey of learning technical, procedural, legal and statutory compliances, and financial and people management skills,' she says.

Brid says there is not much difference in managing a resort of a city or a convention hotel. 'By and large the essence of operations, sales and people-led aspects remain the same. It is just the dynamics of segments that change. A resort hotel will mainly cater towards the domestic leisure segment, groups, conferences—MICE and destination weddings also form an equally important part or mix of our profile. Some years ago resorts were seasonal. But not anymore. The ever-growing demand of travellers and segments have made a place like Goa a 365-day destination, she said.

At the IHG, Shantha de Silva said, quite a few women managers are being readied through an accelerated Express GM development programme. For instance, duty manager Riddhima Nayar, at Crowne Plaza, Greater Noida, was sent to Singapore on an accelerated development programme and within six months was GM of Holiday Inn Express.

'Some managers become GM in as short a span as two years,' de Silva said. 'The programme was developed because we know the younger generation, they will not wait for twenty years to become a GM. In our time and age it took us twenty years to become a GM. The programme is also to support the company's growth. If we have the talent, it will help us to grow quickly to get to a 100 or 150 hotels.

The F&B General Manager

Talk to an owner on how GMs are chosen—and the answer is pretty interesting. Paritosh Ladhani at the Radisson

Collection on the East Gate at Agra says that he wanted to set up a food-focused hotel with several restaurants and hence wanted a GM who was a culinary whiz. And that explains the choice of talented chef Rajat Tuli to run the hotel.

Tuli has introduced a lot of firsts in the culinary scene for Agra, making the property a go-to place for dining for local residents. The hotel boasts a terrace view of the Taj and has a rooftop bar with very interesting cocktails. 'We do molecular cocktails, and are the only ones in Agra to offer these,' said Tuli.

The hotel has six live kitchens, and whole gamut of cuisines ranging from South Asian to Mediterranean and Indian. A tea lounge near the hotel's reception area offers tea and a packed breakfast for early morning visitors to the Taj, a neat innovation.

The kitchen is the most disciplined unit in a hotel—it runs like an army operation, said Tuli, pointing out how it has stood him in good stead as a GM.

Keshav Suri at the Lalit, who has a keen interest in F&B, also points out how chef managers are now a growing trend. At the Lalit, they have created a new role merging services and production. At their Srinagar hotel, the chef has been promoted and is de facto number one.

Collaborations and Talent

General managers spend a lot of time checking out competition. At Aerocity, you will often find the GM of JW Marriott dropping into Andaz or Pullman to see what they are up to. But even as they keep an eye on rivals, Aerocity is also a story of heartwarming collaborations among the GMs of at least four hotels.

Tristan Beau De Lominie, general manager of Pullman and Novotel, describes how the general managers of four hotels got together to pitch for meetings and conference collectively. When first conceived, Aerocity in Delhi, where over a dozen hotels are cheek by jowl, was supposed to have a gigantic convention hall. But that never got off the ground and in the middle of nowhere there were these massive hotels, with guests having no entertainment options in the evenings. Of course, metro connectivity came later and a shopping mall too, but the original conference venue would have helped the hotels because other than being near the airport, the place had no locational advantage—most guests prefer to stay in the heart of the city. That's when the GMs decided to get together and sell all their meeting spaces and rooms collectively for big conferences.

Elsewhere too such collaborations are common. Rajat Tuli describes how he is part of an association of all GMs of Agra and working together to find ways in which they can improve the city.

Wanchoo of the Imperial says he has set up an informal club of sorts where he and other general managers get together—the only condition being they won't talk shop. But he says that camaraderie does not stop anyone from poaching talent.

Talent is a sticky issue in the hotel business. Can the crisis of lack of adequate general manager pool be solved? Literally every chain is investing in training and skilling. But what is needed are more schools of hotel management.

The arrival of the Indian School of Hospitality, a cutting-edge institute to provide talent to the industry, could be a game changer.

While the Institute of Hotel Managements (including the one run by the Taj Group in Aurangabad and the one at Pusa), and institutes such as the Oberoi Centre for Learning and Development or ITC's Welcomgroup Graduate School of Hotel Administration do a great job, they are not enough. The existing IHM capacity, according to industry insiders, is about 10,000-odd seats while the need, if you look at staff-to-room average of even just one, is far far more.

Spotting the gap, former managing director of Starwood Hotels and Resorts, South Asia, Dilip Puri, launched the Indian School of Hospitality that he hopes will create the next generation of leaders for the industry. The vision is to redefine and reimagine hospitality education, he said.

Yateendra Singh, CEO Lausanne Hospitality Consulting, which is partnering the institute says the vision is not to produce masses of hotel management graduates to feed the supply shortfall, but to create 1000 potential leaders. 'Let the market take care of the mass needs, our goal is to produce the 1000 who will influence the course of the industry,' he said.

11

The Big Disruptor

'Play a new game, not the older game, but faster.'

—Seth Godin, American author on marketing
in the digital age

From Kashmir to Kanyakumari, travel anywhere in India and one ubiquitous sign stares out at you from billboards, hoardings on the road and nondescript buildings. You could see the same sign in Japan, China, the Philippines, the UAE and a host of other countries: the jaunty red logo of OYO.

For a hotel brand set up only in 2013, OYO has achieved spectacular, unimaginable scale. In 2018, it had 4,50,000 rooms globally and a presence in 500 cities and its target of 1million rooms appeared to be quite achievable. Its valuation was far more than India's largest hotel company, the over 100-year-old Taj.

And imagine, OYO's founder Ritesh Agarwal was just eighteen years old when he dreamt up this company in 2012. A year later, at nineteen, he registered Oravel Stays Private Limited.

It's a company that has defied all odds, all expectations and all naysayers. There were plenty of people deriding the company right from the beginning. When OYO first came up, legacy hoteliers looked down their noses at the company, saying it was no competition. But when its valuation began to rise and its pricing strategy began to hurt them, legacy hoteliers banded together to criticize the young start-up's practices. They whined about OYO's business model at every forum and demanded regulations against it. Undaunted, Agarwal carried on, tweaking the model here, acquiring a tech company there, and adding innovations bit by bit.

By 2016, hoteliers were beginning to admit that OYO was competition. In August 2016, at the 115th annual general meeting of Indian Hotels Corporation Limited, the Tata Group's then chairman Cyrus Mistry admitted to shareholders that they needed to keep an eye on Ritesh Agarwal's OYO. This spoke volumes about the disruption the young upstart has caused. If further proof were needed, it comes from the fact that OYO's model spawned at least thirty copycats.

When OYO started, it aggregated budget hotel rooms run by independent owners. There were many problems with this model because instead of getting the entire hotel, it would get some rooms, which it branded. The rest of the hotel remained unprepossessing. Also, there was a price disparity between the room sold on OYO and that the budget hotel owner was trying to sell on his own. OYO would be selling at discounts, while the hotel owner would sell at his own rate and nobody would take it. So, their occupancies suffered. Not surprisingly, everyone complained bitterly about OYO's model.

It was a bit akin to when Uber and Ola took off in India, the old black-and-yellow taxi drivers went ballistic. In OYO's case similarly, established hoteliers were annoyed. Unlike the chains who were only looking at converting well-known standalone properties, OYO did not bother with frills or management fees, only going in for standardization and convenience and choosing the franchise route and offering lower rates. The industry had no choice but to start discounting. As one irate hotelier lashed out, 'We were being hit by a technology platform consolidating mom-and-pop establishments that are poor on compliance and selling them like a hotel chain.'

For someone so young, Agarwal handled the criticism maturely. He admits that negative reviews on platforms like TripAdvisor hurt him but he got down to the job of addressing these by auditing guest experiences. He got a team of auditors to go around with a 150-point checklist to review a hotel that had been remodelled as an OYO. He also rapidly changed the aggregating rooms model to own inventories through a franchised route. At every forum he began disowning the aggregator term.

'It's the media that has branded OYO as an aggregator—I would call OYO a branded-hotel franchise model,' he said. But unfortunately, the tag stuck.

If you break it down, OYO's model is surprisingly simple. On the one hand, there are millions of mom-and-pop show kind of hotels all over the country of inconsistent standard and quality. On the other hand, for the common consumer there was a lack of affordable, quality, branded-hotel room supply. OYO looked at the problem from both sides and solved it by putting technology, reach and branding into the hands of tiny nondescript hotels who could now offer rooms in great locations at discounted rates. Basically, OYO went after the millions of small hotels near railway stations, bus stations etc., and renovated and branded them.

Distribution using technology innovatively also helps these hotels. Early on, Agarwal recognized the strength of a mobile platform. The OYO app is perhaps one of the most downloaded app in India. Ninety-five per cent of its bookings come through direct channels so it is one of the few players that has broken the OTA clout and saves enormously on distribution costs. This allows it to invest more in marketing.

Although Agarwal had no experience in hoteliering, he solved two important problems, that of lack of availability faced by consumers with regard to good and affordable rooms and the challenge of discoverability faced by hotel operators bringing innovation into a sector that was steeped in traditional thinking. Very soon, he became a poster boy for India's start-up story, attracting funding easily. Venture capitalists and private equity funds—which had hitherto never looked at the hotel sector—began investing in droves into OYO, thereby infusing the industry with much-needed capital to grow. Even if traditional hoteliers had no faith in OYO's model or its way of doing business, Softbank, Lightspeed Ventures, Sequoia Capital, Hero Enterprises, China Lodging, DSG Consumer Partners, and several others invested in the OYO story in a big way. In 2019, even Airbnb took a stake in OYO.

If OYO opened the keys to new room supply, it also unlocked new consumers. Taking a leaf out of cab aggregator Ola's on-demand model which made cabs accessible and affordable and thus got thousands of new users into the taxi pool, OYO expanded the customer base of branded hotels by making them available, predictable and affordable. Suddenly, backpackers, students, people who stayed with relatives, night-train travellers who just needed a shower and change but were loath to pay huge sums for a hotel room, all began choosing OYO. Voila! A stagnant market that was hovering around 90,000 branded-hotel rooms began growing at a fast clip.

Agarwal says two things have defined OYO's journey. One, constantly being innovative. Two, always keeping in mind how it could bring convenience to the Indian consumer's hotel experience. This is what led to radical things like introducing sunrise (6 a.m.) check-in and a new relationship category by which unmarried couples could book a room.

Says Satbir Singh, founder Thinkstr which helped OYO with its brand strategy, 'Disruption and innovation is in OYO's DNA. We have seen that in the way the company is evolving, in the way they developed offerings like a 6 a.m. check-in, entry for couples in love and so on. The brand has been built on accessibility and they have never shied away from being a budget traveller's first choice.'

OYO also used technology in literally every aspect of the budget hotel business to make it highly efficient. From sourcing supplies centrally to managing housekeepers and setting rates, OYO found a tech solution for a host of processes, helping its owners.

On the customer side, it managed to get a pulse on their needs. It relied heavily on data sciences to study consumer behaviour and deliver to users just the experience they want. OYO records more than 7,50,000 bookings every month. When the analytics team plotted the geo locations of where the bookings originated from, it saw that many of the bookings were happening on highways and road routes, implying that people often book on the way to a destination or at a destination. So, OYO made bookings convenient for last minute check-ins. Similarly, by looking at data of cities that generate most bookings and clusters of feeder cities, it offered targeted supply.

But let's go back to the beginnings.

How in the world did this ridiculously young entrepreneur (is nineteen even an age to start up!) ever have the guts to launch something so audacious?

The Start of OYO

Perhaps it is in his genes. Ritesh himself thinks it is because he is from a small town and so had the occasion to see first-hand how middle India travels. Although his family is originally from north India, Ritesh was born in the southern part of Odisha, near the Andhra Pradesh border. His dad had moved to Odisha for business, running a small FMCG kind of products' provisional store in Rayagada, a very small town next to Koraput.

'I had the opportunity of seeing and learning things that I would probably never have had the exposure to in bigger cities. One of the key things was since it was a small town, everybody would know each other. So even in the early days, when I was in my seventh or eighth grade, I had the opportunity to do very small forms of businesses like sell FMCG products in Dad's business,' he said. Next, he got into selling SIM cards as the telecom sector got booming. Incidentally, the precocious entrepreneur learnt coding at the age of eight.

The youngest of four siblings, Ritesh said he felt good doing all these little gigs as there was always enormous pressure on him. His siblings had all done well educationally and gone to bigger cities to study.

'If you stayed post-tenth grade in the place I was growing up in, it meant that you had not done well enough to go somewhere. And so, because three of my siblings had done well, there was a lot of pressure on me to do well too,' he said.

Most of the people from his town would go to cities like Bhubaneswar, Visakhapatnam and so on for their education. When his turn came, Ritesh told his dad he wanted to go to Kota because he had been seeing front-page advertisements in newspapers about the famous coaching classes of the Rajasthan town that spawned many IIT graduates.

'I felt very curious about it. And I felt that if this is the place where so many good people go to, I should be there,' he said.

Besides, there was his love of coding too, of course. His dad told him that he could go there for two years and they would support him but after that he wanted him to return and run the family business.

Arriving in Kota, Ritesh realized how different the world was from the small place he had grown up in. While he enjoyed his classes, there was a sense of discontent.

'I was continuously remembering my sixth-to-tenth-grade days, when I would sell SIM cards and how I enjoyed that a lot more,' he said.

In 2010, Ritesh read about the IndUS Entrepreneurs (TiE), a networking society for start-ups. Intrigued, he started taking weekend trains to Delhi to attend networking events at TiE. The first one he attended was the TiECon event, an annual jamboree which thousands attend. The buzz is tremendous.

'I just went there and they were so nice to me to let me enter without a card or registration,' he said.

The most exciting thing about the TiE networking events for Ritesh was that everyone was so accessible there and he could chat with several big e-commerce players. You could walk up to anyone. I found that there were so many of these smart people who were working towards transforming our country. Some were solving very conventional problems. Others were talking about unusual e-commerce problems.

Ritesh describes how he met someone who mentioned that he wanted to run an e-commerce site to enable smaller towns to access brands, which is a large problem as well. 'So, I thought now I want to surround myself with only people like these,' he said.

Ritesh started spending more and more time in Delhi only going to Kota for his IIT and other entrance examinations. He rented a barsati (a small terrace pad) in the GK area of Delhi, managing on pocket money from his parents and a small stipend he earned doing odd jobs. His head was buzzing with ideas. When he finished his studies at Kota, he told his dad that he wanted to spend six months in Delhi trying something out before applying to universities.

He had read a lot about Airbnb and also about how during the Commonwealth Games in Delhi (held in 2010), the government was encouraging homestays to meet the supply shortage of rooms. There were so many questions people used to ask, like could they pay by credit card when they reached the property. He also read many complaints about unclean washrooms. He decided he could do something about this.

And the idea of Oravel came to him. He got two interns and built a website to aggregate rooms. The first step before launching, however, was to go and stay in these rooms to see for himself what the issues were.

'For close to three months, every single day I stayed at service apartments, bed and breakfasts, guest houses, small hotels in Delhi,' he said. He accessed the Delhi Commonwealth Games list of lodging places to start off.

But where was the money to go stay at all these places? Was it free?

'I had some savings,' Ritesh replied. 'But I wrote to all these people requesting them to let me stay for free and telling them I was building this thing called Oravel and they could look at the website and so on.'

Very few people let him stay for free. However, many said they could give him a room at 60–70 per cent discount as anyway they had empty rooms.

'That was the time when staying across all these properties I realized how large was the opportunity of just getting the standardization right,' said Ritesh. That was his Eureka moment so to speak.

Soon after, he met Venture Nursery, an accelerator that liked his idea but was more impressed with the effort he had taken to spend three months trying out various B&Bs. Their condition for funding, however, was that he should get himself a cofounder. He also applied for the Thiel Fellowship started by tech entrepreneur Peter Thiel. The fellowship is meant for entrepreneurs under twenty-three and gives selected candidates $1,00,000. He managed to bag it too, one of the first resident Asians to do so.

Around this time, Ritesh went to Rajesh Yadav, an owner of a twelve-room unit he had stayed in, and made him an offer saying that he would help him fill the property. 'Generally, only two or three rooms were being filled. The offer was if we make profit on this unit, we will both share it. If we make losses then I will bear the brunt,' he said. 'He felt that here is a young boy who wants to work hard and the property is empty anyway. So he supported me. The standardization we did was minimum and mostly by getting supplies from Sadar Bazaar,' he added.

This was June 2013. At that time, the website for booking was called Oravel Inns. Initially Yadav's property was called Oravel Inns.

'But he said, "Let's keep the brands separate." So, the property was called OYO Inns,' Ritesh said. But Inns was not really a term that people understood and anyway they were only offering rooms, so the name was changed to OYO Rooms.

This is where Ritesh's story gets a bit hazy. Because his co-founder—yes, he had found one in Manish Sinha, an advertising whiz who had left Bombay and was trying his hand running a homestay in Gurgaon—tells a different story. It was Sinha who coined the name OYO, the inspiration coming from seeing a retail store in Mumbai, and it was he who put together many of the pitches that led to Ritesh becoming a darling of investors and grabbing media headlines. Sinha describes how he was the one who made the presentation at

Lufthansa Runway to Success. 'You can see the videos,' he says. And it was his presence that led to Venture Nursery forking out the initial Rs 30 lakh investment.[1]

That it's a conflicted story, is all that Ritesh is willing to say when quizzed about it. Surprisingly, Sinha, although he felt betrayed, does not have any rancour. He says that Ritesh was always very respectful. Indeed, when you meet Ritesh, the thing that strikes you is how unassuming and passionate he is. Although Sinha's story as well as some of the reported hustles that Ritesh pulled (he allegedly inflated numbers of the listings on his site when pitching to investors and overstated many of his achievements) did come out in newspaper articles,[2] it didn't seem to make a dent on his reputation or appeal to investors. Many probably thought this sort of hustle was a good trait—after all, many a big empire has seen similar beginnings; McDonald's, to name one, where Ray Croc manipulated things to take over the company.[3]

Anyhow, that story soon became water under the bridge and the world moved on.

Meanwhile, back at the first gig that Ritesh had with Yadav—

'The first month was great,' Ritesh said. 'The property was sold out—and mind you, June is off season in Delhi. We booked a decent amount of profits and OYO and Yadav ji shared it.' They had priced the hotel room at Rs 999.

Two months before this happened, Anuj Tejpal, an IIT–BHU graduate who was working with a consulting firm, joined Ritesh.

'Somewhere he had read that Oravel was trying to be India's Airbnb and he reached out saying, "Ritesh, I want to work together", and joined us. If you were to think about OYO, it was actually started by me and Anuj because he was there with me as we moved from the Oravel model all the way to OYO,' says Ritesh, omitting all mention of Sinha.

The OYO room property was ranked highly on TripAdvisor. People recommended it because getting a clean room for Rs 999 was unheard of.

Why Rs 999? There is a story behind that too, dating back to Ritesh's SIM card selling days. 'In the early days of telecom, you had to buy prepaid cards and that would come with validity periods. Then, Airtel for the first time launched what was said to be a no validity lifetime card for Rs 999 and in my SIM card selling days, that was one of the bestselling cards for me. For me, the pricing was slightly superstitious as the Rs 999 price had worked for me then. That is how rooms at OYO Huda City Centre, Yadav ji's property, was priced at Rs 999.

'Interestingly, Yadav was selling his rooms at Rs 1600 per night. I actually decreased the price but it was single occupancy for Rs 999, double occupancy for Rs 1299 and then there was food revenue that had also started coming in. So, the average went back to Rs 1500 only,' Ritesh said.

'If there was a group reservation, we would increase the price. So we did a little bit of pricing experiment in the early days. But because the occupancy grew, it did not matter that the price was lower,' he added. Basically, the pricing was a hit-and-trial method.

Why didn't Ritesh think of interning in a hotel to understand the dynamics of pricing and operations?

'I was naive enough to believe that I could do all these things,' he responded.

But in a way, it turned out to be good, because, as he points out, if he had worked at a hotel, he might have done things the way hoteliers did. Instead, he looked at the problem from a completely different perspective.

'If I had joined a hotel, I would have got training on a $1,00,000 software that is archaic and inconvenient,' he said. 'I believe ignorance was bliss for me. It does not mean that there is nothing to learn on the other side. There is a lot to learn but principally I needed to take a very independent view to be able to build this system,' he added.

This ability to take a dispassionate outsider's view was what stood Ritesh in great stead as he built OYO into a big brand. As he says, he learnt pricing from airlines and taxis rather than established hotels, and consumer branding from companies like Royal Enfield whose messaging was very cult, new age and heavy on signage.

Even in terms of hotel operations, he said that he picks up things from non-hotel experiences. For example, a quick mobile check-in and check-out experience at all OYO receptions was inspired by Uber.

'We said, hey, this driver, if he can use technology so easily, our guys should also be able to use it and checkout should be as easy as getting out of the car. It shouldn't be, oh-I-will-print-papers-and-you-sign-all-of-them; it shouldn't be that difficult,' he said.

The toiletry kits at OYO were inspired by Virgin Airlines, and not other hotels. 'Our first kit was exactly the stuff Virgin Atlantic gives its passengers,' he said.

Ritesh says that this learning from looking at other industries for ideas came from his sojourn in the US as a Thiel fellow. He describes how they were told that emulating from the same industry does not lead to a huge success.

The other big learning was to plan a global company. The Silicon Valley start-ups were not solving just US problems but were building for the world, says Ritesh.

This explains OYO's huge expansion drive into other countries—China, Japan, the Philippines, the UK et al. While the ambition to build a global company is admirable, analysts have questioned its move into unfamiliar markets like London and China.

As it scaled, OYO not just expanded into other geographies but also into allied verticals. It acquired co-working player Innov8, got into homestays in 2017, opened a home-management arm—all of which led one commentator to express his misgivings about OYO's 'egregious excesses'.

Early on, Ritesh also understood that tech would be the biggest differentiator between OYO and conventional hotels, and he says he always has an eye open for an interesting tech company to buy. There has been huge investment in data analytics, in which OYO relies a lot. The idea is to study consumer behaviour and deliver to users just the experience they want.

OYO records hundreds of thousands of bookings every month. When the analytics team plotted the geolocations of where the bookings originated from, it saw that many of the bookings were happening in highways and road routes, implying that people often book on the way to or at the destination. So, OYO made bookings convenient for last-minute check-ins. Similarly, by looking at data for cities that generate the most bookings and clusters of feeder cities, it could offer targeted supply.

Taking a leaf out of several successful apps, OYO also launched a lighter version of its app—OYO Lite. It also looked at frictionless payment, partnering with HDFC bank's PayZapp, a one-click payment solution, as well as mobile wallet Ola Money.

In fact, there have been a host of tech innovations all aimed at enhancing user experience.

So, is OYO a hotel company or a tech company?

'Some people also call us a retail company,' Ritesh countered, with a grin. 'They say that because this is such a fast-usage activity or service that you might even consider it that.'

'The fact that OYO defies bracketing has been a challenge from day one when it comes to hiring,' Ritesh said. 'A lot of tech people join us because they think there is a lot of consumer impact, whereas on the other side, front office guys from hospitality join us saying, "Oh this is a tech company and we would like to be a part of the change."'

However, Ritesh certainly understood all the consumer pain points when it came to hotels.

'If you look at the three different paradigms that decide choice of a hotel, there is location, there is price and there is quality,' he says, adding, 'One or the other is always broken. So if the location and the price are right, quality will be bad. If the location and the quality are right, the price would be high. And if the price and quality are right, then the location would be really far. So, there is never an equilibrium. OYO's ambition is to create that equilibrium by use of talent and technology.'

The problems that Ritesh faced in standardizing the hotels he chose are very different from what the other hotels would face.

'For example,' he said, 'seepage is one of the biggest problems at the converted OYO hotels, which are all mostly old constructions. So, we are understanding the skill set of identifying the seepage and fixing it in the fastest time and with the lowest cost possible so that room doesn't need to be locked for a longer period of time,' he said.

While OYO's revenues are growing, is it booking profits? Will its pricing structure allow it profits? The answer to that lies in the scale. OYO's gamble is that by targeting hotels with low occupancy rates and boosting them up to 80 per cent or so, it would get double the return. And the more it boosts occupancy of OYO properties, the other unbranded similar properties would either be forced out of business or be eager to be absorbed into its fold.

OYO has also been creating new niches. For instance, it has created an OYO Women's Exclusive hotel, an industry first. Now that's innovation. It has also upgraded its offerings, moving up the price chain. It launched OYO Townhouse, which it hopes will open the door to more premium customers. Targeted at millennials, the trendy-looking OYO Townhouse has been designed as a hybrid experience.

'It is 25 per cent hotel, 25 per cent home, 25 per cent shops and 25 per cent cafe,' said Ritesh, describing how OYO Townhouses have an indoor lounge and an outdoor cafeteria. This urban innovation is set in the most unexpected locations, mostly non-commercial residential areas where neighbours get dependent cards to use the hotel facilities.

Targeted at 'millennial-minded' customers, OYO Townhouses offer Netflix in the rooms, smart multipurpose spaces and a bundle of other interesting offerings, including creative menus.

Delhi-based Motherland, co-founded by V. Sunil and Mohit Dhar Jayal, the duo who had earlier brought in American ad agency Wieden+Kennedy to India, has crafted the consumer experience at OYO Townhouse.

'What we are doing at OYO Townhouse is similar to the work we did with Indigo Airlines,' said V. Sunil. 'Motherland is curating the shopping experience at OYO Townhouse with T-shirts, eatables, purses, books and memorabilia carefully sourced from here and there.'

Roping in talented creative professionals like V. Sunil and Satbir Singh of advertising agency ThinkStr has been one of Ritesh's smartest moves.

'While Ritesh himself is a school dropout, OYO has begun to set the bar at IIM professionals while hiring,' said one executive search player. 'That's at the entry level.'

At the CEO level, Ritesh brought in one of India's most successful leaders, Aditya Ghosh, who took low-cost airline Indigo places. Ghosh was then elevated to a board level role and Rohit Kapoor, who was in charge of OYO's real estate business, was made the CEO.

Technology and talent are what will differentiate a company in this age of disruption. And Ritesh has managed to pack his company with an abundance of both. However, analysts worry that OYO could be scaling up too rapidly for its own good.

The debacle of co-working giant WeWork, also a Softbank funded start up, has put the spotlight on OYO. Many feel this hotel chain may go the WeWork way. A worrying aspect for OYO is that in all the focus on technology, it may have lost a bit of focus on the aspects of the customer or the owner. OYO owners have been vocal in their criticism of some of the chain's policies while customers have complained on social media about quality standards. Relationships are what make and break companies in this industry and OYO has to crack that piece. The other problem with OYO's model is its basic burger approach of fast food companies may pall soon as diners crave gourmet offerings.

12

The OTAS—Friends, Enemies or Frenemies

'The world hates change. Yet, it is the only thing that has brought progress.'

—Charles F. Kettering

For this book, I went around asking hoteliers what were the biggest disruptors in their industry. The most common answer was OTAs, online travel agencies.

I heard tirades about them, I heard enthusiastic appreciation, and grudging admissions that they were indispensable now.

Online travel agencies (OTAs) is the name given to travel websites that provide online booking services for hotels, airlines, cars and other travel-related services to users. They started in 1996—more than 200 years after the hotel story started—and probably had far more impact and power scarcely twenty years after coming up. The stupendous growth of OTAs was because of the value they offered to consumers' real-time availability of flight tickets, hotel rooms and price comparison information, prompting decision-making in seconds. It gave rise to the do-it-yourself (DIY) traveller, cutting out travel agents, booking agents and putting a lot of power in the hands of the consumer.

Online travel agencies are regarded as frenemies—friends and enemies—by the hotel industry, who cannot do without them because of the business they bring in. For many of the hotels it's almost 30 per cent of their business. But at the same time, the commissions they charge per booking chips away at their revenues and profits.

It all started in 1995–96 when American Airlines' reservation system Sabre created a website that allowed customers to reserve, book and purchase tickets. It was called Travelocity and run by Sabre executive Terry Jones. Around the same time Microsoft executive Rich Barton pitched the idea of an online travel booking service to Bill Gates and Steve Ballmer. They agreed and Expedia (its name derived from Exploration and Speed) began as a division of Microsoft. Meanwhile, in Europe, a small start-up called Bookings.nl was born in Amsterdam founded by Geert-Jan Bruinsma for lodging reservations. In 1997, in Stamford Connecticut Priceline was founded by Jay Walker and its most revolutionary idea was the name-your-own-price bidding model for consumers. These were the early online travel agencies. In the early days, they were loved by airlines, who could offload unsold inventory on them, and by travellers, who loved the convenience.[1]

So popular did the OTAs become that in no time Expedia had been spun off as a public company. Meanwhile, in Europe, on the lodging front, Booking.nl was growing in size and in 2000 merged with another hotel rooms aggregator site, Bookings Online. The merged entity became Bookings. com, one of the most powerful hotel booking platform in the world.

By 2001, airlines woke up to the fact that the OTAs were beginning to rule the ticket distribution and making huge profits, so four of them banded together and came up with their own offering, Orbitz.com.

By now Expedia was growing and the company that had controlling stake in it bought Hotels Reservation Network, a company set up in 1991 that provided hotel bookings via a toll-free phone network. It became Hotels.com.

More and more hotels that few people knew about became discoverable. But with so many unknown hotels surfacing online thanks to these OTAs, one big problem customers faced was that they were not sure of their quality. A small start-up in Massachusetts came up in 2000 to solve the problem. It came up with a centralized platform where travellers could post recommendations and reviews of hotels anywhere in the world. That was TripAdvisor.

In ten years' time, TripAdvisor became an indispensable website for travellers and a nightmare for hoteliers as one bad review on it could destroy their equity.

Over the years some serious consolidation happened—Travelocity, Hotels.com, Trivago, HomeAway was gobbled up by Expedia, while Priceline picked up Bookings.com, probably one of the best buys that anyone in the travel industry could make. It also owned Agoda, Kayak.com and a host of other aggregators and meta search players. In 2014, Priceline changed its name to Booking Holdings.

Just imagine in 2017, 673.1 million room nights of hotel stay were booked by websites owned by Booking Holdings.

By 2018, the OTA industry had almost become a duopoly, with Expedia and Booking Holdings (formerly Priceline group) controlling the market share. Their models on the hotel room bookings were however different. Expedia focused on merchant revenue. It bought hotel rooms in bulk at a discount, and then sold it to customers at a mark-up. Booking Holdings focused on agency revenue. It earned commission whenever a traveller made a booking on a hotel listed on its website. It did not purchase any rooms. As for TripAdvisor, which introduced a booking option only really late—its revenue came from advertisements.

Globally, hotels and OTAs have been at war ever since hoteliers realized just how much of their potential revenues were being taken away by these online technology players. The OTAs, which ironically were born to eliminate middlemen in the booking chain, had become the single biggest middlemen. They offered attractive discounts and incentives to get customers to keep booking through them. OTAs also connected beautifully with millennials and fast-to-launch apps with great user experience—survey after survey showed that most millennials who are digital natives and look for a good online experience preferred to book via OTAs.

When they started, the OTAs charged commissions that ranged between 5 per cent and 10 per cent. That has risen to 20 per cent and more in many cases. Earlier, there were several OTAs so hoteliers could take advantage of websites with lower commissions but aggressive consolidation, leading to a duopoly, meaning that the online players can call the shots.

Not surprisingly, the OTAs and hotels have been constantly having skirmishes. In India, the story is no different. In November 2018, around 250 hoteliers in Gujarat got together, saying they were going to boycott leading Indian OTA MakeMyTrip because of its excessive commissions, and they would do business only with Yatra, Cleartrip and Booking.com.[2]

But we are getting ahead of the story.

The OTA story in India began a little later than in the West, primarily because Internet penetration was at that time not as high as in the West. Although former ABN Amro executive Deep Kalra's start-up MakeMyTrip (MMT), funded initially by eVentures, began in October 2000, it did not really take off in India as Indians—though they searched the site for fares—were not confident about paying online. Within six months, MMT decided to shift tack and focus on the NRI market looking for tickets to book to and from India. That worked.

In 2005, when the Indian Railways took railway booking online and low-cost airline Air Deccan came up, Deep Kalra decided time was ripe for India. His call was right and MMT blazed a trail in India—between 2005 and 2010, when it went for an IPO listing on NASDAQ, it soared, with its gross merchandise value growing from $30 million to $600 million.

By now players like Yatra and Cleartrip had joined the fray. People in India were getting more and more confident of booking online. Sixty per cent of the airline bookings in India had shifted to online by now. The next frontier was hotel bookings and MMT got into it. There was a reason too—discount wars on airline tickets were at their peak.

Almost all the OTA players in India were gung-ho about hotel bookings. Amit Taneja, the CMO at Cleartrip, optimistically pointed out that the hotel bookings business, unlike airline bookings— which is ruled by seasonality—was pretty much all-weather and throughout the year.

However, getting into hotel bookings in India was easier said than done. In 2015, Deep Kalra points out only 4per cent of hotel bookings in India were done online through OTAs. Global travel research firm PhocusWright had pegged it at 13 per cent but according to MMT, the research firm only looked at upscale categories. If you included the budget segment, online penetration was just about 7 per cent and OTAs had only half the share. Clearly there was huge headroom for growth.

However, there were plenty of challenges too. Unlike the West, where most hotel rooms were chain-owned and there was an assurance of quality, in India that was not the case. For instance, Jessie Paul, CEO of Paul Writer Strategic Advisory, talks about the mismatch in expectation and the actual reality that she faced when she booked a room online. While on the one hand the branded hotels are desperately trying to get the customer directly, bypassing the OTAs, on the other hand, the unbranded hotels—which could have formed the bulk of bookings for OTAs—fail the credibility test.

Kalra listed reasons ranging from poor Internet connectivity to poor discoverability of many hotels and hotels' lack of digital presence. Even many branded hotels in India had antiquated websites that did not support online booking.

While on paper, hotel bookings signalled plenty of opportunity because here was a chance to get the individual hotels up on the platform of the OTAs, their lack of access to technology was an inhibitor. Solution: the OTAs began offering tech tools and support.

But tech was just one part of the story. What OTAs did not factor in was the consumer behaviour of Indians. A peculiar trait of Indians on holiday is not booking in advance. Several hill stations near Delhi as well as places like Goa thrive on walk-ins.

However, despite these challenges, within two years the story was changing. In 2017, a report by Deutsche Bank Ag said that 19 per cent of hotel bookings had moved online and forecast that by 2020, 28 per cent would move online. It said that 78 per cent of these bookings would be done through OTAs.

One of the worries that Indian customers had about booking through OTAs—that of quality of rooms—was addressed by MMT. In 2017, it launched a concept called Assured Hotels, where it certified hotels on parameters like service and product. The other way of breaking consumer resistance to booking online was to offer deals and discounts. Flash sales and last-minute hotel-stay offers were the order of the hour.

However, this had an unexpected fallout. In the whole effort to acquire customers through frenzied discounting, the various OTA players began to hurt each other. By now there were a number of OTAs in India—MMT, Yatra, Cleartrip, Goibibo, not to mention the global players like Expedia and Booking.com, who had checked into India and were leveraging their international clout.

Not only were the OTAs hurting each other but they were hurting hotels. A customer would get far more discounts while booking on an OTA than booking direct through a hotel as the online player was absorbing the losses—don't forget most OTAs were heavily funded.

Two things happened. MakeMyTrip, tired of the discounting war with Goibibo, initiated a merger with it. This happened in 2016. The deal was an interesting one. While MakeMyTrip acquired 100 per cent stake in Ibibo Group, its parent Naspers and Tencent got a 40 per cent share in MMT, becoming the single largest shareholder in the company. Post-merger the MMT—Ibibo entity had as much as 60 per cent market share of India's OTA bookings.

The second thing was that the hotels decided to get aggressive and upped the rewards if you came through their loyalty programmes and booked direct. Some hotels also started looking at ways to use technology to combat the OTAs. Budget hotel player OYO, which received a $1 billion funding in 2018, could use that to offer huge discounts and drive 95 per cent of its bookings to its own channel.

Meanwhile, a completely new competitor popped up— PayTM. The mobile wallet player got into the travel bookings space, disrupting it. Since it owned the payments piece, it could do far more. What Deep Kalra had been warning about for years—that competition would come from a mobile travel agent—came true.

So, the net effect was that the MMT–Ibibo merger, which together controlled 60 per cent of the market in India, could not leverage their market heft. Its marketing and promotional expenses instead of coming down more than doubled.

A report in the *Economic Times* points how post-merger, the company's marketing and sales promotion expenses increased by 139.8 per cent to $115.9 million in quarter ending 30 September 2018.[3]

Meanwhile, international chains were ramping up their online bookings platforms to make it more interesting for the customer to book through them, even without discounts. The OTAs and hotels usually have a price parity understanding, which means the hotel cannot give guests higher discounts than what's offered on the OTA platform. So, they had to get innovative.

Let's take the example of IHG. Shantha de Silva of IHG pointed out how the chain had decided to work with OTAs only for incremental business—first-time bookings—and was trying to migrate repeat bookings on to its own platform. In 2017, he said that IHG's web generated about $4 billion in revenue globally. Of this $1.6 billion dollars came through mobile. Bookings through the IHG app were growing 30 per cent year on year.

'If you go back to history, IHG introduced the first hotel reservations systems in the world in the good old days called Holidesk,' de Silva says, confident that it would be the first hotel chain to come up with a breakthrough Internet model that could take business back from OTAs. While an OTA could only offer the traveller room options like standard, deluxe, premier and so on, what IHG was piloting was the ability to choose the exact room—the floor, near a staircase, room with a view, and so on.

As de Silva explained, 'When a customer books a room, currently he or she can only put a request about wanting a room with a view—it is reactive, but with our reservation system the level of personalization is very high. The customer can pick their own room. This is somewhat akin to the airline model where customers can pick and choose their seats. The possibilities of this are endless for the hotel. Just as an airline could monetize its aisle and window seats and make more money on its front rows, the hotel could possibly have differential rates for each room.

Similarly, if you look at Wyndham's sudden growth in 2018, when it made big market-share gains, the direct cause was its ability to catch OTA users and convert them into booking their own channels. They did this by improving their Reward app, showering loyal guests better experiences and offers.

Most online bookers use OTAs because of their perception that they give better rates. Wyndham successfully combated this perception through a marketing campaign and offering juicy non-monetary incentives.

Even as MMT–Ibibo were battling these elements, Booking.com was increasing its lodging inventory in India by leaps and bounds and increasing its domestic marketing. Booking.com also localized its tools to appeal to Indian customers.

Several hoteliers told me to meet Vikas Bhola, country head of Booking.com, to understand why they felt the foreign OTA was getting a strong grip of the Indian market.

Bhola pointed out that contrary to perception, a majority of reservations on the Booking.com platform is for non-branded hotels, as location is a big parameter when choosing hotels.

'Majorly how we work in search is to create landmarks and list properties around those,' Bhola explained. He added, 'There are many different ways in which customers book, and the platform studied these to offer personalized recommendations based on artificial intelligence. If a customer is more price-sensitive then we will push more discounted properties in front. If the customer tends to choose hotels based on reviews then we push higher rated properties upfront. Also, if the purpose of travel is stated as business then the algorithm will show up a completely different set of hotels. The more you book, the better your experience as the OTA can offer better personalization.'

Bhola said that he was working hard at growing its India listings at 60 per cent annually. 'This year [2017] the focus,' he said, 'is to get more properties in the North-east on to the platform.'

When MakeMyTrip and OYO got into a skirmish in 2015, and the former refused to list the OYO inventory on its platform, again Booking.com gained. It put select OYO inventory on its platform and thereby got to attract budget consumers looking for good deals.

In April 2018, MakeMyTrip, added OYO back to its website and mobile app. However, Treebo and Fab Hotels vanished from the OTA.

All this shows how the fight between the OTAs and the hotels is continuous. To make matters worse, new players like Middle Eastern player Musafir are edging into India.

Today's battles over India's \$2 billion online travel market may not be as bloody. But OTAs are sacrificing profits.

Going forward, the predictions for OTAs are both optimistic as well as dire. On the one hand, newer technology like blockchain poses a threat and can completely disrupt OTAs.

On the other hand, if you look at the online booking figures for India and see the massive headroom for growth, there is hope. According to Morgan Stanley, Indians book only 10–15 per cent of their hotel stays online, compared to 25–30 per cent in China and nearly 50 per cent in the US.

While 500 million Indians have some Internet access, only a minuscule number of these—less than 50 million—transact on OTAs.

13

The Charge of the New Brigade

'I mostly built stuff that I liked.'

—Mark Zuckerberg

Why would somebody with an IIT–IIM background throw up a lucrative job in London with a global consulting firm to start a hospitality venture in India? Ask this of Gaurav Jain, MD and founder of boutique chain resorts, Aamod.

'It is sheer madness,' he admitted, though he looks quite happy with his decision. Jain's personal experience of struggling to find an ideal place to holiday with his family as well as a great interest in tourism is what led him to return to India in 2008 to start Aamod.

'Also, it was a college dream,' he confessed. During his IIM Calcutta days, he and his wife (she was his classmate) actually put together a hospitality project that they pitched to a bank. The project was rejected but his wife got a job with the bank.

For Aditi Balbir, the founder and CEO of V Resorts, who too has an MBA (from ISB, Hyderabad) and a McKinsey in her CV, the jump into a hospitality start-up was partly serendipitous and partly because she is a passionate traveller. The venture capital firm she was working with, Bedrock Ventures, incubated V Resorts as a resorts aggregator. But after some time, when they found the venture not going well, they asked her to step in.

'I also put in some of my own money and took over,' said Balbir, describing how she changed the model totally.

Gone are the days when only those with experience in running hotels could set up a hotel company. Since the dawn of the new millennium, when technology began transforming hoteliering, you could see all sorts of people making a foray into the hotel sector. Also, by now many Indians had become widely travelled and had really good hotel experiences abroad and were discontented with what was offer in India. So, people with nice professional jobs, youngsters barely out of college with that one bright idea to change the sector, businessmen with time and money on their hands and art lovers with a crazy idea—all started setting up hotels.

Another recent trend has seen small regional players getting out of their comfort zones and heading to different geographies. The charge was led usually by the second or third generation of the founders of these regional hotels who saw the opportunity to grow and had the ambition and courage to step out of their safe places.

The demographics of those in the hotel business is slowly changing. There are geeky youngsters like Ritesh Agarwal of OYO. There are also a host of middle-class entrepreneurs, with absolutely no background in hospitality, who are chucking their cushy jobs to enter the space. And there are wealthy youngsters who have lived abroad, travelled a fair bit and feel there are gaps in Indian hospitality they can plug.

Shruti Shibulal, daughter of Infosys founder S.D. Shibulal started off quite conventionally, joining Merrill Lynch in New York after graduating from Haverford College in Pennsylvania. But she had the itch to do something different and a meeting with a former chef at The Park Hotel, who was trying to open his restaurant, afforded the chance. She jumped headlong into the restaurant business as a partner in Caperberry in Bangalore. From restaurants to hotels was but a small step away. And that's how Tamara Hospitality happened, a luxury resort in the Western Ghats in Karnataka, which reinforces the concept of the 'sustainable good life'. Tamara is a developer-operator. It owns the properties it operates. This, according to Shibulal, gives them the advantage of being able to think through the entire lifetime of a project.

Or take Siddharth Gupta, Rahul Chowdhury and Kadam Jeet Jain of Treebo Hotels, a budget chain that uses technology. All three are IIT Roorkee engineering graduates, the former two also MBAs from IIMs and McKinsey consultants. After stints at e-commerce ventures, they launched off into hotels with the idea of offering a comfortable stay at affordable prices and emulating the vast reach of the banyan tree by spreading out all over the country. Although there were others in their category with the same idea, the Treebo founders still believed they could do it differently, focusing very hard on an unbroken customer experience. And the goal of being the most-loved travel network is certainly endearing.

Although there are many competitors in the space that Treebo is in, for some reason it caught the eye of industry veterans. When I went to meet Deep Kalra of MakeMyTrip, he urged me to rename the book as *From Taj to Treebo* as he felt these guys would make a difference. There were some talks of MMT buying stake into the company. At the time of writing this book, an MNC hotel chain was trying to invest in the young Indian company. There were also reports of Treebo and Fab hotels, another young start-up that made a mark merging.[1]

The HVS Anarock India Hospitality Review of 2019 talks of both Treebo and Fab Hotels as no longer being outliers but key players.

Significantly, there were many players who made an entry in this category but several vanished. In 2015, for instance, Mangrove Capital–backed WudStay launched and though its model looked similar to the others, it pivoted quickly, also entering into hostels and retirement homes. The narrative of Prafulla Mathur, its founder, was a convincing one. He said that the brand had the intention of catering to a user's lifespan from student days to post-retirement, describing how a student could be a WudStay hostel customer. Then when she began working, she could be a business traveller, using WudStay hotels, and post-retirement could look at the WudStay's retirement home options. WudStay also acquired another budget hotel aggregator Awesome Stays.

In between, WudStay also sold a pet-friendly hotels proposition. But clearly there was not such a high need for that proposition in the Indian market. The brand had gone practically invisible by 2019.

While some have succeeded and others failed, all these entrepreneurs epitomize the new breed of hoteliers who are bringing in some out-of-the-box thinking and fresh approaches into the sector.

Take Jain of Aamod. He has relived his own pain points and created places that are great for family holidays.

'When we were in England and went on holidays, we never stayed at a large property. We would stay in a barn conversion, a manor house and such accommodation. Nothing was standardized and yet there was high quality of hygiene and service,' he said. But in India, they were hard pressed to find similar places. There was a gap in product that Jain felt he could fill.

Initially, Jain invested in creating such properties. The first one was an ecotourism venture in Shogi, near Shimla, and then one in Dalhousie. But after that he chose to go the management route to expand, adding ten more locations.

Aamod is not averse to expanding abroad and has ventured into Sri Lanka too. 'Our smallest property is four bedrooms and largest is forty-two rooms,' he said, pointing to the diversity of portfolio.

In Balbir's case, V Resorts first started as a resort aggregator but it didn't work.

As she explained, 'It meant just putting a board on a resort and selling it. In 2014, V Resorts pivoted and became a full-fledged management company, with everything from a sales and marketing engine to handling operations. We have a bouquet of services that we offer an owner. How V Resorts is different from other management companies is that it only handles projects that are less than thirty rooms.

We have busted the myth that a small property cannot make money.'

She, like Jain, insists there are many gaps in existing products. 'The market for short breaks is really picking up and people are all the time looking for places to unwind. That's the space we operate in and that's bursting with opportunity,' she said.

'The name V Resorts came about because every property has a great view. That's one thing we insist on when we sign a project—that the guest should get a lovely view,' said Balbir.

If unhoteliers like Balbir, Jain, Mathur and Gupta think they can transform this space, there is another new crop of change-makers in this sector—the children of hoteliers, who have a different vision and approach to their parents.

In 2015, Amruda Nair, the granddaughter of the legendary Captain C.P. Krishnan Nair of Leela Palaces, Hotels and Resorts decided to chart her own route in hoteliering. Although she worked alongside her father, Vivek Nair, at the Leela Group, Amruda branched out on her own, getting together with Doha-based billionaire Sheikh Fasal Bin Qassim Al Thani to create Aiana Hotels and Resorts. The idea was to manage hotels in both the Middle East and India but create properties with an Indian ethos. Perhaps bitten by her family's experiences of owning hotels, Aiana has consciously followed an asset-light strategy.

Among the regional hoteliers, the trend of the GenNext really expanding family brands or taking different positioning and tack is evident.

In India's tourism story, it's the regional hoteliers who have played a big part in opening up virgin destinations or troubled spots. Usually it's the local businessman who sets up a hotel there, and once it is successful and tourists flow in, the big chains arrive.

Take Kashmir, where Umar Tramboo, the young scion of a prominent local business family with interests in cement, set up the Khyber Himalayan Resort & Spa in Gulmarg, only the third five-star hotel in the state and the first in the ski resort. It came up in 2012 when the Valley was just opening up to tourism after years of insurgency.

Or take high-altitude Leh, where the local Abdu family set up the Grand Dragon, a luxurious centrally heated eighty-two-room hotel. The Abdus ran a small hotel in Leh, but it was the vision of Danish Din, the son, who had done his hotel management in Spain and worked at a hotel in Madrid that led to the ambitious hotel. It is unexpected to get such a refined F&B experience at an offbeat place like Leh, but that's the story all across India.

Similarly, Deval Tibrewala is taking his father's legacy forward. Deval's father ran a successful textile store in Shillong but set up Polo Towers in Meghalaya's capital twenty-five years ago to address the lack of good accommodation and dining-out options.

When Deval entered the family's hotel business, he used the group's familiarity with the region to expand by opening a resort at Cherrapunjee. The floodgates to tourism in the Northeast were just opening and his vision was to make this gorgeous day-trip destination into a place where people think of staying. A car rallyist and a caving enthusiast (it's a big adventure sport in Meghalaya to negotiate the labyrinthic limestone caves wading through water), Deval also set up a hotel at the emerging Garo business hill-town of Tura to provide accessible accommodation.

'The flagship Polo Towers,' Deval said, 'is in the social fabric of Shillong, a place where residents would come to unwind, where young couples met and fell in love, where they got married and would come to celebrate their anniversaries and births of their children. And now the children are getting married here.'

So Deval is making changes to appeal to his generation as well, at the same time keeping the old ethos intact.

'Back when the hotel was started by my father, twenty-five years ago, Shillong had no options in good hotels. However, my father really saw the need for an upscale hotel in Shillong when there was only a poorly managed government hotel as accommodation for visitors to Shillong. His vision was to build the best and biggest hotel in Shillong, something that transformed the face of tourism and business in Shillong. And that's just what he did. Today Hotel Polo Towers is Shillong's largest hotel in every respect. Be it the number of keys or the number of restaurants,' said Deval.[2]

The hotel's name was a no-brainer, since it was located in the area called Polo Grounds. Incidentally, there is no polo ground on the spot now, with government buildings and homes all around. But it was the place where chukkers of polo were once played and horse racing was common. That's why the hotel also has the emblem of a stallion.

Since Deval's entry into the business, rooms have been refurbished and F&B completely altered. Now there is Cupcake Factory, an artisan bakery with a selection of fine teas, and an Irish pub that comes alive in the nights.

'I love the incongruity of having an Irish pub in the Scotland of the East,' he grinned.

However, he has kept the character of the hotel intact because, as he points out, it is one of those comfortable places that people who grew up there keep coming to week after week.

'We are equivalent to their third place as Howard Schultz called Starbucks, the first being home and the second being work. Shillong unwinds at Hotel Polo Towers and we are very grateful for having that place in people's hearts,' he said.

'Given this backdrop,' Deval said, 'it is our duty to keep refreshing the hotel and bring it up to date with global trends. I think that a city hotel requires you to be as dynamic as the city that hosts you and it is my responsibility as a hotelier to not only keep evolving with the citizens but also take risks and push forward new ideas that will rejuvenate the city's attitude towards entertainment and eating out,' he said.

So far the Polo Tower had had a monopoly over the area but now that the Northeast is opening up and groups like the Taj and Radisson are making inroads into places like Guwahati, how will it cope? Both these hotels have been given concessional terms by the government and are not really built on a commercial mandate.

'Their presence—however they've come—is a positive sign for the region as they bring in a lot of best practices and expand the talent pool available in the region,' says Deval.

Finally, when the Northeast is teeming with opportunity and is such a virgin area, why is the group opening hotels in Allahabad and Jabalpur?

'As a market, India has a lot of potential at travel hubs and Allahabad and Jabalpur stations have a great many number of travellers using the facilities. Hotel Polo Max Jabalpur is situated inside the Jabalpur railway station and Hotel Polo Max Allahabad inside the Allahabad Railway station. In cities where the train station is the primary driver of the economy, every hotel claims to be ten minutes away from the station. So, when we got a chance to actually open inside the station, we just couldn't let the opportunity go,' he said simply.

'More importantly,' said Deval, 'being confined to one region is not the best way to have a cross pollination of ideas. We have brought our signature brand of Shillong hospitality to Uttar Pradesh and Madhya Pradesh and similarly have brought in ideas from there to our hotels in the Northeast.'

14

The Alternative Accommodators—
Airbnbs, Homestays and
Service Apartments

*'A sense of belonging is one of the most powerful human needs.
Airbnb was built on that need.'*

—Scott Bedbury, brand consultant, BrandStream

In 2007, who could have said that a bed-and-breakfast service started in a loft apartment, because its two inhabitants could not afford the rent, would one day go on to become almost as valuable as the world's largest hotel group Marriott founded in 1927?

Launched as Airbedandbreakfast.com—and soon famous world over as Airbnb—this Silicon Valley start-up born in San Francisco offered 5 million homes in 2018 and could boast of 300 million guest arrivals across 81,000 cities and 191 countries. Its valuation in 2019 was $38 billion. Marriott's valuation in 2019 was $44.9 billion (post its merger with Starwood, mind you).

And yet, ask Indian hoteliers if they regard Airbnb as a disruptor that threatens their business and the answer surprisingly from most is no. They say it is a different segment, the consumers are not the same and so on.

If that were indeed the case, why would an Accor invest in One Fine Stay, a homestay start-up that like Airbnb offered travellers the chance to step into the shoes of a local? Why would India's largest hotel chain, the Taj Group, get into the homestay segment with its Ama Trails and Stays?

Guest houses have always been around. Several other lodging models like homestays, timeshares, service apartments and hostels for backpackers have also been around, but Airbnb's growing global clout and success is what has turned the focus of hoteliers back to alternative accommodation. What Airbnb did was to use technology to disrupt an old lodging category and infuse it with an aspirational status, making it a cool thing to do. It's a status symbol of sorts to stay in a homestay as opposed to a hotel.

Smart hoteliers know that this is something they have to deal with. That competition is not just coming from the rival hotel chain and similar formats, but from completely different products. What better wake-up call than seeing young millennials working in MNCs agitate that they would rather stay at an Airbnb while travelling on work rather than a hotel.

At IBM, interestingly, a change in its HR travel policy was necessitated because its young executives posted a rant on social media about how their employer's policy did not allow them to claim cab fare if they used Uber. From that to

Airbnb is but a short step. And indeed at a corporate travel seminar organized by industry association FICCI, there was a discussion about the need for corporate travel agents to add Airbnb choices.

In early 2019, leading OTA Booking.com reported that there were 1,40,000 listings in India of homes, apartments and other unique places to stay. When Booking.com did a survey of its travellers, it found that 68 per cent surveyed said they would prefer 'Alternative Accommodations'.

Globally, Booking.com ended 2018 with 5.7 million reported listings in its 'Alternative Accommodations' business, up 18 per cent year-over-year. It earned $2.8 billion in revenues from this category in 2018, almost 20 per cent of the company's overall revenue for the year.

In the survey, the top reason that Indians cited for wanting to stay at a homestay was the desire to live like a local. The second was the budget.

Now look at Airbnb's growth in India. At the end of 2018, it had over 45,000 listings in India—6000 of these in Goa alone. Over 1.8 million Indians used Airbnb and between 2017 and 2018, it saw a whopping 78 per cent growth with business travellers especially using Airbnb a lot.

Early on, in its India foray, Airbnb took an unusual tack by tying up with the Self-Employed Women's Association of India (SEWA), a trade union for women workers representing 2 million women living mostly in India's rural areas. SEWA members were encouraged to share their homes on Airbnb, opening up tourism in untouched parts of India. It found that payment was a challenge with the SEWA hosts and worked on the processes.

Another interesting collaboration that Airbnb did in India was with rural artisans in Andhra Pradesh. It worked with the state's tourism board to identify artisans who could throw open their dwellings to tourists.

If it were just different kinds of homestay experiences, hoteliers would not have needed to worry so much. But Airbnb increasingly began to offer consumers very rounded travel experiences. In 2017, Brian Chesky, one of the founders of the platform, flew to New Delhi to launch the Trips platform, with fifteen unusual experiences that guests could book in the capital city through the platform. Among the experiences were a visit to a saree museum and learning how to drape the garment in twenty different ways, a chance to visit a couture house, see a camera museum etc.

Airbnb was moving beyond the home and coming up with fascinating curated experiences for travellers—one that you wouldn't find in any guidebook.

It was certainly providing more and more reason for consumers to think of staying in a home rather than a hotel. Millennials were sold. But in next to no time, even forty-and fifty-year-olds were trying out Airbnbs.

Neha Sharma, a university administrator from Jaipur, who had to constantly come to Delhi to meet officials, told me she was booking Airbnb as it offered better locational advantage. She could pick a place near her official meeting place at half the cost. For an overnight stay, this was ideal.

However much hotels might deny that Airbnb was not affecting their business and it was targeted at a different audience, the hard truth is that people who otherwise would have stayed in a hotel were staying in a homestay.

Apart from the global Airbnb, India has its own rising homestay start-ups. Stayzilla, a homestay aggregator, came up only to shut down. Its model was not tenable. But there are plenty of other boutique homestay chains stealing away possible leisure guests from hotels.

Take Manish Sinha's Unhotel, a company that offers handpicked stays in charming homes across the country. The action is all coordinated from Cinnamon Stays, a red-and-white villa in Gurugram, where he lives with his family and lets out six rooms.

Going by the high TripAdvisor ratings for his properties, Sinha's experiment has been quite successful for somebody who strayed into the world of homestays by accident. But then this digitally savvy former ad professional who has a way with words has infused a lot of creativity into his homestays, enticing websites and travel blogs.

It all began when Sinha who was an advertising professional decided to relocate to Delhi–NCR. It was around the time that New Delhi was getting set to host the Commonwealth Games and the government was urging people to set up bed and breakfasts (B&Bs). Since Sinha got a large house on a pricey rent, he decided to let out a few rooms.

'Nobody came,' he says. 'The location on Sohna Road, Gurugram, was too far.'

But Sinha hung on and when Gurugram exploded as a business hub, Cinnamon Stays, with its quirky rooms, hospitable hosts and engaging dinner conversations became sought after. So lively was the ambience of the place that when Sinha's wife's aunt came to visit them she wistfully wished she could turn her large sprawling home in Varanasi into a homestay too.

Thus was born Granny's Inn in the spiritual city. The Varanasi home was restored and refurbished with modern bathrooms.

Although he wanted to expand, Sinha says he realized that he didn't really want to run homestays around the country. His strength was storytelling. Thus was born the Unhotel, an experiential company, where he weaves stories and experiences for a handpicked bunch of homestays and helps market them.

There are several other new homestay players now. SaffronStays, a premium homestay network, has been adding fifteen homes to its network every month. It is an interesting model as it is premiumizing the homestay segment. According to news reports, at SaffronStays, the average revenue per booking ranges between Rs 20,000 and Rs 24,000, with 75 per cent accounted by room rent and rest from F&B.

Homestays have been around for a while now but it is only post 2015 that efforts to organize the category were somewhat successful. Club Mahindra had attempted it earlier but didn't make much headway. Stayzilla collapsed. But OYO launched a homestay segment, banking on a government policy to help alternative accommodations. OYO Rooms has now become OYO Hotels and Homes.

'After Start up India, Stand Up India, the homestay policy is going to be the next big thing!' exclaimed Ritesh Agarwal, founder and CEO of OYO. He has been part of the discussions with the tourism ministry.

The Ministry of Tourism, which spearheads the Incredible India initiative that seeks to increase the number of tourist footfalls in the country, has been concerned about the shortage in hotel room supply and wants to unlock what it calls idle inventory of citizens' homes.

Accreditation, certification and categorization of homestays are part of the policy being debated in 2018.

According to Anarock Consultants, a leading real estate services company in India, India will need more than 2.5 million rooms across the hospitality industry to meet the snowballing demand by 2020. And that explains the incentives to homestays.

Not only has the government relaxed the licensing rules for people seeking to convert their property into certified homestays but it has been developing a centralized database. Simultaneously, it is working with online aggregators like Airbnb that list homestay properties and introduce ratings, guest houses and bed-and-breakfast options.

Suggestions have been mooted that state governments could exempt homestays from service tax. Not surprisingly, hotels are crying foul. It is an unequal playfield, as many point out, as players like Airbnb often don't have to pay taxes, and have easier time with licenses while hotels have to struggle with these.

However, OTAs have embraced the homestays idea wholeheartedly and listed them.

'People today are looking not just at costs when they choose homestays but authentic experiences,' Deep Kalra, the erudite founder of MakeMyTrip, said.

MMT briefly forayed into homestays with its Rightstay offering. 'The kind of exciting alternative accommodations you are getting in India today—so different from the impersonal guest houses—is a massive change,' said Kalra, forecasting that this category is going to explode.

If Airbnb and other homestays are impacting possible growth of hotels, so are hostels. Changing consumer behaviour has completely changed the perception of hostels. Earlier, only those couldn't afford a hotel would stay in hostels. In today's sharing community-living economy, youngsters who come from well-heeled families love hostels because of the community-living ambience.

Zostel, India's first chain of backpacker hostels, taps into this trend by trying to provide quirky, hygienic and affordable options to young travellers. However, in December 2018, the company launched a new offering Zostel X, aimed at not-so-young travellers not into backpacking but wanting the vibe of a community hostel.

The competition from timeshare players like Sterling Resorts and Club Mahindra as well as service apartments is also not to be scorned at, especially as strong branded players are in both these spaces now.

Singapore-based service residence player, the Ascott, has seen great potential in India and put up two properties in Chennai and one in Gurugram. Typically, service apartments are meant for long-stay guests. But Ascott's two brands in Chennai Citadines in Old Mahabalipuram area and Somerset Greenways in the heart of town at MRC Nagar and flagship Ascott at Ireo City in Gurugram attract transient traffic as well. Over 80 per cent of its guests at Somerset are long stay, but at Citadines the mix is different. Citadines is Ascott's mid-market brand, targeted at the young executive, which is reflected in its airy, vibrant decor with graphic prints on walls rather than paintings. Interestingly, however, soon after it opened at OMR, there were more medical tourists at the property than corporate workers.

Globally, Ascott has a couple of other brands—Quest and the Crest Collection. Keeping up with the times, it has also developed a new brand called Lyf, a radical new concept that promotes co-living and co-working.

Indian firm Lemon Tree Hotels too made a foray in the service residences segment through its management arm Carnation Hotels, opening a 195-key serviced residence in Noida, branded Sandal Suites for Assotech Realty.

According to Rattan Keswani, deputy managing director, Lemon Tree Hotels and Director Carnation Hotels, Sandal Suites has been designed keeping in mind business travellers, long-stay project teams and relocating families. There are tennis courts, squash courts and other recreation facilities at Sandal Suites. Developer Assotech is creating an F&B hub Sandal Street, a sort of mini Cyber Hub, the food complex in Gurugram that is a roaring success, near the complex.

While Ascott's focus is on extended stay guest, Rattan Keswani feels that a pure service apartment model is not economically viable. You need to chase the transient traveller too, he feels. The reason he says this is that now in most Indian cities good condo accommodation is available, with all bells and whistles, where the executive can get security staff and cheaper help. So that is where the model cracks, he says.

Well, with hotels chasing extended-stay guests, and the serviced residences chasing the transient traveller, everything is cannibalizing everything else in the lodging segment. That just increases the complexities of doing business.

III

ROOM FOR GROWTH: STRATEGIES

15

The Wellness Mantra

'A spa hotel? It's like a normal hotel, only in the reception there's a picture of a pebble.'

—Welsh comedian Rhod Gilbert

Tour through the palatial ITC Grand Bharat at Manesar and you will find an entire floor set aside for Kaya Kalp. Does it make business sense for a hotel property to dedicate such a ginormous space for a spa? There are nine treatment suites, hammams, a jacuzzi area, an Ayurveda zone and what not spread over 3200 sq. km. of scented, flower-bedecked expanse at the ITC Grand Bharat.

At the ITC Grand Chola, the spa is spread over 22,000 sq ft. Interestingly it's not a uniform experience at all in the ITC hotels. The effort is to introduce indigenous therapies for indigenous regions. So, at the Chola, the treatment will be more from the southern traditions, while at the Maratha it draws on local treatments. And significantly, ITC has a

Swasthya (healthy) menu for guests who book their wellness packages.

'Adding a spa takes the average room rate (ARR) up by 15 per cent,' says Ritesh Reddy of O2 spa, the largest standalone spa chain in the country, which is now managing the spa offerings of several hotel chains.

There are two routes that hoteliers are taking to wellness. One is that every other hotel puts a spa in its property, whether a business hotel in the city or a resort. Some like ITC manage their spa business with their own brands. If ITC has its Kaya Kalp then Taj has its Jiva Spa (though it has taken a call to have Jiva only at select locales and outsource the management at other hotels). Many hotels outsource wellness; Lemon Tree has outsourced to Tattva, Accor to O2 and OYO to Sarva to set up studios at its Townhouse properties and so on.

The second route is to put up pure wellness-focused properties. This is the piece that is waiting to explode. Though there were early entrants like Ananda in the Himalayas above Rishikesh, Jose Dominic's Kalari Kovilakam in Kerala and Ayurveda-focused chains like Niraamaya that came up later, it still has not seen the explosive growth it could potentially see.

Ingo Schweder, the slenderly built German who co-founded the spellbindingly scenic Ananda in the Himalayas, one of India's best wellness retreats, says that wellness is a $4 trillion economy globally of which the tourism component alone generates more than $562 billion. According to the Global Wellness Institute, wellness tourism is growing faster than all other forms of tourism and it has a higher average length of stay as well as higher spend per tourist.[1]

He says that in the age of increasing lifestyle diseases and smartphone detox, more people are taking wellness trips instead of conventional holidays, with a wellness traveller spending 59 per cent more than an ordinary tourist. While spa properties in scenic locales are ideal for healing holidays, most people end up looking for quick detox breaks at driving distance from cities.

Scenting the opportunity, Schweder, who supervised the development of Oberoi's Raj Vilas, Amarvilas and Udaivilas during the late 1990s and later set up fifteen resort spas for the Mandarin Oriental Hotel Group, became a wellness entrepreneur, with Bangkok as his base.

The ardent yoga practitioner is not only creating a spa empire of his own through a chain of destination wellness resorts, branded GOCO Retreats, but also offers consultancy to big hotel chains.

'We do thirty-five to forty projects every year for the likes of Marriot, Conrad, Bulgari, Ritz Carlton and Emaar,' he said.

In 2018, GOCO Hospitality had a footprint across thirty countries and had big plans for India, including a development in Goa in partnership with a local player to offer an authentic experience.

After Goa, Ingo feels the most promising destination for a spa hotel is Mulshi Lake, near Pune. Certainly, Mulshi is becoming the new go-to place for rejuvenation for stressed-out Mumbaikars, with healing retreats like Atmantan created by Pune-based Nikhil Kapur proving a big draw.

With India's wellness tourism market projected to be one of the fastest growing in the world (50 per cent faster than global tourism), Schweder's interest in the Indian market is understandable.

He is not the only one. Jupiter Capital–promoted Niraamaya too has gone the wellness route as it spotted a gap there and sees better returns there. The group began operations in 2008 by acquiring Surya Samudra in Kovalam and turning it into its flagship property.

'From Rs 4500 we pushed the ARR to Rs 40,000,' Manu Rishi Guptha, CEO, Niraamaya Retreats, pointed out, describing how Ayurveda in extreme luxury is the group's core proposition. And that is the gap in the market that it has aimed to address.

After that, it created a resort in Thekkady and in 2018 opened one in Kumarakom.

'Two more resorts in Kerala—one in Fort Kochi and one in Munnar—will complete the Kerala circuit of Niraamaya,' said Guptha, pointing out how they have Rs 400 crore invested in the state.

There is immense opportunity, as Guptha points out, because stress and bad health are high in the Indian subcontinent and the need for wellness is growing. Also there is no off-season in wellness, he points out. However, Niraamaya is only playing at the higher end.

'I believe, for the moment, wellness will be targeted more towards the upper echelons primarily because in a country like India there are far too many people at the bottom of the pyramid who are still struggling but in the years to come, each and every person would start thinking of wellness,' Guptha said. He, however, points out that while there would be only 1 or 2 per cent of people in India who would right now be keen on wellness; in countries like the US, the UK and Germany, 75 per cent people already think of wellness and their spending powers are much higher than that of Indians.

GOCO's Ingo feels, however, that democratization of wellness holidays is a big trend.

'Wellness,' he said, 'will no longer be the preserve of the well-heeled or the 40-plus age group. Baby boomers generate 74 per cent of global traffic in wellness trips. But a shift is happening as the millennial generation is very focused on fitness and staying healthy.'

Several Indian players have already realized the potential of wellness and are raking in the returns. According to a Hotelivate report, Clafouti Beach Resort, Carnoustie Ayurveda and Wellness Resort, and Moksha Himalaya Spa Resort in Shimla, and the Manasa Yoga Retreat in Jammu and Kashmir are some properties that operate in a niche space and at a higher price point than typical non-wellness resorts.

The tariffs at wellness resorts are fairly high because supply is low. But things are bound to change.

'I believe that as the marketplace becomes more efficient and more people in the space start talking about the need to fill the gap that is becoming ever wider than the efficiency would creep in. Maybe ten to fifteen years from now, it would be a demand-supply–driven thing but right now, for the next few years, I definitely believe that there would be a scarcity of supply, and the demand would be higher which will keep the prices high,' said Guptha.

Significantly, MNC hotel chains like Hyatt are getting into the wellness space. Hyatt's acquisition of Miraval, a provider of wellness experiences, is part of that strategy.

The American chain also acquired Exhale, another player in the wellness space.

Several hotels have invested in huge wellness programmes at their properties.

Spas are one way of course. Yoga classes, health centres are all part of the course. At Starwood's Westin, the entire hotel brand is centred on the well-being positioning. The signature look of the hotels is green and leafy, with detoxifying plants placed strategically in lobbies, rooms and corridors. There are yoga mats in every room. The six pillars of the well-being movement at the hotel are Sleep Well, Eat Well, Move Well, Feel Well, Work Well and Play Well.

At the Khyber Hotel in Gulmarg, a lot of investment has gone into its spa. The hotel has a gigantic spa wing complete with a heated indoor swimming pool and has tied up with global brand L'Occitaine. With three single treatment rooms and two couple suites, each with its own private steam chamber, the spa aims to bring to life the invigorating climate of Gulmarg.

'People are now travelling around the world to pursue activities that enhance their overall well-being, thus seeking authentic experiences like spa, wellness treatments or rejuvenation,' Umar Tramboo, the man behind the luxurious hotel, said.

Given that spas have proved so lucrative, why have few hotels decided to build a spa brand? The answer is provided by Ritesh Reddy.

'The imperative to outsource,' said Reddy, 'is because hotels measure everything by the space allocated for a service and the revenue it fetches them. At many hotels,

23 per cent of space allocation to a spa got them less than 0.2 per cent of revenue—so they felt it made better sense to outsource. For the outsourced partner, it was easier to drive in footfalls to the hotel spa since it had the scale and could offer discounts.'

Spa tourism is also growing in India because states like Kerala, which are big on Ayurveda, have done numerous campaigns around it. Incredible India 2.0 campaign has laid special emphasis on globally showcasing the country's spiritual and wellness traditions.

The Spa of Tomorrow

GOCO retreats are in Bali, Thailand and Germany, but it's when he talks about the Glen Ivy Hot Springs development in California that Schweder gets a gleam in his eyes. Spread over 20 acres, with nineteen indoor and outdoor pools, seventy-two treatment rooms, pulling in 1,70,000 visitors every year, it's altogether on another scale. Schweder describes how GOCO plans to develop a wellness community on the adjacent land, which is surrounded by organic orchards, a golf course, mountains and a nature preserve. Wellness communities, he forecasts, will soon become a big thing, with cities built and branded around concepts of health and sustainability.

As for the spa of tomorrow, that's still evolving. Online booking site Hotels.com worked with futurists to see what the world of hospitality would look like in 2060 and it forecasts that spas will no longer be about mud baths and massages. Instead, the hotel spa of the future could be a longevity clinics based on DNA analysis.

So, once you check into Spa 2.0, you will receive personalized prevention treatments, prediction and health enhancement programmes designed to refresh your health and understand your future health risks. These will use the latest genetic medicine treatment, mind-refreshing drugs, brain fitness and prevent disease/s it predicts.

16

The Loyalty Card

'If I could go back one moment in time, it would be five minutes before the person who invented the first loyalty programme so that I could beat him over the head.'

—Pascal Vincent Doyle, former chairman of the Jurys Doyle Hotel (now rebranded as the Doyle collection)

An old joke doing the rounds in marketing circles is that there are more loyalty points floating around in the world today than money. And that cash has no memory, but points have.

Airlines were the first to have pioneered loyalty programmes. It all began on 1 May 1981, when American Airline started its frequent flyer programme AAdvantage to counter competition from low-cost airlines People Express. But today every marketer from literally every sector—hotels, petrol companies, credit card companies, telcos, restaurants, e-commerce players, mobile wallets and even that neighbourhood mom-and-pop store rewards you for spending. Ajay Kelkar, founding partner at Hansa Cequity, calls loyalty programmes the hardest working tool in a marketer's armoury. Each time you shop, you get a discount for your next purchase, incentivizing you to return. To put it crudely, marketers bribe you—with rewards to stay with them.

Of course, if you meet marketers they will go to great lengths to say that rewards is not the term they use, but rather, the preferred word recognition. As Deepa Harris Misra, the former marketing head of the Taj Group, explains, 'It is not a transactional relationship any more. It is far deeper.'

Some believe that hoteliers are making the loyalty tool sweat most. They certainly have been on a recruitment overdrive to make their guests sign up for their programmes. In 2018, Hilton Honours had more than 70 million members. The InterContinental Group had 100 million and was the highest until they were overtaken by the Marriott Starwood combine. After they combined their loyalty programmes—a really messy unification—Marriott Starwood had 110 million members in 2018.

The reason hotels are big on loyalty programmes is simple. For most hotel chains with a strong programme—be it Starwood (now Marriott) or Taj—40–50 per cent of their occupancy comes from their loyalty card members. Year-on-year the growth is 10 per cent.

In the bruising battle the hotel industry is currently fighting with the OTAs, the loyalty card is one way of getting the customer to book direct and save on commission. A precondition for loyalty card members is you get deals in hotels only if you book direct.

At Accor India, for instance, over 50 per cent of the business comes through loyalty programmes and it contributes significantly to occupancies.

'In India,' says Arif Patel, 'Accor has crossed the 1 million mark in members—the more hotels open, the more there is recruitment into the programme.'

The second and more important reason for hotels to invest in loyalty programmes is that it gives them an immense amount of behavioural information about their guests.

As Sebastien Bazin, global CEO of Accor during one of his visits to India explained: 'For fifty years, we were responding to the demands of guests. But now we have to anticipate their expectations. This is where our worldwide loyalty programme gets important—the more you know your customer, you are able to provide them what they want without them asking you.

For most marketers and hoteliers today, personalization—providing customized service—is a big thing. For this, data is very important, which the loyalty programme provides. Marriot Hotels even has a vice president in charge of personalization.

At the Adobe Summit in Las Vegas during the hospitality track, Devin Sung, VP Personalization for the chain, asked, 'Why do business travellers often zero in on the same hotel they stayed last time, and choose the same airline over and over again?'

'It's because the fear of the unknown can lead to stress,' he explains. 'Predictable data points can make travel less stressful. It's a known route. The service is familiar. You know where things are. They are locked in your head.'

By providing the exact experience that the guest wants, the hotel can get him or her to stay over and over again. Personalization induces loyalty.

Forget personalization, the data from loyalty programmes helps hoteliers spot trend changes at the right time.

'Thanks to technology and the access to information, we are learning what our guests want,' Bazin said. In the last forty years, people wanted comfort, good bedding, fire security system, a good shower. Today they want emotions, experience, leisure, they want to see objects, they want interesting colours, design, so today hotels are far less standardized than in the past. This is a good thing as it forces hoteliers to be innovative,' he added.

A Tricky Card

However, loyalty is a very tricky card to play. If you reward the customer too much, you end up hurting your balance sheet. On the other hand, if you make it too tough to redeem points and claim benefits, then you don't earn any loyalty.

Remember the era of blackout dates—festive holidays and peak travel dates—when hotels would not allow you to redeem your points. The fine print had many conditions.

A lot of people who launched loyalty programmes started looking at P&L value, and how you cut costs on it. 'So, they started shifting goalposts to earning miles or rewarding,' says Sandeep Mittal, MD, Cartesian Consulting. 'This proved to be a self-goal.'

But over the years, lessons have been learnt. The Taj, which has been chopping and changing its Inner Circle loyalty programme and even entered into an alliance with Shangri La Hotels' Golden Circle programme, has really dived deep into it. It identified four types of customers—the evangelists who swear by the products they are using and rarely change; the deal-seekers who keep looking for offers they can leverage; the value-difference seekers, who seek comfort and recognition, and are high touch-and-feel people; and, finally, the simple samaritans, who are happy if they get peace and convenience, and are process-driven.

It accordingly tailored its loyalty programme and its services. As Harris explained, 'A brand has to cater to all these diverse sets of customers, and meet all their articulated and unarticulated needs to command loyalty.'

The race for scale by hotels is closely interlinked with the loyalty card. The more hotels you have, the more chances guests will sign up for your loyalty programme and opt to stay at your hotels. If you have hotels in every city in India, and at convenient locations, you will try to get your office to book you in that hotel every time. IHG, which has 100 million members, had a portfolio of over 5500 hotels in 2008, including InterContinental Hotels & Resorts, Kimptom, Crowne Plaza, Holiday Inn, Holiday Inn Express and more.

This is why when foreign chains first arrived in India, they were racing to reach the 100-hotel mark. Given the massive global footprint of global hotels, enrolling into their loyalty programme and staying as much as possible with them benefits Indian customers. They can use the points earned in domestic stays during overseas trips. Compared to 5500 hotels that an IHG has, or 4400 hotels of an Accor or 7000 hotels of the merged Marriott–Starwood combine, a Taj Hotel, even with its tie-up with Shangri La, can offer only a network of around 200 hotels.

Indian guests are now as savvy as their American counterparts in extracting the most out of their loyalty cards. As Deepika Arora of Wyndham Hotels said, 'An interesting article I was glancing through said that 77 per cent of the Indian travellers know how to earn and redeem the miles. It shows that the point junkies are growing in this market.'

Accor's Arif Patel concurred. He says loyalty cards are now being sought after by people from tier-two and tier-three towns and that India has become a mature market where customer understanding about points-based programmes is quite high.

'As a result,' Arora said, 'hoteliers are now going in for affiliations to make the loyalty programme more rewarding for guests. Most have tie-ups with airlines. Wyndham had a partnership with Jet Airways, for instance, in terms of mile points extended. Ditto with Accor and others.'

'Taj's partnership with Shangri La is a good one,' Arif Patel felt as he said they complement each other. 'One is looking for inbound customers and the other for outbound.'

This may be wishful thinking, but Patel feels that just as the airlines have a One World Alliance or a Star Alliance and code sharing arrangement, a similar alliance could work in the hospitality sector too.

Wyndham also invested lots in simplifying its loyalty programme. If you have 15,000 points you can get a night in a hotel. So it is as simple as for every dollar you spend, you earn 10 points. You spend five nights in a hotel you are upgraded to a tier above.

'The simplicity of our programme has caught a whole lot of attention,' Arora said. 'Also, since many of Wyndham properties are in the mid-market segment, the chain is making it easy for my customers to use its hotels. I am not making my loyalty programme aspirational for them. I am making it more usable for them. So that is probably one of the biggest differences between the Wyndham loyalty program vis-à-vis any other, she said. According to her, in other hotels' loyalty programmes you encourage collection of points to be aspirational enough to be staying in that big nice hotel that you have been dreaming about.

Changing Philosophy

While Wyndham's loyalty programme might work for its customer base, for luxury operators, a free night stay or upgrade really does not become a selling proposition.

At loyalty marketing forums and hospitality conferences, the Oberoi is often talked about. Why? Because it had steadfastly refused to have a loyalty programme, and yet it has sticky customers. It's the Apple of the hotel world. Apple too steadfastly refused to discount, counting on its status.

At the luxury level, the experience sought by customers is far more. So, a Taj is doing things like arranging a special birthday meal for its loyal guests, creating experiences like a theatre show, or exhibitions.

Thanks to big data, brands now have the most exhaustive behavioural information about customers.

'From being push-based marketing, loyalty programmes have today become a service,' says Kelkar. That's the change in philosophy we are seeing today.

Meanwhile, there are some interesting twists and challenges to the loyalty programmes of hotels. Some of the OTAs have their own loyalty schemes. So, the loyalty is migrating from the hotels to the channels. To woo them the hotel has to come up with more innovations. It's a constant see-saw battle.

In fact, in 2014, tired of seeing customers migrate to OTAs, mid-market chain Lemon Tree had tried a gimmicky money-back offer wherein guests who check in at any property in the chain get vouchers for the same amount as their billing amount. During their next stay, those vouchers could be redeemed on services like salon, food and beverage, laundry, etc.

While most players offer a free membership loyalty programme, India's fastest growing budget hotels operator OYO has created a paid loyalty rewards programme, OYO Wizard. It is available in three tiers—Wizard Blue (Rs 99 for a six-month membership), Wizard Silver (Rs 199 for a one-year membership) and Wizard Gold (Rs 399 for a two-year membership). You get instant cashbacks on check-ins. Over 6000 hotels under OYO's 9000 hotels portfolio in India are part of the programme. Every fourth room in India is booked by a Wizard member on OYO today. Clearly, loyalty is paying for OYO.

While Arif Patel might contend that the customer coming through loyalty programmes pays more and is more valuable, Saurabh Gupta, who heads the India region for Preferred Hotels, a global distribution company that helps independent hotels, differs. He says that the most loyal customer is often least profitable for a property. They don't pay top dollar.

'They get the best suites, they get free airport drops and other freebies,' he points out. According to him, a loyalty programme is beneficial to the operator—in this case a Marriott or an Accor—but not to the owner of a particular property.

Who does the loyalty programme belong to? It's the operator brand. Who is paying for the deficit in rates or the value-added services—it's the owner of a property.

'For the owner, it becomes labour,' he contended.

There's a germ of truth in what Gupta says. Look at how Starwood Preferred Guest (SPG) used to run, as explained by its former India head Dilip Puri.

'When Starwood signs a management contract with a hotel, SPG is part of the contract. The hotel pays a small fee to SPG—a fund in the US managed by Starwood—for every guest. Each time a customer earns points for staying at a Starwood property, those points are credited to her unique account. These points also sit in the fund in the US, along with the fees that the hotels in the Starwood network pay,' he said.

'Now if an Indian customer redeems the points in a hotel in Hong Kong, the stay is free for the customer. For the hotel in Hong Kong, there is no loss by giving a night's stay free as it gets reimbursed for it from the SPG fund. But remember the fee the hotel has already paid, so there is a cost there,' he added.

The trickiest part is the fund manager's, as the fund has to be really finely balanced—the money accrued as fees should be more than the cash outgo from handing out rewards, plus shrewd investments have to be made to grow the fund.

But Puri says that SPG was pretty scientific. It studied what the redemption patterns are and what gets carried forward. Often loyalty funding is also used for loyalty promotions. All that is taken into account.

Many loyalty funds have come a cropper because they are not managed well. But as Preferred's Gupta himself admits, there is the other side of the coin too—if a well-executed loyalty programme can yield a lot of benefits, especially in getting a first-time guest coming from another channel to repeat.

But his contention is that for owners, using a loyalty programme of a distribution partner like Preferred is better. That's because in the iPrefer programme, it's not the operator's brand that is being marketed, but the owner's brand. Suppose after five years the contract with the operator breaks up, the valuation of the owner's property will go down. On the other hand, the hotel chooses to be stand alone and just signs up for a loyalty programme with a distribution partner, even if you break up five years later, the hotel's brand value is not shaken.

Essentially, what emerges is that there are lots of benefits to loyalty programmes. It's an important and necessary tool for hoteliers. However, it's a very tricky tool too.

Some prescriptions that those who have been operating loyalty programmes for a long time give are:

1) Keep it simple—Easy-to-earn and easy-to-burn works best. Redemption should be a mix of discounts on rooms and services as well as experiential offerings that delight, such as concert tickets.

2) Regular communication on offers is a must. At the same time, the communication should not be spammy.
3) Don't break promises—Nothing angers a customer more than being shown fine print and conditions. Be transparent.
4) Add in a social layer—Having loyal guests is great but if the guest is endorsing you constantly on social media through TripAdvisor feedback etc., add in extra rewards.
5) Coalitions deliver more—Increase the spread through alliances and partnerships but at the same time make sure the hotel's brand is not getting diluted in the mix.

Going forward, Arif Patel feels loyalty programmes may not be as strong a card.

'The peak years were the 1990s and the 2000s,' he said. 'It will be all about experience now. However, the coming of blockchain—an incorruptible digital ledger of transactions linked using cryptography—could disrupt loyalty.'

To put it simply, he explains that what blockchain will enable is that if X has 100 points, Y 200 and Z 500, none of them could get much of those points but blockchain will enable them to pool those points and allow one person to claim them.

Phocuswright, a travel research authority, pointed out blockchain's potential to improve hotel loyalty programmes and several interesting use cases. The blockchain-on-a-blockchain system, data sharing from different places such as customers' cryptocurrency wallets, will enable a far more complete and authentic profile of guests, giving clues on their purchasing behaviours. It can also enable better cross-promotions.

Blockchain-based loyalty platform Loyyal has already started showing the way. Emirates Airlines has used Loyyal to add ride-sharing service Careem to its loyalty network.

That's just one small example. Blockchain tokens could replace points in a loyalty programme and that will put more power in the hands of the consumer. Why? Because loyalty points usually reside with the issuing company's system. And the company can devalue points, or points could just simply disappear as with JetPrivilege points when the airline went bust. Blockchain tokens on the other hand reside with the consumer.

The world is changing.

17

Banking on Banquets—
The Taste of Things

'Chefs should always do what makes them happy and what works for their customers. But they should not fool themselves into believing that theirs is the only way forward.'

—Vir Sanghvi

It's unusual for a five-star hotel's fancy restaurant to wander out of its property. Especially when it has an iconic signature dish that has been wowing people and drawing them into the hotel. So, in December 2018, when the China Kitchen at the Hyatt Regency at Bhikaji Cama Place in New Delhi, known for its Peking Duck, opened at the CyberHub in Gurugram, it created quite a buzz. For Amitesh Jatia, owner of the hotel, however, it seemed a win-win decision to take the restaurant brand associated with the Hyatt and monetize it as a standalone.

A month before Fairfield by Marriott's launched in Bangalore, a giant food truck sporting eye-catching banners of the hotel's restaurant could be seen moving all over the city. Through this mobile kitchen, the global hospitality chain was creating buzz for Fairfield's all day restaurant Kava Grill and Lounge.

For a no-frills business hotel—which globally does not extend its menu beyond a basic breakfast—expending so much effort to market what looked like just another 24-hour coffee shop seemed unusual.

Now visit the IHG hotels like Crowne Plaza, Holiday Inn and Holiday Inn Express. At the Crowne Plaza in Delhi's middle-class suburb of Rohini, there is Chao Bella, a unique combination of Indian and Italian. Another brand specifically made for India is Five Spices.

Why has IHG bothered to create these restaurants? Well, MNC chains are just following the aroma of money when it comes to hoteliering in India—a country where F&B often outstrip room revenues in a trend that is completely contrary to Europe and the US.

Noted food critic Marryam Reshii said, 'Restaurants and spas are calling cards for a hotel.' As she explained, 'They are often a hook to attract a guest to a hotel. She gave the example of how The Lodhi in Delhi got in Manish Mehrotra's Indian Accent, arguably one of India's most inventive restaurants, into its premises. It is now a calling card for the Lodhi.

Indian hoteliers such as ITC and Taj had got a whiff of this years ago and changed their marketing menu by creating memorable culinary brands. In India, the celebrity chef was non-existent until these two chains allowed their kitchen maestros full creativity. Chef Hemant Oberoi at the Taj hotels was perhaps better known than any general manager at the chain's properties.

But the foreign hoteliers were quick to latch on to this winning recipe also. They invested in detailed research into the dining habits and food preferences of Indians, and many of them have tasted success with their new eateries.

Hyatt has always tried to whip up a culinary storm— if its China Kitchen in Delhi has been a hit from the start then it tried to create a bigger impact with the ritzy vertical restaurant the Flying Elephant at its Park Hyatt property in Chennai. Or take the Pullman in Aerocity, which has done zany things at its restaurants.

'F&B has played a very important role in positioning our hotels in India,' said a Marriott executive. 'If you look at the JW Marriott in Aerocity, it has really tried hard with its restaurants. For Marriott, across the country, at least 40 per cent of its revenues comes from F&B.'

'The India hotels of IHG clock an average of 47 per cent F&B revenues,' Douglas Martell told me once, pointing out that this is even higher than the Asian average of 40 per cent. In Europe IHG ekes barely 15 per cent from F&B. Certain locations such as Crowne Plaza Rohini yield as high as 60–70 per cent F&B revenues especially during the wedding season.

Ditto for the Lalit, Bangalore, which is a standout F&B performer for the Lalit Suri Hospitality Group, raking in 70 per cent of the hotel's revenues, according to Keshav Suri, executive director of the group.

Clearly, with such high percentage of revenues coming from F&B, everyone's had to dish out innovations to make

sure they don't miss out. A Marriott which never offers room
service delivery in any other countries is forced to do so here,
after its consumer surveys. Rajeev Menon, chief operations
officer for Marriott International in South East Asia, once
said, 'Ninety-six per cent of the people we talked to wanted
some room service delivery.'

ITC Hotels was the first on the food lane in perfecting an
F&B–centric approach at its hotels.

Describing how the chain invested in creating many
iconic Indian restaurant brands—Dum Pukht, Bukhara,
Dakshin—Nakul Anand, executive director of ITC hotels,
said, 'First we were not known for our food. But today our
F&B is on par with our rooms. The minute it realized that
the food tastes of India were globalizing, it set about creating
Oriental and Occidental brands (Pan Asian, West View, and
more recently Japanese fare at Edo and Italian at Ottimo
Cucina). Our aim is to create globe's finest Indian and India's
finest global restaurant brands.' He points out how the group
invested in making even its coffee shops—Pavilion, Madras
Pavilion, Cubbon Pavilion, Peshwa Pavilion and so on—
into brands.

While ITC had always been ahead on the food curve, it
was noted food writer, the late Jiggs Kalra, who strengthened
the hotel chain's positioning. Vir Sanghvi in his tribute to
the king of the kitchens in his 'rude food' column in the
Hindustan Times.[1] describes how Jiggs persuaded ITC that all
great restaurants needed to be helmed by chefs.

'He worked closely with Manjit Gill (who was then
executive chef of the Maurya) to create a new restaurant to be
called Dum Pukht. The inspiration came from the Lucknow

style of cooking (mainly biryani) in steam but Jiggs and Manjit worked together on many new dishes,' wrote Sanghvi.

In India, the chefs have mostly been kept hidden and never allowed to get bigger than the hotel brand. Contrast this to the West. At Las Vegas, it's the name of the famous chefs that is on the walls of the hotels—Gordon Ramsay et al. That is changing slowly in India.

Taj was also an early leader in creating an F&B pull but interestingly followed a slightly different approach. It got in well-known international F&B brands such as Wasabi by Morimoto, even as it created its own specialty brands, a move that Leela Group has also emulated. For its showpiece Chanakyapuri hotel, Leela has got in two iconic New York based restaurants, modern Japanese cuisine Megu and French gourmet Le Cirque.

'In some ways getting these "foreign" F&B brands is an image-building exercise for these hotels as these are go-to destinations for the well-heeled,' said food critic Marryam Reshii.

For the Taj, a large part of the credit for its great F&B goes to Camellia Panjabi who interacted closely with guests and told chefs what to put on their menus. She created legendary restaurants such as Golden Dragon in the Bombay Taj, Paradise Island and Karavalli in Bangalore. Camellia also used Jiggs' expertise to rejig menus at Taj's restaurants.

Each hotel had their own strategy. ITC needed a very powerful focus on regional Indian cuisine, as the group's whole ethos was 'made in India'. If you look at the WelcomGroup logo, it is a namaste. The global cuisine destinations it was creating at its hotels could only be side dishes, while for the others, the global restaurants they got to their hotels were the main course and a style statement, adding to the snob value and pull factor. It also helped that bill averages were Rs 5000 per person here at these fancy global restaurants. Said a Leela spokesperson, 'Luxury dining restaurants are no more "occasion" restaurants. It is a part of today's lifestyle.'

The realization that they could increase average ticket price size slowly crept into every hotelier— hence the frenetic race to create great F&B. Lalit Hotel, which when it had first started—in its early Bharat Hotels avatar—had cut a dash with its rooftop Thai restaurant Blue Elephant in Delhi but then floundered. Now it is regrouping, betting on brands such as Baluchi and Oko. In Bangalore, Keshav Suri pointed out, some innovative F&B offers like Gourmet Express, Theater Konnection etc. have kept the F&B business of the unit always in the news. He adds that the Bangalore hotel has the largest event space in the city and hence the revenues from events are quite strong. And that is the key!

Banking on Banquets

When hoteliers talk about F&B contributing over 40 per cent of their revenues, they don't mean from restaurants alone. For almost all hoteliers, banqueting contributes 50 per cent of the F&B revenues today—for some, it could be 70 per cent. The bet is it will contribute even more, especially as India is seeing an explosion of great standalone restaurants that is stealing the footfalls from hotel restaurants.

Douglas Martell points out that Crowne Plaza Rohini F&B revenues zoom during the wedding season, and is seeing good year-on-year growth.

'Growth of the wedding market is reflective of the growth of wealth in India,' he observed. 'MICE too is growing at a very fast clip. MICE is probably our biggest opportunity. We are making sure our hotels are now redesigned around conference facilities,' Martell added.

He also feels that there is more potential in mid-market MICE than luxury-market MICE. Also, smaller meetings and training programmes that require smaller, cheaper places are now in demand, spelling huge opportunity for the mid-market players such as Lemon Tree, Fairfield, Courtyard by Marriott and Holiday Inn Express.

For Marriott, banquets contribute nearly 60 per cent of F&B revenues and going forward they see more yields coming this route. But all hotels are doing other things too to drive up F&B revenues.

Nightclubs, Social Zones and More

Today's traveller is a social creature who does not like to be confined to rooms. So the attempt is to enslave the traveller by offering all forms of entertainment in-house. And if you can get the local city folks in too, why not—it all keeps the till ringing.

Which is why nightclubs—once an integral part of Indian hotels in the swinging 1960s and 1970s—are now roaring back with new, bling avatars. Take Kitty Su at the Lalit, rather edgy and risqué in its merchandise. Or the way The Park has re-energized Someplace Else.

Keshav Suri admitted, 'Kitty Su is giving mileage to the group, generating high footfalls and adding to the rooms and the F&B revenue.'

Subtle changes are happening in lobbies too. Gone are the days when you could walk into a five-star lobby and do your meetings in air-conditioned comfort without ordering a thing. Suri candidly admits they noticed this and introduced a tea service at the Bangalore hotel lobby. Others have done so too—a case in point is the Ambassador (a Taj SeleQtions property) in Delhi.

Similarly, health clubs are driving footfalls for F&B outlets at outlets. When you open up health club membership to neighbourhood residents, soon people trip in to use the gym and stay on to have breakfast at the coffee shop.

Spoil the Party

All this is undoubtedly exciting, but what could spoil the F&B party for hoteliers is the strong competition from external standalone options.

Gone are those days when if you had to celebrate an event in style, you drove to the five-star hotel in town and partied at the finest restaurant. And the only safe discotheques were at hotels. Today the lounge bars, pubs and coffee shops all are exciting F&B destinations. Auma, SetZ and Cavalli Café at the Emporio Mall or a Masala Library are places where the well-heeled like to be seen. Even the 24-hour coffee shops, where many a corporate deal has been sewn, have to work much harder as executives on the move now do meetings in chai bars, coffee outlets and elsewhere.

Samir Kuckreja, founder and CEO, Tasanya Hospitality, a consultancy firm, felt that when it comes to innovation, restaurants at Indian hotels have not done enough. But food critic Marryam Reshii pointed out that they are trying to rope in home cooks to offer something different. However, the danger with the home-cooks trend is that quality can be patchy.

18

The Sweet Spot in the Middle

'The success of any hotel is the rate it can charge. When rates go up in mid-market, it will become sexy.'

—Dilip Puri, former managing director,
Starwood Hotels and Resorts

In the late 1990s and early 2000s, when Anil Madhok's Sarovar chain started, it was one of the first branded mid-market chains in India. Mid-market was a barren landscape in India's hotel scenery till then.

Cut to 2017–18, around 59 per cent of India's branded room inventory was in the budget or mid-market space. No longer was India the outlier inverse pyramid market—more hotels in upscale and luxury. What caused the shift?

Well, ever since the downturn began in 2009 or so, hoteliers had been lyrically extolling the virtues and potential of the mid-market and economy segment. There was so much unaccommodated demand that every chain leapt into this space. From the Taj Group (Ginger) and ITC (Fortune) to foreign chains such as InterContinental Hotel Group (Holiday Inn Express), Accor (Ibis, Formule 1, Novotel) and Marriot (Fairfield) and to Lemon Tree and Sarovar, everyone had winged into mid-market. Even a Starwood, clearly focused on luxury, followed the herd and brought its Four Points by Sheraton brand here.

But the mid-market story has had its highs and lows, successes and failures and several learnings along the way.

Come 2015 and the mood was elegiac among mid-market hoteliers. Except for a few mid-market operators, many were struggling. Notably, Keys, a mid-market brand for India launched by billionaire Nicholas Berggruen's private equity fund, saw some of its top management—especially the founding team who had shares—quit and rumours were it was about to fold up. It eventually did not and picked up but not after some course correction. Premier Inn, the wildly successful mid-market brand in the UK, was so bruised that it exited.

Ginger Hotels went through so many renovations and iterations that everyone felt that mid-market was a loser's market.

But there were many who did exceedingly well in the mid-market too. Sarovar stood firm. Lemon Tree played the segment well. However, it was Accor's Ibis, which grew slowly and steadily, that seemed to have got a total grip on the mid-market.

'In this segment, unlike the upscale and luxury, the band of profitability is very narrow and the margin for error is really low,' said Ashish Jakhanwala, MD and CEO of SAMHI Hotels, which owns several mid-market hotels, including

Fairfield by Marriott and Formule 1. 'So those who made mistakes were severely punished.'

Jakhanwala said that the problem was both cyclical and systemic. Cyclical issues were due to collision of supply increase and drop in demand growth over past years. This took many by surprise, especially investors who had underwritten their investments during peak cycle. Systemic issues are because of poor knowledge of business and in some cases poor intent.

To get the return on capital employed (ROCE) is to predict and take strategic investment. Do this sensibly, especially when land cost is high.

'Many players followed a land bank model and paid for it,' said Rattan Keswani, deputy managing director at Lemon Tree Hotels. 'We don't land bank. If a location makes sense for future, we will do it in future. We see no reason to invest in a parcel and keep it,' he added.

The other mistake that many mid-market and even budget hotels made when the room rates refused to harden was to invest heavily in F&B and banqueting, taking a lead from upscale hotels. With occupancies low (averaging 58 per cent), the idea was to get non-room revenue up. However, that strategy was not always successful.

'It was a completely flawed approach,' Shwetank Singh, vice president—development and asset management, Interglobe Hotel (a joint venture between Accor Asia Pacific and Interglobe Enterprises), which runs Ibis, felt. 'With a tight operating structure, your cost of running a mid-market hotel room per day is around Rs 300. So a room can get you a profit margin of 80–85 per cent, which no F&B investment can. In F&B, you will get a maximum of Rs 40 for every Rs 100 you spend—where is the comparison with room margins?' he queried. 'Yes, in some markets like Punjab, you can get good returns from banqueting, but if you are bringing in F&B, it's additional manpower cost, and while it's a spurt in topline, the impact on bottomline is not all that great,' he added.

'Utility, manpower and F&B are three main costs (constituting up to 75 per cent) of operating a hotel,' Singh said. 'Ibis,' he said, 'has one of the tightest labour ratios of 0.5 (for every 100 rooms, a staff of 50) and that cannot be flexed any further, nor can you turn utilities on and off . . . so all hinges on the room rate.'

'Many of the foreign chains entering India just did not anticipate the high cost of utility services here,' said Jakhanwala. 'Here you need a whole separate area to house utilities that range from power back-up, water filtration units and so on. In addition, India is just not a self-service market, so manpower requirements are higher than global.'

The reasons that British chain Premier Inn failed in India were unfortunate and mostly to do with a run of bad luck with partners. It did a project internally to see which market it could expand into and decided to head to Middle East and India. In the Middle East, it entered into a joint venture with Emirates, which was a great partnership and worked to a great extent. In India, they homed in on Emaar MGF. Emaar had a fantastic land back—almost 8500 acres.

But Emaar went in for an IPO around this time and it completely lost interest. The expected cash flows did not happen and Emaar's calculation was that hospitality had a long gestation. So in that joint venture, very few projects happened between promise and reality. One was Delhi, which was actually Emaar

MGF's own land parcel. The other was Bangalore Whitefield and the third one was Pune. And then that meltdown crisis happened and it made matters worse. At this point Premier Inn's parent Whitbread bought the entire 49 per cent stake from Emaar. But a precious year and a half had been wasted.

Looking back at Premier Inn's journey, Shwetank Singh, who was with the British group before he moved to Ibis, said that the number one factor was that though it had all the credentials, what it didn't have was an international mindset.

'They probably didn't understand the nuances of a different market. And number two, I think the world is full of examples of companies who have been incredibly successful but they want to try something new and then they start judging the new baby also with the same parameters of the old,' he analysed. 'Premier Inn fell in the classic innovation trap. They wanted success too quickly.'

Kabir Kewalramani, managing director of Berggruen Holdings, the investors behind Keys, blamed the chain's woes squarely on discounting wars.

'The problem is with rate. And the problem lies at the top. In Bombay you can get a five-star hotel room for Rs 6500 or so. As a result, four stars have to bring down rate below that and so on,' he said.

Exactly the same issues that have plagued the low-cost airlines troubled the mid-market hotel players. High capital costs, long development time and gestation cycle, and poor room rates are directly impacting the return of capital employed (ROCE), making investors impatient and piling on the pressure on the hotel operators. In panic, many discounted the rates, which eroded chances of profitability further.

Caught in a Crossfire

The mid-market and budget operators did not anticipate the strange situation that they would be competing not only against the unorganized segment (non-branded hotels and guest houses) but also upscale hotels that dropped rates so dramatically. Or that online travel agencies (OTAs) would end up aggravating their rate woes by championing the unorganized sector.

'It was not a level playing field against the unorganized sector,' said P. Mohankumar, former managing director and CEO of Roots Corporation, which runs Ginger Hotels. According to him, branded hotels invest a lot in regulatory compliances (nearly 140 licences), including fire safety, sprinklers, CCTV cameras and continuous training of staff, all of which take time and money. Branded players come with a cost.

'There is a certain price point one can operate at, below which it doesn't make economic sense,' he continued. 'On the other hand, this segment is a very price-sensitive one and a few hundred rupees can swing a consumer's choice. So branded hotels whose development costs are Rs 35 lakh per key were competing against hotels built at barely Rs 17 lakh per key while the difference in room rates they charge are barely Rs 200 or so.'

But wouldn't superior quality and service ensure footfalls?

'In the short term, no, and by the time the customer wisens up, it might be too late,' said Jakhanwala.

What the hotel operators did not factor in was the unexpected role played by OTAs who had thrown up hitherto undiscovered standalone hotels, offering far lower rates. Also many operators cribbed that OTAs charge a higher commission from hotels than they do from airlines. So the hotels had to launch their own tech platforms, invest in loyalty programmes to get customers on their own and try and cut out the OTAs. Lemon Tree announced last-minute flash sales a la the OTAs and money-back offers if a customer booked direct.

'The fight,' said Keswani, 'is who gets the eyeball, and who retains the eyeball. In the interim, if I get the eyeball to stay with me, I am still happy.'

Amit Taneja, chief revenue officer, Cleartrip, admitted that as a percentage the commission it charges from hotels is higher. 'But our cost is linked to transaction so it is fair. Plus we give global visibility and bring down the cost of customer acquisition for a hotel that has far less marketing spends than an airline,' he said.

But more than the OTAs, it was platforms like OYO Rooms, which put tech, reach and branding into the hands of tiny hotels that gave sleepless nights to big hoteliers.

When the initial opportunity in the budget segment was spotted, the calculation was that there were 850 million domestic travellers crisscrossing between many of India's tier-two and tier-three towns who were in sore need of good hotels. The premise was correct. But what the big chains did not factor in was that the corporate costs of branded hotels are so high that investing in a sub-100-room hotel in these towns made no sense. But build anything above a 120-key hotel in these towns and filling up the rooms would be a struggle. This is where small domestic operators like grabbed advantage.

Ginger, which initially expanded into Agartala and Pantnagar, had to restrategize and focus on developing properties in micromarkets of metros and tier-one towns. In 2018, Ginger again went back to the drawing board and decided to make its hotels more premium, exit the budget positioning and go higher up the value chain.

Those running mid-market and budget operations also did not factor in the strange rules of hoteliering in India. In India, regulatory measures for the hotel industry were originally designed for five-star hotels—so they have quixotic rules like mandatory car parking facility for any hotel that has over fifty rooms.

'Ninety per cent of our guests come in taxis—there is really no need to invest in such car parking facilities. Every inch of construction is cost of capital,' J.B. Singh of InterGlobe Hotels pointed out.

'Rather than support the growth of the budget-hotel segment, which builds affordable tourism infrastructure in the country and caters to the masses, the regulators classified hotels above Rs 200 crore as infrastructure. This indicates either apathy or poor knowledge of what is required for growth of tourism in India,' said Jakhanwala.

But as Rattan Keswani pragmatically said, 'In this business, some things you have to factor in are: Will land be cheaper? No? Will government consider infra status for projects below Rs 200 crore and help us? No idea.'

The only way out then was to innovate. Investing in F&B has clearly not worked.

'Building meeting spaces can raise occupancies by a good 10–15 per cent,' says Shwetank Singh.

Many hoteliers were forced to go back to the drawing board and come up with fresh ideas to tackle these challenges. Lemon Tree, for instance, decided that where land cost is high and a mid-market rate will just not work, it will build an upscale hotel. So in Aerocity, it created a Lemon Tree Premier, with an attached Red Fox to it, so that at one go, it can accommodate two different price points.

Sarovar, which runs Hometel, launched a Hindi website, perhaps the first hotel chain to do so in an attempt to expand its domestic customer base.

The other course correction that many mid-market operators did was to look at buying rather than building. The cost of development for a branded budget of a mid-market hotel works out to Rs 30–35 lakh per key excluding land cost.

'My personal experience is that so many hotels are up for sale, so why build now,' pointed out Shapath Parikh, Director Parikh Inn, which runs Fortune Park Centre point at Jamshedpur.

All these course corrections helped the mid-market players.

Now, let's look at what Ibis did right. In January 2019, the French premium economy brand opened its nineteenth hotel in India in Kolkata's Rajarhat area. There were many statements it made with the launch, starting with the hotel's multicoloured facade.

'We are breaking away from the traditional monochrome exteriors of the past,' pointed out Jean-Michel Cassé, COO, AccorHotels, India and South Asia. New design features included wider windows, tweaks to the furniture in the room to suit current user behaviour and a revamped menu to cater to younger palates.

'Every new design we are making, we are innovating,' said J.B. Singh, president and CEO of Interglobe Hotels, the JV between Interglobe Enterprises and Accor Asia-Pacific, which runs the Ibis brand in the Indian subcontinent, explaining how even as a current hotel is being launched, back in the Gurgaon headquarters, the team is busy creating a new design with many tweaks for the fifth hotel down the line.

'This way, the brand remains fresh, contemporary and relevant to changing customer expectations. The target,' Singh said, 'was to have a new design for every third hotel in the line.'

The ultimate focus of these design tweaks is to enhance consumer experience. At the same time, offering more value to the consumer should not come at a higher cost to the guest.

How do you design better and better customer experiences, maintain your pricing and yet continue to remain profitable?

'That is the big challenge,' says Singh, describing the journey of innovation that is going into the making of Ibis 2.0. He maintains that in the ten years of Ibis in India, with every new hotel it launched, it understood the building and operating structures so well and automated the processes so much that it totally cracked the code on cost arbitrage. Every inch of the hotel building area was studied so that wasteful areas could be eliminated, energy efficiency increased by using sustainable materials and design could be localized and personalized.

As for operations, a host of little things make running the hotel more efficient and sustainable. For instance, there are no wasteful soap bars and mini shampoo bottles in the bathroom, which are thrown away after single use or taken away by guests. Instead there are dispensers. Instead of disposable mineral water bottles, there are refillable glass water-bottles. The breakfast menu has been shrunk, making it simpler and more appealing to young guests with some regional offerings too.

Interestingly, globally the Ibis brand is piloting a host of design innovations following an Ipsos study it commissioned across six countries to study customer expectations. Eighty per cent of respondents said they would like to see a more social hotel where even non-staying guests would feel welcome. After that survey, Ibis set about transforming itself, creating living spaces that are flexible and open to the local community and there is increased social interaction.

Ultimately, keeping the customer at the centre of the experience helps a brand grow.

19

The Luxury Experience

'We're ladies and gentlemen serving ladies and gentlemen.'

—The Credo at Ritz Carlton

The definition of luxury is changing.

'Luxury is different things to different people now,' says Frits van Paasschen, former head of Starwood and author of *Disruptor's Feast*.

For some, luxury is defined by things that are scarce. There was a time when going to exotic locations was itself a luxury. Few could afford to visit the Maldives, Bhutan or Machu Pichu. Today, so many people do that. For someone else, luxury may be serenity, which is becoming increasingly difficult to find. For many millennials, luxury is experiencing something new that is sustainable, ethical and has purpose.

As so many different definitions of luxury pop up, hoteliers have had to reinvent themselves to please one category or the other of luxury seekers.

Time was when luxury meant Belgian chandeliers, spectacular decor and hedonism—the finest of wines, fish and caviar. But today's luxury clientele is satiated with all that. Vir Sanghvi, India's foremost hotel critic, wrote in a column about his own changing tastes—how jaded with such offerings, he moved to hip hotels, the likes created by Ian Schrager, considered the father of boutique properties, or Andre Balazs, the man behind the Standard Hotels in the US, which incidentally were far from standard, at least in their culinary experiences.

Sanghvi wrote that after a point he tired of the hip hotels fad too, and began seeking something else. Several hotels are realizing that there is no point trying to catch the fads and sticking to classic, timeless and simple. You can't go wrong there. Taj's focus on Tajness was part of that realization.

Today's trends are so far removed from the hedonism of the past that the luxury traveller could be vegan and earthy. In India especially, a surprising fact is that many hoteliers miss out on the fact that most billionaires in the country are vegetarian. The smartest food-based luxury hotel in the country, ITC, caught on to that when it set up the Royal Vega at the ITC Grand Chola in Chennai.

If those are some new trends in luxury, the other big trend is that many more people today can afford luxury hotels. For hotels, meanwhile, there has been such an explosion of ritzy properties to cater to the growing numbers of the rich, that there is a price war.

'Luxury is at a discount today,' said Ashish Jakhanwala, MD and CEO of SAMHI hotels, when asked what the top trend for luxury hospitality today was.

For the top luxury hospitality chains, as if battling price pressures were not enough, a host of other disruptors are conspiring to give them nightmares. Airbnb, for one. Just trawl through Airbnb's luxury homestays and you will find at least 300 luxurious apartments in Paris. From spectacular hilltop villas in Italy to historical corner lofts in New York's happening Manhattan district, there is top-notch accommodation available for around €1000 in Europe or $1500 in the US. In India, according to Airbnb, there are several luxurious farmhouses on the network and celebrity cricketers number among those choosing the stay option.

So what are the hospitality majors doing? They have no choice but to reinvent themselves and come up with some unforgettable experiences to hook the luxury traveller and to differentiate themselves.

Experiential, Exclusive and Eco-friendly are the three Es that drive the luxe hospitality business today. Jose Dominic of the CGH Earth Group was ahead of his times when it came to catering to the three Es. He had been offering eco-friendly luxury to the discerning traveller, who is looking to experience local life.

'Luxury has to go hand in hand with sustainability,' he stressed. 'Sustainability is seen as being inconvenient and more expensive. But this is not true,' he said. 'Sustainability requires responsible tourism, which includes local community and also includes responsibility of consumers. Luckily, this is the era of the conscious traveller,' he said.

As for exclusivity, his chain came up with a radical new offering—a one-key hotel in Kerala. Chittoor Kotraram, the tiny palace that the rajah of Cochin, Rama Varma, built for himself in order to be close to the Guruvayur Temple, was converted into a hotel. But only for one family. Chittoor can accommodate just six people, so only one family or a group could get a booking.

And there are lots of dos and don'ts for guests booking the property. They need to enter barefoot and stay that way. The menu is rather sparse—only one item a day! And yet people book a stay in this unique hotel, where the promise is you will be treated like a Kerala King for the sheer novelty of the experience.

ITC hotels have also been taking the sustainable, eco-friendly tack to woo the conscious traveller.

Off the highway at Manesar and past sleepy villages, through the picturesque Aravali ranges and out of nowhere, quite literally, rises a palace-like structure replete with domes and royal pavilions. This is ITC Hotel's lavishly laid out 300 acres golf retreat, the ITC Grand Bharat, which showcases a slice of all that is rich and fine in India.

But as you sit down to dine at the Pavilion, one of the restaurants here, the menu delivers a shock—it has warning alerts on it. There are traffic signal lights against the fish on the menu, indicating which piscine species are overfished (red light), which are under threat (orange light) and which are in abundance (green light). For instance, the Indian salmon is red-lighted as overfished; anchovy, pomfret, mackerel and red snapper are flagged as under threat; while sole fish, tuna etc. get an approving green light. The choice is left to the diner. But a nudge is delivered to make a wise choice.

The Choose Wisely programme piloted at this property is just one of the examples of the ways in which ITC introduces responsible luxury to its guests. Incongruent though luxury without waste and sustainable luxury may seem at such an opulent setting, ITC Hotels has been riding on this philosophy in all its properties for some time. At the Grand Bharat, responsible luxury is showcased to the hilt whether it is in the way it sources ingredients and produce for its restaurants from nearby villages, the way it serves slow food, the huge effort taken to minimize carbon footprint or the way it provides sustainable livelihood to the locals. Or the way it is moving from linear production systems to circular ones—for example, the plastic bottles used here are sent to a company in Rajasthan that recycles them as garments!

'We believe that values are shifting at a deep level due to the curse of the excess and the need to endorse luxury that is deep rooted and meaningful,' says Nakul Anand, executive director ITC, in charge of hospitality, describing how the chain decided to move some years ago from a business-as-usual approach to business that cares.

Several years ago, Starwood Hotels created a whole new brand called Element that is eco-friendly and green to the core.

'Being green and sensitive to the environment is no more a nice thing to do, it is an essential thing to do,' says Dilip Puri, former managing director of Starwood.

As for the experiential, several hotels are creating memorable stuff. When Andaz, Hyatt's lifestyle brand hotel, opened in Delhi, it crafted a theme '401 reasons to fall in love with Delhi'. The theme came about because the hotel has 401 rooms. For two and half years now, all through the construction phase, its German general manager Heddo

Siebs rode around Delhi in his Royal Enfield trying to dig out the quaint odds and ends in India's capital. The result of his expeditions: In each room, there is a piece of art or artefact that gives the guest a tantalizing reason to explore Delhi. Room 373, for instance, has a lovely painting depicting Haus Khas village, while in another room there is an artwork made with the silver foil that lines the top of Indian mithai. All the works of art are synchronized with a coffee-table book that is placed in each room, strategically open at the page that matches the room number.

Besides the rooms, the hotel created an exciting Juniper bar, seeking to bring gin back in fashion. A unique food outlet, AnnaMaya, is a food hall rather than a restaurant, with shelves selling artisanal products and carts piled with vegetables, where guests could dine as well as shop.

Not luxury in the conventional sense, but certainly appealing to the millennial mindset that seeks the out of the ordinary.

At the Taj, meanwhile, the track the venerable chain has taken is to play on heritage, provenance, storied craftsmanship, restorative ethics and authentic experiences. The welcome experience at some of the Taj hotels is entrancing. At the Falaknuma Palace in Hyderabad for instance, an old-fashioned buggy greets visitors at the gate and ferries you up the hilly incline, where as you mount the stairs at the entrance, a shower of rose petals falls on you.

Almost every chain is now playing on heritage and digging out historical nuggets and memorabilia. For instance, at St Regis New York, guests are treated to Bloody Mary lunches. After all, the cocktail—also called the Red Snapper—was invented in the King Cole Bar here eighty years ago.

'Today, the luxury traveller is not only financially capable but is also a global citizen, design and tech savvy, a foodie, and constantly looking for new and unique experiences. So, this segment will continue to command and drive change the world over, said Umar Tramboo, MD of Pinnacle Resorts, which has created the rather exotic boutique hotel Khyber Himalayan Resorts and Spa in the ski town of Gulmarg.

Food rituals are certainly one of the biggest drivers of luxury hotels. At the Khyber, an elaborate tarami—Kashmiri feast served at weddings—is one of the big experiences for guests staying here. At the tea zone, Chaikash, guests can taste local saffron tea while looking at the mountain ranges.

At the Taj Mansingh, every month offers a different exotic cuisine experience, from Japanese to Colombian, with master chefs from those countries travelling down.

Many hotels do epicurean journeys, delving into a region's heritage. At ITC hotels, the chain has taken enormous pains to make sure that the food served mimics the cuisine of the region. So the Grand Chola in Chennai will go all out to serve Chettinad and other cuisines.

Some hotels go so far as to arrange dinners at local homes of celebrities—say a Bollywood star in Mumbai or a socialite. Eating at a local's house is in fact one of the big trends today to hook travellers.

Riding on Weddings

For luxury hotel operators, weddings are a golden egg. The Taj Group's chief revenue officer Chinmai Sharma makes no bones about the fact that the group is pitching hard to host luxe weddings at its palace properties, especially the Umaid Bhawan in Rajasthan, already a hot favourite with big industrialists. India's richest family, the Ambanis, hosted their daughter Isha Ambani's wedding at the palace. Bollywood celebrity Priyanka Chopra also had her wedding there.

The Taj puts in a lot of time studying trends and even has something called a wedding barometer.

'Weddings are becoming more and more exclusive, the size of the wedding groups is reducing and they are becoming highly experiential events,' says Sharma.

There's a reason of course why literally every luxe player is seen at wedding extravaganzas such as these. In an otherwise sluggish market, weddings are perhaps the only growth drivers. As somebody said, weddings are the only recession-proof market in India.

Taj's Chinmai Sharma says that according to their calculations, the trackable spend at luxe weddings is somewhere around Rs 1000 crore. According to Swarovski's head in India, Vivek Ramabhadran, there are at least 500 weddings in India where over Rs 10 crore is spent.

According to Kotak's report *Top of the Pyramid*, on the luxury market in India, spends at weddings in India are event higher. They hover around Rs 20 crore to Rs 40 crore at weddings hosted in India and are far higher at exotic destination weddings.

The fashion among A-listers in India is to do exotic destination weddings set in Venice or Puglia in Italy, Chantilly in France or island locales in Asia. But now Indian hotels are pulling out all the stops to attract the big weddings here.

According to consultancy firm HVS Anarock, personalization is the key to the future success of destination weddings in India. Apart from themes, there is a steady demand for newer locations from to-be couples who are also scouting for waterfront properties with helipads and pillarless ballrooms. At the same time, the pull of ancient forts remains high. Several of the newer hotels coming up are building with an eye to the wedding market.

Rajasthan, Goa and Kerala are the top three wedding markets in India but hotels in Mahabalipuram down south and Mussoorie up north are joining in.

'The rising appetite for destination weddings is unquestionably a boon for the Indian hospitality industry,' notes HVS Anarock. According to its data, 2018 saw the Indian hotel industry witness a countrywide RevPAR growth of 9.6 per cent over 2017, a large part of this fuelled by weddings.

Strangely enough India's hotel industry has been skewed more towards urban business hotels than towards leisure and resorts. Hotelivate report *The Ultimate Indian Hospitality Report* points out how leisure hotels command higher RevPar than their urban equivalents. It compared the rates of twenty branded leisure properties with twenty branded urban properties in the same scale—the RevPar of Rs 9235 in 2017–18 at the leisure properties was 1.6 times that of their urban counterparts.

The lack of serious investment in luxurious leisure resorts in India so far is understandable—most A-listers choose to holiday abroad than within the country. But it is a bit of a chicken and egg situation. They choose to do so because there are limited choices in India while hotels refuse to develop virgin destinations because they feel demand is low. Given India's massive coastline, there certainly is immense opportunity. It is up to the industry to make the first move.

IV

ENTER THE BOTLER:
THE FUTURE OF HOSPITALITY

20

Bots, Botlers, Blockchain and Beyond

'The new definition of insanity is to do same things and expect different results.'

—Frits van Paasschen, former head of Starwood Hotels

What will travel and hospitality in 2030 be like?

The pandemic, which brought the hotel industry to a standstill for several months, has shown how difficult it is to predict the future. Who would have imagined in 2019, that an epidemic could wreck a centuries-old industry?

The world is changing in such momentous ways that anything can disrupt this industry. Just imagine if the Hyperloop—ultra-fast transportation that zips you to a city and back in next to no time—becomes a reality, will there be such a need to stay in hotels on business? Work on the Hyperloop is speeding up and the futuristic transport solution could be a reality sooner than we think. You could take a business trip and return the same day.

Will there be only leisure hotels then?

That's clearly not a scenario that hoteliers want to think about, though they are thinking a lot about the future now. The point one is trying to make is that disruption is coming from not just within the industry, but from seemingly unrelated events such as a global pandemic, new innovations or even climate change.

Every new path-breaking technology could impact hotels in some way or the other.

Technology Impact

As far back as 2014, Phil McAveety, chief brand officer of Starwood Hotels—this was before the merger with Marriott—had painted a scenario where a guest would send a 3D print scan of his shoes and the hotel would have gym shoes the exact size ready and waiting in the room when he checks in.

The other trends he outlined, including checking into a hotel through a smartwatch, sending voice-activated requests for car pick-up and robots as valets, are all a reality already. At the St Regis Hotel in New York, as you brush your teeth you could press a remote and the mirror in the bathroom turns into a television. At an Aloft hotel in Cupertino, you might be served tea by a robot butler quaintly named Botlr.

At the Starwood Experience Centre in Stamford, Connecticut, where the hotel chain creates mock-up rooms for all its brands, you get a sense of some of the changes happening inside hotels. At the Aloft mock-up room, for instance, there is no television but a projector on top of the bed and a smartphone dock at the bedside. The guest of the future will be bringing his own entertainment is what the chain anticipated, and this could change the room interiors.

Apps in the hands of travellers allow them to directly communicate with front desk, housekeeping and concierge staff. Nakul Anand, executive director, ITC, felt that travellers will increasingly want to be in control, and hotels have to hand this over. So, typically, many of the services you would ring for will all migrate to within the room.

Technology is clearly one of the biggest drivers of change in the hotel experience today. 'Companies that don't embrace technology as an enabler will disappear,' said Dilip Puri. Artificial intelligence will allow guest experience to become so much better. Chatbots are already making the booking experience easier.

All trends point to the latest kid on the technology block, blockchain, disrupting the hotel industry. Blockchain is a growing list of linked digital records using cryptography that has already begun to change thinking about online distribution of hotel rooms.

Currently, all hotels depend a great deal on OTAs that use technology to connect consumers with hotel chains. Every hotel has to invest in technology—booking engines, property management systems and channel managers—to connect to the OTA system. In a blockchain-based system, hotels can use any device to connect directly to a blockchain and there on to consumers, eliminating expensive OTAs. It is a distribution landscape that is very creative. And it could especially benefit smaller hotels. Google and Amazon could get into this technology. Several blockchain-based platforms have come up and early movers like CitizenM Hotels have logged on to it.

Technology is also going to impact operations—the way hotels source their supplies, for instance. Currently, many hotels stock 30 per cent extra inventory of some supplies, keeping in mind damage and theft. What if there comes a time when there is a way to do everything in real time?

Consumer Behaviour

But there are other trends, too, shaping the future of hospitality. As Frits van Paasschen, the former head of Starwood, author of the thought-provoking book *The Disruptor's Feast*, pointed out, the consumer could be a disruptor.

Consumer profiles, tastes, needs, expectations are all changing. Even before the pandemic, every hotel chain from Marriott and Intercontinental to Taj and ITC had been studying the changing consumer and new guest expectations, and beginning to redo their services accordingly. For instance, a study by the Intercontinental Group found that the big travellers of tomorrow would be from different places compared to the present. More travellers would originate from emerging economies like Brazil, Russia, China, India and parts of Asia. These new global explorers have very different needs from American and European travellers, and hotels would need to gear up accordingly.

That's why IHG introduced HUALUXE Hotels & Resorts, a hotel brand designed by the Chinese for the Chinese within its portfolio. Others like Accor adapted their offerings too—Accor's Grand Mercure Mei Jue brand focuses on the Chinese traveller's expectations. According to Jean-Michel Cassé, it is a matter of time before a hotel tailor-made for Indian guests comes up.

The pandemic has shown how changes in consumer behaviour can shape the hotel trends of the future. Health and hygiene has become a huge priority with guests. Rather than stay at a hotel populated by many, there are several people who are now looking to book a place that caters to a single family or individual—and hence, homestays and rented villas have become the first choice of many.

The trend of Work From Home—and Work From Anywhere—has impacted the hotel industry in a big way too. It has opened up new opportunities. Even if the world returns fully to offices, the choice of remote work is here to stay, and employees are taking advantage to stay in scenic resorts and work. Many a hotel chain that were focused on business hotels in busy metros are now quickly adding leisure hotels in scenic places.

MICE (meetings, incentives, conferences and exhibitions) took a big hit during the pandemic. Globally, MICE was an $808 billion industry in 2019. But when the world shut down and virtual meetings reigned, the events industry came to a standstill.

India has only a minuscule 0.5 per cent share of the MICE sector, though it leads when it comes to organizing big fat weddings, which is a huge business for hotels. Although the corporate world found a way to network and do business through webinars and virtual summits during the pandemic, and many feel this way of doing events is here to stay, there is no replacement for face-to-face meetings. The Kerala Travel Mart organized in May 2022 saw 1500 delegates congregate in Kochi and 55,000 face-to-face business meetings, which augurs hope for both the events industry and the tourism and hospitality industry.

The big fat Indian wedding is a big growth opportunity for hotels. In fact, this is what helped beleaguered hotels bounce back post-pandemic.

Even a flower delivery start-up like Ferns N Petals has realized the potential in weddings and created two 'wedding hotels'—Udman and The Opulent—in Delhi, designed and sold mainly for marriages.

Additionally, according to figures from the US Inland Revenue Department, the trends are the growth in women travellers (30 per cent of Chinese millionaires are women, while in the US there are now more female millionaires aged 18–44 than male), so expect rooms specially designed with a feminine touch for women guests. As companies go for massive gender-diversity programmes, with targets of having at least 30 per cent of their employees as women, more business travellers could be women.

The millennial cohort is a demographic that has already altered many a hotel's offering. Shared spaces and community activities are all geared towards millennial guests. But Gen Z—those born in the mid-1990s to early-2000s—is rising and that's another cohort with a very different personality. This group loves to stay in hostels and this has given rise to a host of branded hostel chains—Zostel and goStops are two that are growing fast.

At the same time you can't leave out older guests' preferences, so hotels will have to balance all their offerings to cater to many generations.

Another growing set of consumers is the woke brigade—guests who passionately care for the environment, are worried about climate change, are activistic in nature and will stay only in places where everything is ethically sourced or made. Witness the way Marriott has already committed to reduce plastic usage in its hotels. Or the way Taj has put into place an ambitious programme called Paathya, a sustainability-driven initiative.

Personalization

You can get the consumer grouped and bunched in cohorts—from a geography or a particular generation or gender—but within these groups, each consumer is still unique. Rising individuality is a big trend and hotels will have to cater to each guest differently.

The more agile hotels have already appointed heads of personalization. Marriott, for instance, has a VP personalization. At the Adobe Summit in Las Vegas, a session was devoted to personalization at hotels. Melissa Lemberg, global partner, IBM Interactive Experience, described here how IBM's Watson understands different types of data and has the ability to draw a personality trait of a customer. IBM Watson coupled with the Adobe Experience Manager allows hotels to do extreme personalization. How it works is that by trawling through social feeds (Twitter, Instagram, Facebook, and so on) as well as a host of available data on the web, the personality graph of a customer who is booked to stay is generated. This gives clues to likes and dislikes, taste in books, food and attitudes. So a proactive hotel could add shows and movies the guest likes to the TV in her room and delight her.

Besides this, hotels will have to do away with rigid 2 p.m. check-in norms and do personalized 24-hour flexible check-ins, get the bed and pillow preferences right, breakfast choices anticipated, temperature setting in rooms at the exact level the consumer wants, and so on. Many of these are already being done, but it will get to a really intense level. There are websites that allow you to book a room for just four hours—soon you could book rooms for just an hour. This could totally disrupt hotel operations, for how do you manage housekeeping schedules, then?

Scout New Opportunities

During the pandemic, when repeated lockdowns forced hotels to close their doors, they had to find ways to engage with the absent guests. Food emerged as one of the top ways they could cater to their customers. Many chains got into the unchartered terrain of doorstep food delivery, started creating DIY meal kits and even experimenting with concepts such as chefs on hire, where anyone could rent a five-star hotel chef for a day at home. Many chains rolled out very interesting financial packages that would tempt the guest out of the cocoon of their homes and sample a stay at a hotel. For instance, high-end wellness resort chain Niraamaya rolled out pay now, stay later schemes.

While adversity got the creative juices of the hotel chains flowing, the important lesson here is that they need to keep thinking out of the box and keep rolling out innovative schemes, even in good times.

Overtourism

Frits van Paasschen talks of overtourism as a big trend. Some destinations have got so much hotel supply and so many tourists spilling into it that the destination will completely go out of fashion. Hotel consultant Manav Thadani agreed. 'As key markets near oversupply and saturation, lesser-known destinations will see interest from brands and consumers alike,' he said.

The trick is in getting the next big destination right. Hainan in China is a big bet. Soon there will be more hotels in Hainan than in Hawaii, said the global head of development of a big hotel chain.

In India, taking this bet is very difficult going by the experience of several developers. When Bekal in Kerala opened up, pushed by the state government, the Lalit and a few others invested in the destination. For thirteen years nothing happened because the promised infrastructure never came up. Now, the Lalit is trying to open up Chitrakoot as a new destination in Madhya Pradesh. But the same infrastructure problem remains as nearby Khajuraho, a heritage site, suffers 40 per cent occupancy because flight, road and rail connectivity is very poor.

While there is no shortage of new destinations in India, there is the additional problem of government red tape. Jose Dominic's problems of coping with the government interference at Bangaram Island is a case in point. If VIPs visited, access to the island would be cut off, and so on.

Hotel Formats

Hotel formats are already being radically changed. There are pod hotels, innovations from space-starved Japan that cater to travellers on a budget and limited needs. The first pod hotel in Mumbai has already got terrific reviews from travellers, who visit the business capital for just a day and need only a place to sleep in at night. Both Jean-Michel Cassé of Accor and Navjit Ahluwalia of Hilton feel that big box hotels are going to explode in India. At Las Vegas, the Venetian run by the Intercontinental Group combined with the Palazzo has over 7000 rooms. Genting Highlands in Malaysia has 7351 rooms. In India, by contrast, anything over 500 rooms is considered massive.

ITC has taken the lead in setting up the biggest hotels in India, with the Grand Chola in Chennai, and the Royal Bengal Sonar combined property in Calcutta that together has 693 rooms. A 1000-room hotel was not yet a reality in India in 2018 but come 2023, we could have that. The advantage of a big box format is that it can tap into the huge opportunity for MICE. This is something that has just not been exploited well in India.

Hoteliers can really experiment with formats if they put some creative thought to it. Frits van Paasschen pointed to the world's first ice hotel that came up in north Sweden and the reason it came up. He started with an ice sculpture show. Then an ice gallery. But nobody was turning up. In desperation he created an ice hotel and for some reason, it was successful. Now, there are many ice hotels.

Closer home, in India, there is an art hotel in Mumbai, where every room is a canvas. Plenty of hotels have art in their lobbies and rooms, but boutique hotel LeSutra, located quite close to the sea face, has made art its very raison d'être. Over 120 painters, forty sculptors and fifteen designers have created this exotic little getaway in Mumbai's posh Khar neighbourhood. This quaint, charming place draws its inspiration from mythology and from the three gunas—tamas, rajas and sattva—and tells the story of Ravana, Krishna and several characters from Indian epics.

'It is a big challenge for a large organization to do things unconventionally,' said van Paasschen. 'But it is an imperative to do so.'

Casino hotels could be the next big opportunity in India. The country's rules prohibit casinos on land—so the first casino hotels have sprung up on ships on the Goa coast. At the Deltin Royale, the casino experience is quite memorable. Spread over four levels and 40,000 square feet, the ship attracts over a thousand footfalls on many days. It has been conducting poker tournaments to drive traffic. Occupancy at the 106-room Deltin Suites remains high as guests check in there to be ferried to the floating casino. At several hotel conventions in India, one has been running into representatives from MGM hotels who have been checking out the country in the belief that it will be only a matter of time before regulations change and casino hotels are allowed.

Post-pandemic, the hotel format has come into question more than ever before as the lodging environment has become quite complex. The fear of travel has not gone away completely and people want hotels that are within drivable distance. Camper homes or caravan holidays have become popular. One-key villas—where the entire property can be rented by a guest—is something that travellers are seeking in the era of social distancing. Hotel chains are responding to these new demands.

Consolidation

Consolidation is a big trend globally and in India as hoteliers feel that adding scale could insulate them. Also, it is an easier way to get innovative if you acquire a hotel chain or a digital disruptor or a niche player that is doing interesting things.

Marriott Starwood was the biggest consolidation in the hotel industry. But all other international chains too have been on an acquisition spree to cover all possible flanks. Just look at the list of acquisitions Accor made between 2016 and 2017 to get an idea of how various bases are being covered to counter disruption. In July 2016, it acquired John Paul, world leader in the concierge market. In February 2017, it acquired TravelKeys, a luxury-villa rental expert. In March 2017, it entered into an agreement with Brazil Hospitality Group, Brazil's third-largest hotel company to manage its hotels. Now, match this acquisition to the trend found by BCG that Brazil would contribute huge numbers to global travel. In March 2017 itself, Accor also got into bed with Rixos Hotels for a bigger foothold in the upper upscale market. The same month it bought Potel et Chabot, a luxury catering and reception planning company. In April 2017, it bought

Availpro, which creates software suites for hotels. The same month it also bought VeryChic, a digital platform for private sale of luxury hotel rooms, apartments, cruises and packages. In May 2017, it bought Noctis, an events and entertainment company in France. In July 2017, it created global headlines with its acquisition of onefinestay, an Airbnb competitor and then grouped some of its previous buys—Travel Keys, Squarebreak, etc.—into the onefinestay brand. In October 2017, it bought Mantra and Orient Express, adding to its hospitality offerings. The same month it also acquired Gekko, a specialist in hotel distribution.

This is by no means an exhaustive list, mind you—but it shows how agile hotel chains are thinking. In India, Accor has been sniffing around budget hotel chain Treebo to buy a 40 per cent stake in it.

Indian chains have been slower to acquire but things are beginning to change now. LemonTree hotels acquired Keys. OYO has been a very agile acquirer, buying into a variety of companies, including Amsterdam-based vacation rental firm Leisure Group.

Can being agile stop hotels from being acquired? If you look at Starwood, it's really tough to say.

As Frits van Paasschen pointed out, 'At Starwood, we worked hard to avoid being devoured by digital disruptors. Disruptors were eating away at our business model from all directions. There were the online travel agencies—Booking, Expedia, CTrip, and the like—as well as peer-to-peer lodging companies, most conspicuously Airbnb. Online reviews, such as Tripadvisor, were eroding the signalling value of brands. At the same time, there were so many digital start-ups promising to solve travellers' and hotel owners' problems.

In the end, Starwood's sellout happened not because it could not keep pace with digital disruption—it was one of the few chains doing so admirably—but because the board and the leadership could not see eye to eye on many things. So, strong corporate governance and leadership are essential elements as well in taking a hotel chain's story forward. Or even exiting at the correct time.

As van Paasschen pointed out, 'It may seem like a subtle distinction, but combining with Marriott is not the same as being made obsolete by a digital disruptor. Starwood's brands are well-positioned to compete in the digital marketplace. My only regret is that we could have played our hand in consolidation earlier, when our relative position was far better. Our strengths became headwinds in 2015, when the US dollar had strengthened, and the emerging markets slowed.'

Watch out for Trend Lines

Closing advice from van Paasschen to hoteliers is to keep a strong watch on trend lines. Automation, growing inequity, rising nationalism, protectionism and climate change all have a bearing on the hotel business. A sustainable hotel, for instance, will do far better in the future.

Bibliography and webliography

An overview of hospitality, tourism and hotel industry, http://shodhganga.inflibnet.ac.in/bitstream/10603/72868/12/12_chapter%201.pdf

Seth, Pran Nath. *Successful Tourism: Fundamentals of Tourism.* Sterling Publishers, 2006.

Devendra, Amitabh. 'The Hotel Industry in India the Past and the Present', *Journal of Hospitality Financial Management,* vol. 9: Issue 1, Article 7. Available at: http://scholarworks.umass.edu/jhfm/vol9/iss1/7

Sankar, *Chowringhee.* Translated by Arunava Sinha. Penguin India, 2007.

Rinku Paul and Puja Singhal. *Daughters of Legacy.* Penguin Random House India, 2018.

Tomsky, Jacob. *Heads in Beds: A reckless memoir of hotels, hustles and so called hospitality.* Anchor, 2012.

Karkaria, Bachi. *Dare to Dream: The Life of Rai Bahadur Mohan Singh Oberoi.* Penguin India, 2010.

Notes

1. Behind the Glitter—Cast of Characters

1. Refer to https://www.sarafhotels.com/about
2. Hitender Rao, 'Venod Sharma's corporate interests behind his quit-Cong gameplan', *Hindustan Times*, 6 March 2014, https://www.hindustantimes.com/chandigarh/venod-sharmas-corporate-interests-behind-his-quit-cong-gameplan/story-EDOOskhoqM3ZiqNkA69G1H.html

    'The money, power that back Manu Sharma,' NDTV, 11 November 2009, https://www.ndtv.com/india-news/the-money-power-thatback-manu-sharma-404659

    From interviews during author's visit to the hotel at the time of its launch.
3. Tanvi Dubey, 'At the helm of the MBD group, Sonica and Monica take forward their father's legacy', Yourstory, 29 September 2015, https://yourstory.com/2015/09/mbd-group-sonica-monica-malhotra.

    Author's interviews with Ms Malhotra.
4. Author's interview with Saurabh Gupta of Preferred Hotel.
5. Indian Hotel Survey 2016-2017, https://hotelivate.com/hotel-finance/indian-hotel-industry-survey-2016-2017/

6. Anumeha Chaturvedi, Vinod Mahanta, 'Leela shareholders
    back sale to Brookfield', *Economic Times*, 27 April 2019, https://
    economictimes.indiatimes.com/markets/stocks/news/leela-
    shareholders-back-sale-to-brookfield/articleshow/69067922.cms

7. Arvind Chhabra, 'Badal family's poultry farm that became
    Sukhvilas resort: An island of luxury amid deprivation',
    Hindustan Times, 13 December 2016, https://www.
    hindustantimes.com/punjab/sukhvilas-an-island-of-luxury-
    amid-deprivation/story-UjXVKcsnjEsk2V89sHZToL.html

2. All Keyed Up—Setting the Context

1. 'In terms of rooms OYO is the world's third largest hotel
    chain', Livemint, 10 July 2019, https://www.livemint.com/
    companies/start-ups/in-terms-of-room-count-OYO-is-now-
    world-s-third-largest-hotelchain-1562763503806.html

2. World Travel and Tourism Council: Travel & Tourism
    Economic Impact 2019 India; downloadable at https://www.
    wttc.org/economic-impact/country-analysis/country-data .

3. 'Dry way on the highway: Supreme Court's 2016 ban on liquor
    sales comes into effect today', *India Today*, 1 April, 2017,
    https://www.indiatoday.in/india/story/supreme-court-liquor-
    ban-on-highway-968917-2017-04-01

4. Anumeha Chaturvedi, 'FCM Travel Solutions and KPMG
    release white paper on business travel in India', *Economic
    Times*, 23 January 2017, https://economictimes.indiatimes.
    com/industry/services/travel/fcm-travel-solutions-and-
    kpmg-release-white-paper-on-business-travel-in-india/
    articleshow/56734073.cms

5. Anumeha Chaturvedi, 'SAMHI to rebrand Premier Inn as
    Fairfield by Marriott', *Economic Times*, 20 September 2017,
    https://economictimes.indiatimes.com/industry/services/
    hotels-/-restaurants/samhi-to-rebrand-premier-inn-as-
    fairfield-by-marriott/articleshow/60760278.cms

6. Shweta Ramsay, 'Owner-Manager relationship: Are
    Indian owners becoming assertive?', Hospitality Biz India,

8   September 2014, http://www.hospitalitybizindia.com/
     detailNews.aspx?aid=20154&sid=5

7.   P.N. Venugopal, 'Demolition orders for Banyan Tree luxury
     resort', *Down to Earth*, 17 September, 2015, https://www.
     downtoearth.org.in/news/demolition-orders-for-banyan-tree-
     luxury-resort-41860

8.   Author's interviews with Accor spokespeople.

9.   Bidya Sapam and Anirudh Laskar, 'Brookfield to buy Leela hotels
     for ₹4,500 crore,' Livemint, 17 December 2018, https://www.
     livemint.com/Companies/vf1N6CiyNlpNWUlgn0ELBN/
     Brookfield-to-buy-Leela-hotels-for-4500-crore.html.

3. Laying the Foundation—History and Evolution

1.   Kevin D. O'Gorman, 'Origins of the commercial hospitality
     industry: From the fanciful to factual', *International Journal of
     Contemporary Hospitality Management*, October 2009

2.   Ibid.

3.   'The Treasury Building & Spence's Hotel: the connection',
     Heritage structure of Bengal (blog), 10 March 2013, http://
     heritagestructurewb.blogspot.com/2013/03/the-treasury-
     building-of-kolkata.html

4.   Soumitra Das, 'How a Bengal Town is Embracing Its Danish
     Past,' 18 March 2018, https://thewire.in/history/how-a-
     bengal-town-is-embracing-its-danish-past

5.   'As Connemara Prepares for Makeover, Let's Recall the
     Scandal That Ended the Career of the Man After Whom the
     Historic Hotel is Named', *BWHotelier*, 22 April, 2016, http://
     bwhotelier.businessworld.in/article/As-Connemara-Prepares-
     for-Makeover-Let-s-Recall-the-Scandal-That-Ended-the-
     Career-of-the-Man-After-Whom-the-Historic-Hotel-is-
     Named/22-04-2016-97581/

6.   S. Muthiah, *A tradition of Madras that is Chennai—The Taj
     Connemara*, 2008.

7.   J. Clarke, 'Like a huge birdcage exhaled from the
     earth: Watson's Esplanade Hotel, Mumbai (1867–71), and its

place in structural history', *Construction History: The International Journal of the Construction History Society*, vol. 18, pp. 37–78.

8. 'Watson, you are a forgotten soul', *Times of India*, 23 June 2005, https://timesofindia.indiatimes.com/india/Watson-You-are-a-forgotten-soul/articleshow/1150820.cms

9. T.V. Mahalingam, 'How Mumbai's Watson's Hotel faded into shades of oblivion', Economic Times, 7 July 2012, https://economictimes.indiatimes.com/industry/services/hotels-/-restaurants/how-mumbais-watsons-hotel-faded-into-shades-of-oblivion/articleshow/14727929.cms?from=mdr

10. Elaine Derby, *Grand Hotels: Reality and Illusion*, London: Reaktion Books, 2002;
Bachi Karkaria, *Dare to Dream: The Life of M.S. Oberoi*, Penguin Books, 1992.

11. 'Nanda takes the Claridges cake', *Times of India*, 6 April 2003, https://timesofindia.indiatimes.com/city/delhi/Nanda-takes-the-Claridges-cake/articleshow/42602669.cms

12. Anumeha Chaturvedi, 'Indian hotels, Claridges in JV Talks', 25 August 2018, https://economictimes.indiatimes.com/industry/services/hotels-/-restaurants/indian-hotels-claridges-in-jv-talks/articleshow/65537418.cms?from=mdr

13. Devendra, Amitabh, 'The Hotel Industry in India—The Past and the Present', *Journal of Hospitality Financial Management*: vol. 9, Iss. 1 (2001), http://scholarworks.umass.edu/jhfm/vol9/iss1/7

14. Suman Layak, 'Halls of fame', *Business Today*, 10 July 2011, https://www.businesstoday.in/magazine/cover-story/taj-group-of-hotels-among-100-year-old-companies/story/16486.html

15. Malini Goyal, 'Two Unlikely Maharajas', *Forbes*, 24 August 2009, http://www.forbesindia.com/article/work-in-progress/two-unlikely-maharajas/3352/1

4. The Badshahs and Sultans

1. Sandipan Deb, 'Did Kerkar rob the Taj?', *Outlook*, 13 October 1997, https://www.outlookindia.com/magazine/story/did-kerkar-rob-the-taj/204385

2. N. Sundaresha Subramanian, 'From Fonseca to Taj Mansingh', *Business Standard*, 25 January 2013, http://www.business-standard.com/article/companies/from-fonseca-to-taj-mansingh-112082900064_1.html;

Vir Sanghvi, 'A hotel's tale: How the Taj became the Taj', *Hindustan Times*, 12 November 2016, http://www.hindustantimes.com/brunch/a-hotel-s-tale-how-the-taj-became-the-taj/story-mn7d1sLUb2K8EL2wtMRrDN.html

3. Sandipan Deb, 'Did Kerkar rob the Taj', *Outlook*, 13 October 1997, https://www.outlookindia.com/magazine/story/didkerkar-rob-the-taj/204385

4. Robin Abreu, 'Ratan Tata proves his supremacy by ousting Ajit Kerkar from Taj Group of hotels', *India Today*, 15 September 1997, https://www.indiatoday.in/magazine/economy/story/19970915-ratan-tata-proves-his-supremacy-by-ousting-ajit-kerkar-from-taj-group-of-hotels-830570-1997-09-15

5. Aveek Datta, 'Rakesh Sarna exits; Cyrus Mistry's sympathisers gradually leaving Tata group', *Forbes*, 28 May 2017, http://www.forbesindia.com/article/special/rakesh-sarna-exits%3B-cyrus-mistrys-sympathisers-gradually-leaving-tata-group/47099/1;

Kala Vijayaraghavan and Arijit Barman, 'Taj boss Rakesh Sarna quits after ghost of sexual harassment haunted stint', *Economic Times*, 12 July 2019, https://economictimes.indiatimes.com/industry/services/hotels/-/restaurants/rakesh-sarna-resigns-as-ihcl-md-and-ceo/articleshow/58859676.cms?from=mdr;

Arijit Barman, Vinod Mahanta and Kala Vijayaraghavan, 'Sexual harassment case against Taj CEO Rakesh Sarna made it tougher for Cyrus Mistry', 12 July 2019, https://economictimes.indiatimes.com/news/company/corporate-trends/sexual-harassment-case-against-ihcl-boss-rakesh-sarna-may-have-added-to-cyrus-mistry-woes/articleshow/55361051.cms?from=mdr

6. Suman Layak, 'Room for growth: Indian Hotels MD Puneet Chhatwal's key to unlock value', *Economic Times*, 24 February

2019, https://economictimes.indiatimes.com/industry/services/
hotels-/-restaurants/room-for-growth-indian-hotels-md-
puneet-chhatwals-key-to-unlock-value/articleshow/68130109.
cms?utm_source=contentofinterest&utm_medium=text&
utm_campaign=cppst

7. Ritwick Mukherjee, 'Amid rumours Nita Ambani attends EIH
    AGM', *Asian Age*, 15 August 2019, https://www.asianage.com/
    business/in-other-news/150819/amid-rumours-nita-ambani-
    attends-eih-agm.html

8. Information shared by an Oberoi executive.

9. Habib Rehman: *Borders to Boardroom: A Memoir*, Lotus,
    2014.

10. Vir Sanghvi, 'The Last Emperor', *Hindustan Times*,
    23 March 2009, https://www.hindustantimes.com/india/the-
    last-emperor/story-Q9UK3OgvwLq7vlHUIFBbLO.html

11. Habib Rehman, 'In the Shadow of the Great Maurya', *Borders
    to Boardroom: A Memoir*, Lotus, 2014.

12. Soumonty Kanungo, 'The Metamorphosis of ITC under Yogi
    Deveshwar', Livemint, 23 June 2016, https://www.livemint.
    com/Companies/M4IEWEGmFelQIu3UJ8s1XN/The-
    metamorphosis-of-ITC-under-YC-Deveshwar.html

5. The Women's Touch

1. 'Lalit Suri Lived Life in the Fast Lane', *Hindustan
    Times*, 10 October 2006, https://www.hindustantimes.
    com/india/lalit-suri-lived-life-in-the-fast-lane/story-
    Z8RWts20bH83egAiQqfMBP.html

2. Kishore Singh, 'Lalit Suri: The uncrowned hotel king', Rediff.
    com, 4 April 2005, https://inwww.rediff.com/money/2005/
    apr/04spec.htm

3. Chitra Narayanan, 'Eyes on the destination', *Business Today*,
    27 September 2017

6. The Global Goliaths

1. Arun Kumar, 'Accor, Emaar MGF to spend $300 m in 100-hotel plan for India', *Hindustan Times*, 27 November 2006, https://www.hindustantimes.com/india/accor-emaar-mgf-to-spend-300-m-in-100-hotel-plan-for-india/story-i8nK9eGbP8liXBgQG78UKO.html

2. Leslie Tan and Paul Gordon, 'Bloomberg, Hilton DLF to spend $1.5 billion in Indian venture, Livemint, 16 May 2007, https://www.livemint.com/Money/4pg09T5hU9JG50nZOZuo8N/Hilton-DLF-to-spend-15-bn-in-Indian-venture.html;

    'DLF buys out Hilton's 26 pc stake in hospitality JV', *Economic Times*, 11 December 2011, https://economictimes.indiatimes.com/industry/services/hotels-/-restaurants/dlf-buys-out-hiltons-26-pc-stake-in-hospitality-jv/articleshow/10995169.cms?from=mdr

3. T.E. Narasimhan, 'Intercontinental Hotels to sell stake in JV with Duet India' *Business Standard*, 22 April 2017, https://www.businessstandard.com/article/companies/intercontinental-hotels-to-sell-stake-in-jv-with-duet-india-117042200348_1.html

4. 'India tops international overnight visitors to Dubai in 2018', *The Hindu BusinessLine*, 27 February 2019, https://www.thehindubusinessline.com/news/variety/india-tops-international-overnight-visitors-to-dubai-in-2018/article26382395.ece

5. Moulishree Srivastava, 'Lebua Hotels to open Four Luxury Properties in India', Livemint, 23 April 2013, https://www.livemint.com/Companies/nfQi3aDupE8sUfqF3HqgVN/Lebua-Hotels-to-open-four-luxury-properties-in-India.html

7. The Intrepid Explorers

1. Interview with the author.
2. Chitra Narayanan, 'Leaves, Shoots and the Green Hotel', *The Hindu MetroPlus,* 5 July 2017.

3. In June 2021, Bhatia tragically died at the age of forty-eight. One has to wait and see how the family—especially brother Gaurav—takes forward the ambitious hotelier's dreams.

8. The Owners: Visible and Invisible

1. Chitra Narayan, 'The new inn-keepers', *The Hindu BusinessLine*, 11 January 2018, https://www.thehindubusinessline.com/specials/india-file/the-new-innkeepers/article9686780.ece
2. Derived from hotel industry reports. Most foreign chains have an asset light model whereby they don't own the hotels they manage. Increasingly, Indian chains are adopting the same model too.
3. 'Accor to manage Jaipur Exhibition & Convention Centre', *Economic Times*, 25 March 2015, https://realty.economictimes.indiatimes.com/news/industry/accor-to-manage-jaipur-exhibition-convention-centre/46583712

11. The Big Disruptor

1. Ashish Mishra, 'Will the real Ritesh Agrawal stand up?', Livemint, 7 January 2015, https://www.livemint.com/Companies/7CN7u5d4i3bfYgBAZLdLpM/Will-the-real-Ritesh-Agarwal-please-stand-up.html
2. Ibid.
3. Ray Kroc, *Grinding it Out: The Making of McDonald's*, USA: MacMillan;

    Adam Chandler, 'How Ray Kroc Became an American Villain', *Atlantic*, 26 January 2017, https://www.theatlantic.com/business/archive/2017/01/ray-kroc-mcdonalds-america/514538/

12. The OTAS—Friends, Enemies or Frenemies

1. Dennis Schaal, 'The definitive oral history of online travel', Skift, https://skift.com/history-of-online-travel/;

Michael V. Copeland, 'The Man who Escaped Microsoft and Took a Whole Company with Him', Wired, 6 October 2013, https://www.wired.com/2013/06/rich-barton-empowers-people-and-picks-fights-very-profitably/

2. 'Ahmedabad hoteliers boycott MakeMyTrip & Goibibo on heavy commission, discounts', Times of India, 5 December 2018, https://timesofindia.indiatimes.com/business/india-business/ahmedabad-hoteliers-boycott-makemytrip-goibibo-on-heavy-commission-discounts/articleshow/66947579.cms

3. Biswarup Gooptu and Taslima Khan, 'MakeMyTrip–IBIBO merger: How Combined entity continues to struggle with problems', Economic Times, 26 January 2018, https://economictimes.indiatimes.com/small-biz/startups/features/makemytrip-ibibo-merger-how-combined-entity-continues-to-struggle-with-problems-old-and-new/articleshow/62658501.cms

13. The Charge of the New Brigade

1. Chitra Narayanan, 'Clouds, Caves and Chukkars, The Hindu MetroPlus, 13 September 2017.

2. Shrutika Verma and Mihir Dalal, 'Treebo and FabHotels initiate merger talks', Livemint, 18 October 2018, https://www.livemint.com/Companies/0gMWtBwyEmvH3F17NE2hwK/Treebo-and-FabHotels-initiate-merger-talks.html

15. The Wellness Mantra

1. Chitra Narayanan, 'When Wellness Meets Wanderlust', The Hindu MetroPlus, 15 March 2017.

17. Banking on Banquets—The Taste of Things

1. Vir Sanghvi, 'Rude food by Vir Sanghvi: The legend of Jiggs Kalra', Hindustan Times, 25 June 2019, https://www.hindustantimes.com/brunch/the-legend-of-jiggs-kalra/story-SoFBO5Vl1cNAwjcBhLJgoL.html